1909 ... STREET
CHICAGO, ILLINOIS 5941

Bloom's Modern Critical Views

Bloom's Modern Critical Views

WILLIAM FAULKNER
New Edition

Edited and with an introduction by
Harold Bloom
Sterling Professor of the Humanities
Yale University

BLOOM'S
LITERARY CRITICISM
An imprint of Infobase Publishing

Bloom's Modern Critical Views: William Faulkner, New Edition

Copyright © 2008 by Infobase Publishing

Introduction © 2008 by Harold Bloom

Bloom's Literary Criticism
An imprint of Infobase Publishing
132 West 31st Street
New York, NY 10001

Library of Congress Cataloging-in-Publication Data
William Faulkner / [edited by] Harold Bloom. — New ed.
     p. cm. — (Modern critical views)
   Includes bibliographical references and index.
   ISBN 978-0-7910-9786-1 (hardcover)
   1. Faulkner, William, 1897–1962—Criticism and interpretation. I. Bloom, Harold.

   PS3511.A86Z9856853 2008
   813'.52—dc22
   [B]
                                          2007033754

Contributing Editor: Amy Sickels
Cover designed by Takeshi Takahashi
Cover photo AP Images
Printed in the United States of America
Bang EJB 10 9 8 7 6 5 4 3 2 1

Contents

Contents

Editor's Note

My Introduction sets aside the attempts to Christianize or render normative, socially or morally, the primordial Faulkner of his major phase: *As I Lay Dying, The Sound and the Fury, Light in August, Absalom, Absalom!*

Irving Howe, a "liberal" critic in the mode of Lionel Trilling, gives moderated praise to *The Wild Palms*, underestimating (in my judgment) the remarkable "Old Man" heroic narrative.

In what might be called T.S. Eliot's last stand, the obdurate Cleanth Brooks interprets *Absalom, Absalom!* as essentially Christian tragedy.

The Hamlet, Faulkner's grandly comic Snopes saga, is acutely read by Michael Millgate as what it is: an ironic and allegorical vision of the triumph of Flem Snopes, who now governs us from Washington, D.C.

David Minter, Faulkner's distinguished literary biographer, gives a highly useful account of *The Sound and the Fury*, tracing the difficult process of the book's inception.

In an ambitious essay on *Light in August*, Eric J. Sundquist brings together the book's experimental narrative form and the bloody violence that makes the slaughter of Joe Christmas a veritable apocalypse of American racial hatred and our mad addiction to violence, at home and abroad.

The illusory image of "the Negro" in *Absalom, Absalom!* is questioned by Thadious Davis, who calibrates Faulkner's uncanny power to blood this abstraction.

Faulkner's uneasy relationship to all women, including his own female characters, is charted both by Dianne Luce Cox and by Deborah Clarke. Cox centers on the violated Temple Drake of that perpetual shocker, *Sanctuary*, while Clarke explores Faulkner's gingerly visions of motherhood in *The Sound and the Fury* and *As I Lay Dying*.

Judith Bryant Wittenberg boldly confronts the superb *Go Down, Moses*, a narrative made up of short stories that rivals *The Hamlet* as Faulkner's most Dickensian gallery of diverse characters.

The Town and *The Mansion* complete the Snopes saga begun in *The Hamlet*, and the trilogy is seen in its "textual" terms by Owen Robinson.

In this volume's final essay, Jay Parini engagingly gives us the biographical context for *As I Lay Dying*, Faulkner's finest and most original achievement.

HAROLD BLOOM

Introduction

I

No critic need invent William Faulkner's obsession with what Nietzsche might have called the genealogy of the imagination. Recent critics of Faulkner, including David Minter, John T. Irwin, David M. Wyatt, and Richard H. King, have emphasized the novelist's profound need to believe himself to have been his own father, in order to escape not only the Freudian family romance and literary anxieties of influence, but also the cultural dilemmas King terms "the Southern family romance." From *The Sound and the Fury* through the debacle of *A Fable*, Faulkner centers upon the sorrows of fathers and sons, to the disadvantage of mothers and daughters. No feminist critic ever will be happy with Faulkner. His brooding conviction that female sexuality is closely allied with death seems essential to all of his strongest fictions. It may even be that Faulkner's rhetorical economy, his wounded need to get his cosmos into a single sentence, is related to his fear that origin and end might prove to be one. Nietzsche prophetically has warned that origin and end were separate entities, and for the sake of life had to be kept apart, but Faulkner (strangely like Freud) seems to have known that the only Western trope participating neither in origin nor end is the image of the father.

By universal consent of critics and common readers, Faulkner now is recognized as the strongest American novelist of the twentieth century, clearly surpassing Hemingway and Fitzgerald, and standing as an equal in the sequence that includes Hawthorne, Melville, Mark Twain, and Henry

1

James. Some critics would add Dreiser to this group; Faulkner himself
curiously would have insisted on Thomas Wolfe, a generous though dubious
judgment. The American precursor for Faulkner was Sherwood Anderson,
but perhaps only as an impetus; the true American forerunner is the poetry
of T.S. Eliot, as Judith L. Sensibar demonstrates. But the truer precursor
for Faulkner's fiction is Conrad, inescapable for the American novelists of
Faulkner's generation, including Hemingway and Fitzgerald. Comparison to
Conrad is dangerous for any novelist, and clearly Faulkner did not achieve a
Nostromo. But his work of the decade 1929–1939 does include four permanent
books: *The Sound and the Fury, As I Lay Dying, Light in August,* and *Absalom,
Absalom!* If one adds *Sanctuary* and *The Wild Palms,* and *The Hamlet* and *Go
Down, Moses* in the early forties, then the combined effect is extraordinary.

From Malcolm Cowley on, critics have explained this effect as
the consequence of the force of mythmaking, at once personal and local.
Cleanth Brooks, the rugged final champion of the New Criticism, essentially
reads Faulkner as he does Eliot's *The Waste Land,* finding the hidden God
in the normative Christian tradition to be the basis for Faulkner's attitude
towards nature. Since Brooks calls Faulkner's stance Wordsworthian, and
finds Wordsworthian nature a Christian vision also, the judgment involved
necessarily has its problematical elements. Walter Pater, a critic in a very
different tradition, portrayed a very different Wordsworth in terms that seem
to me not inapplicable to Faulkner:

> Religious sentiment, consecrating the affections and natural
> regrets on the human heart, above all, that pitiful awe and
> care for the perishing human clay, of which relic-worship is
> but the corruption, has always had much to do with localities,
> with the thoughts which attach themselves to actual scenes
> and places. Now what is true of it everywhere, is truest of it
> in those secluded valleys where one generation after another
> maintains the same abiding place; and it was on this side, that
> Wordsworth apprehended religion most strongly. Consisting, as
> it did so much, in the recognition of local sanctities, in the habit
> of connecting the stones and trees of a particular spot of earth
> with the great events of life, till the low walls, the green mounds,
> the half-obliterated epitaphs seemed full of voices, and a sort
> of natural oracle, the very religion of those people of the dales,
> appeared but as another link between them and the earth, and
> was literally a religion of nature.

A kind of stoic natural religion pervades that description, something
close to the implicit faith of old Isaac McCaslin in *Go Down, Moses.* It

seems unhelpful to speak of "residual Christianity" in Faulkner, as Cleanth
Brooks does. Hemingway and Fitzgerald, in their nostalgias, perhaps were
closer to a Christian ethos than Faulkner was in his great phase. Against
current critical judgment, I prefer *As I Lay Dying* and *Light in August* to
The Sound and the Fury and *Absalom, Absalom!*, partly because the first two
are more primordial in their vision, closer to the stoic intensities of their
author's kind of natural piety. There is an otherness in Lena Grove and the
Bundrens that would have moved Wordsworth, that is, the Wordsworth of
"The Tale of Margaret," "Michael," and "The Old Cumberland Beggar." A
curious movement that is also a stasis becomes Faulkner's pervasive trope
for Lena. Though he invokes the imagery of Keats's urn, Faulkner seems to
have had the harvest-girl of Keats's "To Autumn" more in mind, or even
the stately figures of the "Ode to Indolence." We remember Lena Grove
as stately, calm, a person yet a process, a serene and patient consciousness,
full of wonder, too much a unitary being to need even her author's variety
of stoic courage.

The uncanniness of this representation is exceeded by the Bundrens,
whose plagency testifies to Faulkner's finest rhetorical achievement. *As I
Lay Dying* may be the most original novel ever written by an American.
Obviously it is not free of the deepest influence Faulkner knew as a novelist.
The language is never Conradian, and yet the sense of the reality principle
is. But these is nothing in Conrad like Darl Bundren, not even in *The Secret
Agent*. *As I Lay Dying* is Faulkner's strongest protest against the facticity of
literary convention, against the force of the familial past, which tropes itself
in fiction as the repetitive form of narrative imitating prior narrative. The
book is a sustained nightmare, insofar as it is Darl's book, which is to say,
Faulkner's book, or the book of his daemon.

II

Canonization is a process of enshrining creative misinterpretations, and
no one need lament this. Still, one element that ensues from this process
all too frequently is the not very creative misinterpretation in which the
idiosyncratic is distorted into the normative. Churchwardenly critics
who assimilate the Faulkner of the thirties to spiritual, social, and moral
orthodoxy can and do assert Faulkner himself as their preceptor. But this
is the Faulkner of the fifties, Nobel laureate, State Department envoy, and
author of *A Fable*, a book of a badness simply astonishing for Faulkner. The
best of the normative critics, Cleanth Brooks, reads even *As I Lay Dying* as a
quest for community, an exaltation of the family, an affirmation of Christian
values. The Bundrens manifestly constitute one of the most terrifying visions
of the family romance in the history of literature. But their extremism is
not eccentric in the 1929–1939 world of Faulkner's fiction. That world is

founded upon a horror of families, a limbo of outcasts, an evasion of all values other than stoic endurance. It is a world in which what is silent in the other Bundrens speaks in Darl, what is veiled in the Compsons is uncovered in Quentin. So tangled are these returns of the repressed with what continues to be estranged that phrases like "the violation of the natural" and "the denial of the human" become quite meaningless when applied to Faulkner's great fictions. In that world, the natural is itself a violation and the human already a denial. Is the weird quest of the Bundrens a violation of the natural, or is it what Blake would have called a terrible triumph for the selfish virtues of the natural heart? Darl judges it to be the latter, but Darl luminously denies the sufficiency of the human, at the cost of what seems schizophrenia.

Marxist criticism of imaginative literature, if it had not regressed abominably in our country, so that now it is a travesty of the dialectical suppleness of Adorno and Benjamin, would find a proper subject in the difficult relationship of the 1929 business panic and *As I Lay Dying*. Perhaps the self-destruction of our delusive political economy helped free Faulkner from whatever inhibitions, communal and personal, had kept him earlier from a saga like that of the Bundrens. Only an authentic seer can give permanent form to a prophecy like *As I Lay Dying*, which puts severely into question every received notion we have of the natural and the human. Darl asserts he has no mother, while taunting his enemy brother, Jewel, with the insistence that Jewel's mother was a horse. Their little brother, Vardaman, says: "My mother is a fish." The mother, dead and undead, is uncannier even than these children, when she confesses the truth of her existence, her rejecting vision of her children:

> I could just remember how my father used to say that the reason for living was to get ready to stay dead a long time. And when I would have to look at them day after day, each with his and her single and selfish thought, and blood strange to each other blood and strange to mine, and think that this seemed to be the only way I could get ready to stay dead, I would hate my father for having ever planted me. I would look forward to the times when they faulted, so I could whip them. When the switch fell I could feel it upon my flesh; when it welted and ridged it was my blood that ran, and I would think with each blow of the switch: Now you are aware of me! Now I am something in your secret and selfish life, who have marked your blood with my own for ever and ever.

This veritable apocalypse of any sense of otherness is no mere "denial of community." Nor are the Bundrens any "mimesis of essential nature."

They are a super-mimesis, an over-representation mocking nature while shadowing it. What matters in major Faulkner is that the people have gone back, not to nature but to some abyss before the Creation-Fall. Eliot insisted that Joyce's imagination was eminently orthodox. This can be doubted, but in Faulkner's case there is little sense in baptizing his imagination. One sees why he preferred reading the Old Testament to the New, remarking that the former was stories and the latter, ideas. The remark is inadequate except insofar as it opposed Hebraic to Hellenistic representation of character. There is little that is Homeric about the Bundrens, or Sophoclean about the Compsons. Faulkner's irony is neither classical nor romantic, neither Greek nor German. It does not say one thing while meaning another, nor trade in constants between expectation and fulfillment. Instead, it juxtaposes incommensurable realities: of self and other, of parent and child, of past and future. When Gide maintained that Faulkner's people lacked souls, he simply failed to observe that Faulkner's ironies were Biblical. To which an amendment must be added. In Faulkner, only the ironies are Biblical. What Faulkner's people lack is the blessing; they cannot content for a time without boundaries. Yahweh will make no covenant with them. Their agon therefore is neither the Greek one for the foremost place nor the Hebrew one for the blessing, which honors the father and the mother. Their agon is the hopeless one of waiting for their doom to lift.

III

Faulkner writes tragic farce rather than tragedy, more in the mode of Webster, Ford, and Tourneur than that of Shakespeare. In time, his genius or daemon may seem essentially comic, despite his dark houses and death drives. His grand family is Dickens run mad rather than Conrad run wild: the hideous saga of the Snopes, from the excessively capable Flem Snopes to the admirably named Wallstreet Panic Snopes. Flem, as David Minter observes, is refreshingly free of all influence-anxieties. He belongs in Washington, D.C., and by now has reached there, and helps to staff the White House. Alas, he by now helps to staff the universities also, if not the entire nation, as his spiritual children, the Yuppies, have reached middle age. His ruined families, burdened by tradition, are Faulkner's tribute to his region. His Snopes clan is his gift to his nation.

IRVING HOWE

The Wild Palms

Most of Faulkner's influential critics have agreed that *The Wild Palms* is a failure and that its two intersecting stories—"Wild Palms" and "Old Man"—need not be printed together as they were in the original edition. In his *Portable Faulkner* Malcolm Cowley reprints "Old Man" by itself; other editors and publishers have followed his lead. I propose to question this view, both as regards the structure and value of the novel. By looking somewhat closely at their plots, it should be possible to see whether the two parts of the book are genuinely bound together through theme and atmosphere.

A study in middle-class romanticism, "Wild Palms" is probably the most depressing and painful narrative Faulkner has ever written, if only because the self-destruction of its characters proceeds from a desire in itself admirable. The story opens at the point where the disintegration of its leading figures is almost complete. Charlotte Rittenmeyer, a young woman of powerful ego and compulsive sexuality, and Harry Wilbourne, a rather pliant hospital interne, leave New Orleans after a brief, intense love affair. Charlotte abandons a conventional marriage, Harry the promise of a conventional career. Together they seek a life beyond the city, uncertain whether their rebellion is against bourgeois norms or the very fact of society itself. This confusion of purpose is to be a major source of their troubles, for only if controlled by a precise awareness of both goal and limits could their flight possibly succeed. Soon their behavior seems a painful demonstration of how perilous the romantic

From *William Faulkner: A Critical Study*, pp. 233–242. Chicago: Ivan R. Dee. © 1991 by Irving Howe.

view of life can be, how violently it can exhaust and then consume those who are most loyal to it—romantic in this instance signifying a refusal to live by any terms except those which cannot be enforced. As Charlotte tells Harry:

> "Listen; it's got to be all honeymoon, always. Forever and ever, until one of us dies. It can't be anything else. Either heaven, or hell; no comfortable safe peaceful purgatory between for you and me to wait in until good behavior or forbearance or shame or repentance overtakes us."

Charlotte is not a fool; if she were, "Wild Palms" could not build up to the tension it does. She can be so fanatically self-destructive as to demand "all honeymoon, always," but she can also express her outlook in terms that are more impressive: "'They say love dies, between two people. That's wrong. It doesn't die. It just leaves you, goes away, if you are not good enough, worthy enough. It doesn't die; you're the one that dies.'"

The two young people believe they are turning to a blazing sensuous life, an utter purity of instinct and touch. Their relationship is eagerly, programmatically physical; only the clash of bodies, they feel, is an act free of social deceit. Charlotte wants no disabling or melting tenderness. She makes love to Harry by "striking her body against him hard, not in caress but exactly as she would grasp him by the hair to wake him from sleep." The comparison is acute. Vital enough to strain for a release of suppressed energies, courageous and admirable in her readiness to take chances, Charlotte deceives herself only in supposing that an unencumbered act of natural living, an embrace of the sun, can be a sufficient means toward personal fulfillment.

Charlotte and Harry wander off to Chicago; they have difficulty in finding work but that is not their most vexing problem. What really troubles them is that in rejecting the impersonal of the city and the deadness of middle-class existence they cannot find a way of life that might transcend the violence of their rejection. They trap themselves in a frozen gesture of protest, beyond which they cannot move. As soon as they begin eating regularly they wonder if they are not in danger of sliding into bourgeois complacence. To avoid this danger they abandon the city, moving to a desolate mining camp in Utah. Faulkner is crucially involved in this flight, for he has nothing in common with the middle-aged wisdom—perhaps merely middle-aged resignation—which would sneer at it. He is always ready to extend his sympathy to anyone who lives to the limit of power or desire. Yet he is also perceptive enough to see that the flight of Charlotte and Harry is fundamentally incoherent; and in a biting passage he shows the civilization from which the lovers had fled seeping into the remote mining camp—Harry is cheated of his wage, he has to perform an illegal abortion on the supervisor's wife: again, the moral ugliness of the city.

Destitute, the lovers drift south, back to the Mississippi basin, where Charlotte reveals herself to be pregnant and Harry performs his second abortion, this time a failure. Now, in the opening scene of the novel, the couple is living in penniless inertia, Charlotte resentful and broken, Harry a cartoon of the independent man he had hoped to become. When Charlotte dies after the botched abortion, Harry is taken off to prison, there to nurture memories of love, in safety and emptiness—yet not total emptiness, for in some desperate way he remains faithful to the vision he could not live by. In jail he experiences a moment of overwhelming, perhaps fulfilling, reflection:

> . . . and in the night he could face it, thinking *Not could. Will. I want to. So it is the old meat after all, no matter how old. Because if memory exists outside the flesh it won't be memory because it won't know what it remembers so when she became not then half of memory became not and if I become not then all of remembering will cease to be.—Yes*, he thought, *between grief and nothing I will take grief.*

Thrusting its characters into a fierce, somewhat muddled yet ultimately impressive struggle against reality, "Wild Palms" elevates that struggle to a principle of life: "Love and suffering are the same thing . . ." the value of love is the sum of what you have to pay for it . . ." But the story also complicates and partly abandons this romantic view. The destination of flight proves as unacceptable as its starting point, perhaps because finally there is not so much difference between the two. Neither society nor isolation can satisfy Charlotte, and Harry's satisfaction is but a dependency of hers. Living too rigidly by a preconceived code, which transforms her passion for freedom into a mode of self-tyranny, she destroys both herself and her lover. The destruction, as I say, is impressive, far more so than the usual run of adjustments; still, it is destruction. So streaked is the life of Charlotte and Harry with the neurotic colors of the world they refuse, so fanatical is their fear of a settled existence, that they render themselves unfit for the natural haven to which they would retire. In the most extreme rural isolation they continue to live by the standards of the city, and at the end it is Harry's ineptness at abortion, a technique of civilization, which causes their catastrophe. Between the city from which they would escape and the natural world they dream of finding, there is no intermediate area of shade and rest. The act of rejection having consumed their energies, nothing remains for the act of living.

A simpler story, "Old Man" concerns an unnamed Mississippi convict. "About twenty-five, flat-stomached, with a sunburned face and Indian black hair and pale, china-colored, outraged eyes," this tall convict, as he is called, is one of Faulkner's natural men. Limited in mental power, he is superbly in control of his immediate environment and endowed with a fine, even over-acute sense of moral obligation. He has, however, grown so accustomed to the harsh security of the prison farm that he does not take his freedom when he can.

Brought with other convicts to the Mississippi River to help control a flood, the tall convict is instructed to rescue a woman perched on a cypress snag and a man stranded on a cotton-house roof. Rowing furiously, he finds the woman, who is far gone in pregnancy, and through his instinctive skill in adapting himself to the river they manage to drift crazily down the flood waters. Neither intimacy nor affection sweetens the life of convict and woman; two people thrown together, they must cooperate if they are to survive, but more they will not do. It is a kind of honesty, free of the language of romanticism.

The woman, helped by the convict, has her baby. At the first mouth of the river they end their journey, settling in Cajun country where the convict becomes the partner of an alligator hunter and again, with his marvellous affinity to natural life, proves highly successful. For the first time freedom tempts him: "*Yes. I reckon I had done forgot how good making money was. Being let to make it . . . I had forgot how it is to work.*" But a malicious twist of circumstances forces him to leave the alligator country and return to the prison area. "Yonder's the boat," he tells the prison guard, "and here's the woman. But I never did find that bastard on the cotton house." A final cut of injustice, the climax of "Old Man" is the sentencing of the convict to ten more years for "attempted escape." What impresses him more than this injustice, however, is his memory of how difficult it was to rid himself of the pregnant woman during his time of freedom. As in most Faulkner novels, freedom proves to be elusive, and when found, limited.

Simply sketched, these are the plots of "Wild Palms" and "Old Man." Faulkner has divided each story into five parts, alternating a part from one with a part from the other. To follow the pattern of the novel, envisage an interweaving of the following sections:

"WILD PALMS"	"OLD MAN"
1. Failure of abortion, Charlotte close to death.	2. Convict leaves for flood.
3. Flashback: Charlotte and Harry leave New Orleans.	4. "Lost" in flood.
5. Flashback: drifting from country to Chicago.	6. Drifting with pregnant woman on flood waters.
7. Flashback: haven in a mining camp.	8. Haven with Cajun.
9. Charlotte's death, Harry's imprisonment.	10. Return to prison.

Is this crossing of stories mechanical and arbitrary? That Faulkner may have composed them separately and then spliced them together is not very important; the problem is, why did he connect these two stories in so unusual a way? He has said that "I did send both stories to the publisher separately and they were rejected because they were too short. So I alternated the chapters of them." But he has also referred to *The Wild Palms* as one story of "two types of love," and has recently declared that he wrote "Old Man" to bring the other story "back to pitch" by contrast with its "antithesis." The remark is very shrewd, for "Wild Palms" by itself is almost intolerably painful and needs very much to be brought "back to pitch."[1]

Even a glance at the above pattern of the novel should show some rough parallels between the two stories. There is the possibility that if taken together they will yield a dissonant irony or "counterpoint" which neither could yield alone. The possibility that any two stories by the same writer could be made to yield interesting contrasts and continuities cannot be denied; but at stake here is a relation much more detailed and intimate. Each story charts an escape from confinement to a temporary and qualified freedom and then to an ultimate, still more confining imprisonment. Two opposite intentions— one derived from extreme romanticism, the other a grudging response to circumstances—lead to the exhaustion of both intern and convict, and in that exhaustion there is a kind of common fate. Coincidence this may be, but the correspondences and joined oppositions between the two stories are so numerous and suggestive that we are obliged to take them seriously, as elements of a literary design.

Both the intern and the convict are socially homeless men who discover how intractable the world can be and how little one's hopes and ideas can move it. They are radically different men, but in the end the differences do not count for much. The convict is more resourceful and creative than the intern, perhaps because he is able to float upon the wave of circumstance rather than to dash himself against it. Where the convict helps bring new life into the world, though admittedly life for which he has no more than an abstract responsibility, the intern can only abort and that unsuccessfully. In "Old Man" the life principle does rise to a rueful sort of triumph, yet it brings neither resolution nor satisfaction: it is a triumph that simply keeps the circle of existence turning. In "Wild Palms" a diseased hunger, not merely for life but also for clamping a rigid scheme upon life, becomes the catastrophe.

Still, in noting such contrasts we should not succumb to any pat assumption that Faulkner favors the convict over the intern, primitivism over civilization, nature over the city. The survival of the convict, ambiguous triumph though it may be, has been purchased at the price of a self-denial of personality, a rather awesome suppression of natural desires, and a loss of the vision of freedom—none of which either the characters of "Wild Palms" or Faulkner himself could tolerate. If in some sense the convict proves to be more durable than the intern, there is no reason (except an indulgence in literary primitivism) to ignore the cost of that durability. At the end both men are trapped, and the familiar distinction between will and fate, character and circumstance tends to be dissolved into an ironic perception of their gradual merger.

Faulkner, I think, lends conditional assent to the rebellion of Charlotte and Harry, but with the tacit warning that rebellion becomes suicidal if pressed to a fanatic grasping for total freedom. "Old Man," with a good many sardonic qualifications, proposes a counter-term of acceptance, but this too is carried to an extreme by the convict. Rebellion and acceptance, by the end of the book, shrink in importance beside the overwhelming fact of exhaustion.

In both stories the imprisonment of the leading character is at least partly due to excesses of conscience and ideal, and Faulkner's implicit conclusion—one may decide—is that our emotional economies thrive best on restraint. But when reading the novel itself, this is hardly the impression one is left with. The idea of restraint as a possible resolution seems, for this book, too distant and contained, inadequately rooted in the actual happenings, not a genuine option. At some points it may dimly visit us, but the true and overpowering energy of the book is directed toward another idea: that a suffering man encounters his fate through a total fulfillment of his chosen task. Both intern and convict are caught up in floods, the one a flood of passion, the other a flood of nature, the one a flood wilfully sought after, the other a flood that cannot be escaped. It hardly matters, the novel seems to say, which kind of flood a man lives through; in the end it will break him, and his humanity will be marked by the fullness, the courage of his struggle against it.

The Wild Palms points to the gap between aspiration and realization, the way in which the incommensurable becomes man's fate; and it suggests that this fate cannot be avoided through rebellion or acceptance, aggression or passivity. In the world of this novel, as perhaps in the world of all Faulkner's novels, emotion exceeds possibility, response fails situation, and for the welling of human passion there is never a properly receptive object. It is perceptions such as these which lie behind the strain and fury of Faulkner's prose, and which it is the function of the double plot in *The Wild Palms* both to release and qualify.

By starting "Wild Palms" near its climax, Faulkner magnifies its painfulness, for once he turns to trace the history of Charlotte and Harry it is impossible to feel any hope for them. "Old Man," beginning at its chronological outset and sweeping forward with a humorous and rhythmic equanimity, serves as emotional ballast. The two stories, it should be noted, are of unequal merit and interest, "Old Man" being much superior simply as a piece of writing and "Wild Palms" touching upon problems that are likely to seem more urgent to a modern reader. "Old Man" releases Faulkner's gifts for the fabulous, a mode of narrative in which a human action can be subsumed under, and gain magnitude from, an imposing event in nature. "Wild Palms," because so much of the behavior of its two lovers is caused by a wilfulness bordering on stupidity, cannot reach the tragic limit toward which it strains. Uncertain in its treatment of Northern locale, the story suffers even more seriously from a grating hysteria, an eagerness to hoard and multiply pain, and Faulkner's desperate—yet in some ways admirable—involvement with the two lovers. But whatever one's judgment of the stories, they do sustain each other through a counterpoint of response and should be printed, as they were offered, together.

Probably of little use to anyone but himself, Faulkner's device of alternating sections of the two stories may be judged a *tour de force* that partly succeeds. The novel can hardly be considered one of Faulkner's major works: it will not bear comparison with *The Sound and the Fury* or *Light in August*. But neither is it the negligible effort or outright failure it is too often taken to be. A serious, occasionally distinguished book which contains some admirable parts and is arresting in its general scheme and intent, *The Wild Palms* merits our respect.

NOTE

1. *Interviewer*: "Are the two unrelated themes in *The Wild Palms* brought together in one book for any symbolic purpose? Is it as certain critics intimate a kind of esthetic counterpoint, or is it merely haphazard?"

Faulkner: "No, no. That was one story—the story of Charlotte Rittenmeyer and Harry Wilbourne, who sacrificed everything for love, and then lost that. I did not know it would be two separate stories until after I had started the book. When I reached the end of what is now the first section of *The Wild Palms*, I realized suddenly that something was missing, it needed emphasis, something to lift it like counterpoint in music. So I wrote on the *Old Man* story until *The Wild Palms* story rose back to pitch. Then I stopped the *Old Man* story at what is now its first section, and took up *The Wild Palms* story until it began to sag. Then I raised it to pitch again with another section of its antithesis, which is the story of a man who got his love and spent the rest of the book fleeing from it. . . . " *Paris Review*, Spring 1956.

CLEANTH BROOKS

History and the Sense of the Tragic

*A*bsalom, *Absalom!*, in my opinion the greatest of Faulkner's novels, is probably the least well understood of all his books. The property of a great work, as T. S. Eliot remarked long ago, is to communicate before it is understood; and *Absalom, Absalom!* passes this test triumphantly. It has meant something very powerful and important to all sorts of people, and who is to say that, under the circumstances, this something was not the thing to be said to that particular reader? To the young Frenchman who had served in the *maquis*, to the young writer in New York interested in problems of technique, a little weary from having given his days and nights to the prose of Henry James, to the Shrevelin McCannons all over Canada and the United States with their myths of the South compounded out of *Uncle Tom's Cabin* and *Strange Fruit*—to all these *Absalom, Absalom!* had something to give. That is important, and I do not mean to disparage it. Yet the book has its own rights, as it were, and in proportion as we admire it, we shall want to see not merely what we can make of it but what it makes of itself. In any case, the book is more than a bottle of Gothic sauce to be used to spice up our own preconceptions about the history of American society.

Harvey Breit's sympathetic introduction to the Modern Library edition provides a useful—because it is not an extreme—instance of the typical misreading that I have in mind. Mr. Breit writes:

From *William Faulkner: The Yoknapatawpha Country*, pp. 295–324, Baton Rouge: Louisiana State University Press. © 1990 by Cleanth Brooks.

It is a terrible Gothic sequence of events, a brooding tragic fable.... Was it the "design" that had devoured Sutpen and prevented him from avowing the very thing that would have saved the design? Was it something in the South itself, in its social, political, moral, economic origins that was responsible for Sutpen and for all the subsequent tragedy? Quentin can make no judgment: Sutpen himself had possessed courage and innocence, and the same land had nourished men and women who had delicacy of feeling and capacity for love and gifts for life.

These are questions which the typical reader asks. Shreve, the outsider, implies them. But it is significant that Quentin does not ask them. The questions are begged by the very way in which they are asked, for, put in this way, the questions undercut the problem of tragedy (which is the problem that obsesses Quentin). They imply that there is a social "solution." And they misread Sutpen's character in relation to his society and in relation to himself.

It is the quality of Sutpen's innocence that we must understand if we are to understand the meaning of his tragedy, and if we confuse it with innocence as we ordinarily use the term or with even the typical American "innocence" possessed by, say, one of Henry James' young heiresses as she goes to confront the corruption of Europe, we shall remain in the dark. Sutpen will be for us, as he was for Miss Rosa, simply the "demon"—or since we lack the justification of Miss Rosa's experience of personal horror, we shall simply appropriate the term from her as Shreve, in his half-awed, half-amused fashion, does.

Faulkner has been very careful to define Sutpen's innocence for us. "Sutpen's trouble," as Quentin's grandfather observed, "was innocence" (p. 220). And some pages later, Mr. Compson elaborates the point: "He believed that all that was necessary was courage and shrewdness and the one he knew he had and the other he believed he could learn if it were to be taught" (p. 244). It is this innocence about the nature of reality that persists, for Sutpen "believed that the ingredients of morality were like the ingredients of pie or cake and once you had measured them and balanced them and mixed them and put them into the oven it was all finished and nothing but pie or cake could come out" (p. 263). That is why Sutpen can ask Quentin's grandfather, in his innocence, not "Where did I do wrong" but "Where did I make the mistake . . . what did I do or misdo . . . whom or what injure by it to the extent which this would indicate? I had a design. To accomplish it I should require money, a house, a plantation, slaves, a family—incidentally of course, a wife. I set out to acquire these, asking no favor of any man" (p. 263).

This is an "innocence" with which most of us today ought to be acquainted. It is par excellence the innocence of modern man, though it has not, to be sure, been confined to modern times. One can find more than a trace of it in Sophocles' Oedipus, and it has its analogies with the rather brittle rationalism of Macbeth, though Macbeth tried to learn this innocence by an act of the will and proved to be a less than satisfactory pupil. But innocence of this sort can properly be claimed as a special characteristic of modern man, and one can claim further that it flourishes particularly in a secularized society.

The society into which Sutpen rides in 1833 is not a secularized society. That is not to say that the people are necessarily "good." They have their selfishness and cruelty and their snobbery, as men have always had them. Once Sutpen has acquired enough wealth and displayed enough force, the people of the community are willing to accept him. But they do not live by his code, nor do they share his innocent disregard of accepted values. Indeed, from the beginning they regard him with deep suspicion and some consternation. These suspicions are gradually mollified; there is a kind of acceptance; but as Quentin tells Shreve, Sutpen had only one friend, Quentin's grandfather, General Compson, and this in spite of the fact that the society of the lower South in the nineteenth century was rather fluid and that class lines were flexible. Men did rise in one generation from log cabins to great, landed estates. But the past was important, blood was important, and Southern society thought of itself as traditional.

That Sutpen does remain outside the community comes out in all sorts of little ways. Mr. Compson describes his "florid, swaggering gesture" with the parenthetical remark: "yes, he was underbred. It showed like this always, your grandfather said, in all his formal contacts with people" (p. 46). And Mr. Compson goes on to say that it was as if John L. Sullivan "having taught himself painfully and tediously to do the schottische, having drilled himself and drilled himself in secret . . . now believed it no longer necessary to count the music's beat, say." Yet though Sutpen's manners have been learned painfully, Sutpen has complete confidence in them. "He may have believed that your grandfather or judge Benbow might have done it a little more effortlessly than he, but he would not have believed that anyone could have beat him in knowing when to do it and how" (p. 46).

Mr. Compson is not overrating the possession of mere manners. More is involved than Miss Rosa's opinion that Sutpen was no gentleman. For Sutpen's manners indicate his abstract approach to the whole matter of living. Sutpen would seize upon "the traditional" as a pure abstraction—which, of course, is to deny its very meaning. For him the tradition is not a way of life "handed down" or "transmitted" from the community, past and present, to the individual nurtured by it. It is an assortment of things to be possessed, not a manner of living that embodies certain values and determines men's conduct. The fetish objects are to be gained by sheer ruthless efficiency.

(Sutpen even refers to "my schedule.") Thorstein Veblen would have understood Sutpen's relation to traditional culture. Sutpen is on all fours with the robber baron of the Gilded Age building a fake Renaissance palace on the banks of the Hudson. The New York robber baron's acquiring a box at the opera did not usually spring from a love of music, and one is tempted to say that Sutpen's unwillingness to acknowledge Charles Bon as his son does not spring from any particular racial feeling. Indeed, Sutpen's whole attitude toward the Negro has to be reinspected if we are to understand his relation to the Southern community into which he comes.

It would seem that the prevailing relation between the races in Jefferson is simply one more of the culture traits which Sutpen takes from the plantation community into which he has come as a boy out of the mountains of western Virginia. Sutpen takes over the color bar almost without personal feeling. His attitude toward the Negro is further clarified by his attitude toward his other part-Negro child, Clytie. Mr. Compson once casually lets fall the remark that Sutpen's other children "Henry and Judith had grown up with a negro half sister of their own" (p. 109). The context of Mr. Compson's remarks makes it perfectly plain that Henry and Judith were well aware that Clytie was indeed their half-sister, and that Clytie was allowed to grow up in the house with them. This fact in itself suggests a lack of the usual Southern feeling about Negroes. Miss Rosa is much more typically Southern when she tells Quentin, with evident distaste, that Clytie and Judith sometimes slept in the same bed.

After Sutpen has returned from the war, Clytie sits in the same room with Judith and Rosa and Sutpen and listens each evening to the sound of Sutpen's voice. When Sutpen proposes to Rosa, he begins, "'Judith, you and Clytie—' and ceased, still entering, then said, 'No, never mind. Rosa will not mind if you both hear it too, since we are short for time'" (p. 164). Clytie is accepted naturally as part of the "we." She can be so accepted because acceptance on this level does not imperil Sutpen's "design." But acceptance of Charles Bon, in Sutpen's opinion, would. For Sutpen the matter is really as simple as that. He does not hate his first wife or feel repugnance for her child. He does not hate just as he does not love. His passion is totally committed to the design. Not even his own flesh and blood are allowed to distract him from that.

As for slavery, Sutpen does not confine himself to black chattel slavery. He ruthlessly bends anyone that he can to his will. The white French architect whom he brings into Yoknapatawpha County to build his house is as much a slave as any of his black servants: Sutpen hunts him down with dogs when he tries to escape.

The trait that most decisively sets Sutpen apart from his neighbors in this matter of race is his fighting with his slaves. Sutpen is accustomed to stripping to the waist and fighting it out with one of his slaves, not with rancor, one supposes, and not at all to punish the slave but simply to keep fit—to prove to himself and incidentally to his slaves that he is the better man. Some of Sutpen's white neighbors come to watch the fights as they might come to watch a cockfight. But it is significant that they come as to something extraordinary, a show, an odd spectacle; they would not think of fighting with their own slaves. To Miss Rosa, Sutpen's sister-in-law, the ultimate horror is that Sutpen not only arranges the show but that he enters the ring himself and fights with no holds barred—not even eye-gouging.

Sutpen is not without morality or a certain code of honor. He is, according to his own lights, a just man. As he told Quentin's grandfather with reference to his rejection of his first wife: "suffice that I . . . accepted [my wife] in good faith, with no reservations about myself, and I expected as much from [her parents]. I did not [demand credentials], as one of my obscure origin might have been expected to do. . . . I accepted them at their own valuation while insisting on my part upon explaining fully about myself and my progenitors: yet they deliberately withheld from me one fact which I have reason to know they were aware would have caused me to decline the entire matter" (p. 264). But Sutpen, as he tells General Compson, "made no attempt to keep . . . that [property] which I might consider myself to have earned at the risk of my life . . . but on the contrary I declined and resigned all right and claim to this in order that I might repair whatever injustice I might be considered to have done [in abandoning my wife and child] by so providing for" them.

Moreover, Sutpen is careful to say nothing in disparagement of his first wife. Quentin's grandfather comments upon "that morality which would not permit him to malign or traduce the memory of his first wife, or at least the memory of the marriage even though he felt that he had been tricked by it" (p. 272). It is Sutpen's innocence to think that justice is enough—that there is no claim that cannot be satisfied by sufficient money payment. Quentin imagines his grandfather exclaiming to Sutpen: "What kind of abysmal and purblind innocence would that have been which someone told you to call virginity? what conscience to trade with which would have warranted you in the belief that you could have bought immunity from her for no other coin but justice?" (p. 265).

Sutpen thinks of himself as strictly just and he submits all of his faculties almost selflessly to the achievement of his design. His attitude toward his second wife conforms perfectly to this. Why does he choose her? For choose he does: he is not chosen—that is, involved with her through passion. The choice is calculated quite coldbloodedly (if, to our minds, naïvely and innocently). Ellen Coldfield is not the daughter of a planter. She does not possess great social prestige or beauty and she does not inherit wealth.

But as the daughter of a steward in the Methodist church, she possesses in high degree the thing that Sutpen most obviously lacks—respectability. Mr. Compson sees the point very clearly. He describes Mr. Coldfield as "a man with a name for absolute and undeviating and even Puritan uprightness in a country and time of lawless opportunity, who neither drank nor gambled nor even hunted" (p. 43). For Sutpen, respectability is an abstraction like morality: you measure out so many cups of concentrated respectability to sweeten so many measures of disrespectability—"like the ingredients of pie or cake."

The choice of a father-in-law is in fact just as symbolically right: the two men resemble each other, for all the appearance of antithetical differences. Mr. Coldfield is as definitely set off from the community as is Sutpen. With the coming of the Civil War, this rift widens to an absolute break. Mr. Coldfield denounces secession, closes his store, and finally nails himself up in the attic of his house, where he spends the last three years of his life. No more than Sutpen is he a coward: like Sutpen, too, his scheme of human conduct is abstract and mechanical. "Doubtless the only pleasure which he had ever had . . . was in [his money's] representation of a balance in whatever spiritual counting-house he believed would some day pay his sight drafts on self-denial and fortitude" (p. 84).

This last is Mr. Compson's surmise; but I see no reason to question it or to quarrel with the motive that Mr. Compson assigns for Coldfield's objection to the Civil War: "not so much to the idea of pouring out human blood and life, but at the idea of waste: of wearing out and eating up and shooting away material in, any cause whatever" (p. 83). Mr. Coldfield is glad when he sees the country that he hates obviously drifting into a fatal war, for he regards the inevitable defeat of the South as the price it will pay for having erected its economic edifice "not on the rock of stern morality but on the shifting sands of opportunism and moral brigandage" (p. 260).

Some critics have been so unwary as to assume that this view of the Civil War is one that the author would enjoin upon the reader, but William Faulkner is neither so much of a Puritan nor so much of a materialist as is Mr. Coldfield. The truth of the matter is that Mr. Coldfield's morality is simply Sutpen's turned inside out. Faulkner may or may not have read Tawney's *Religion and the Rise of Capitalism*; but on the evidence of *Absalom, Absalom!* he would certainly have understood it.

Sutpen is further defined by his son, Charles Bon. Bon is a mirror image, a reversed shadow of his father. Like his father, he suddenly appears out of nowhere as a man of mystery: "a personage who in the remote Mississippi of that time must have appeared almost phoenix-like, fullsprung from no childhood, born of no woman and impervious to time" (p. 74). Like his father, Bon has an octoroon "wife," whom he is prepared to repudiate along with his child by her. Like his father, he stands beyond good and evil. But Bon is Byronic, rather than the go-getter; spent, rather than full of pushing vitality; sophisticated, rather than confidently naïve.

Sutpen is the secularized Puritan; Bon is the lapsed Roman Catholic. Whereas Sutpen is filled with a fresh and powerful energy, Bon is world-weary and tired. Bon is a fatalist, but Sutpen believes in sheer will: "anyone could look at him and say, *Given the occasion and the need, this man can and will do anything*" (p. 46). Bon possesses too much knowledge; Sutpen on the other hand is "innocent." The one has gone beyond the distinction between good and evil; the other has scarcely arrived at that distinction.

The father and the son define the extremes of the human world: one aberration corresponds to—and eventually destroys—the other. The reader is inclined to view Bon with sympathy as a person gravely wronged, and he probably agrees with Quentin's interpretation of Bon's character: that Bon finally put aside all ideas of revenge and asked for nothing more than a single hint of recognition of his sonship. Faulkner has certainly treated Bon with full dramatic sympathy, as he has Sutpen, for that matter. But our sympathy ought not to obscure for us Bon's resemblances to his father, or the complexity of his character. Unless we care to go beyond Quentin and Shreve in speculation, Charles Bon displays toward his octoroon mistress and their son something of the cool aloofness that his father displays toward him. If he is the instrument by which Sutpen's design is wrecked, his own irresponsibility (or at the least, his lack of concern for his own child) wrecks his child's life. We shall have to look to Judith to find responsible action and a real counter to Sutpen's ruthlessness.

These other children of Sutpen—Judith and Henry—reflect further light upon the character of Sutpen—upon his virtues and upon his prime defect. They represent a mixture of the qualities of Sutpen and Coldfield. Judith, it is made plain, has more of the confidence and boldness of her father; Henry, more of the conventionality and the scruples of his maternal grandfather. It is the boy Henry who vomits at the sight of his father, stripped to the waist in the ring with the black slave. Judith watches calmly. And it is Judith who urges the coachman to race the coach on the way to church.

Henry is, of the two, the more vulnerable. After Sutpen has forbidden marriage between Bon and Judith and during the long period in which Henry remains self-exiled with his friend Bon, he is the one tested to the limit by his father's puzzling silence and by his friend's fatalistic passivity. But he has some of his father's courage, and he has what his father does not have: love. At the last moment he kills, though he kills what he loves and apparently for love. It is the truly tragic dilemma. Faulkner has not chosen to put Henry's story in the forefront of the novel, but he has not needed to do so. For the sensitive reader the various baffles through which that act of decision reaches us do not muffle but, through their resonance, magnify the decisive act.

Henry's later course is, again, only implied. We know that in the end—his last four years—he reverted to the course of action of his grandfather Coldfield, and shut himself up in the house. But there is a difference. This is no act of abstract defiance and hate. Henry has assumed responsibility, has acted, has been willing to abide the consequences of that action, and now, forty years later, has come home to die.

If it is too much to call Henry's course of action renunciation and expiation, there is full justification for calling Judith's action just that. Judith has much of her father in her, but she is a woman, and she also has love. As Mr. Compson conjectures: "And Judith: how else to explain her but this way? Surely Bon could not have corrupted her to fatalism in twelve days. . . . No: anything but a fatalist, who was the Sutpen with the ruthless Sutpen code of taking what it wanted provided it were strong enough. . . . [Judith said] *I love, I will accept no substitute; something has happened between him and my father; if my father was right, I will never see him again, if wrong he will come or send for me; if happy I can be I will, if suffer I must I can*" (p. 121). It is Judith who invites Charles Bon's octoroon mistress to visit Bon's grave. It is Judith who, on his mother's death, sends to New Orleans for Bon's son and tries to rear him. Some years later she also tries to free him (as Quentin conjectures) by promising to take care of his Negro wife and child if he will go to the North to pass as white, and Quentin imagines her saying to him: "Call me Aunt Judith, Charles" (p. 208). But Quentin's conjectures aside, we know that Judith did take him into the house when he was stricken with yellow fever, and that she died nursing him. The acknowledgment of blood kinship is made; Sutpen's design is repudiated; the boy, even though he has the "taint" of Negro blood, is not, turned away from the door.

Both Henry's action, the violent turning away from the door with a bullet, and Judith's, the holding open the door not merely to Bon, her fiancé, but literally to his part-Negro son; are human actions, as Sutpen's actions are not. Both involve renunciation, and both are motivated by love. The suffering of Henry and Judith is not meaningless, and their very capacity for suffering marks them as having transcended their father's radical and disabling defect.

Faulkner has not put the contrast between the children and their father explicitly nor with quite this emphasis. In the first place, it is Sutpen's story that he is telling (or rather it is Sutpen's story that Quentin and Shreve are trying to recreate). The stories of Judith and, particularly, Henry are dealt with only obliquely. But the Judith, who, in the hard and poverty-stricken years after the war, learns to plough like a man and who collects the dimes and quarters in the rusty can to pay for the headstone for Charles Bon's grave and who asks Bon's son to call her Aunt Judith is a very different person from the dreamy and willful girl to whom Henry introduced Bon at Sutpen's Hundred. And on the night when Quentin and Miss Rosa break into the decaying mansion and find Henry, who has come home to die, what looks out from Henry's eyes is not "innocence." Faulkner does not name it, but he does dramatize for us Quentin's reaction to it. At the least, it is knowledge, a fearful knowledge bought with heroic suffering.

One must not alter the focus of the novel by making wisdom won through suffering the issue. But the consequences entailed upon Judith and Henry have to be mentioned if only to discourage a glib Gothicizing of the novel or forcing its meaning into an over-shallow sociological interpretation.

Miss Rosa feels that the Coldfields are all cursed; and certainly the impact of Sutpen upon her personally is damning: she remains rigid with horror and hate for forty-three years. But it is Miss Rosa only who is damned. Judith is not damned; nor am I sure that Henry is. Judith and Henry are not caught in an uncomprehending stasis. There is development: they grow and learn—at however terrible a price. Uncle Ike in "The Bear" also inherits a curse: an ancestral crime that, for him at least, involves the necessity for renunciation and expiation. I cannot see that the "curse" inherited by Judith and Henry is essentially different in nature or that the general moral pattern in *Absalom, Absalom!* differs radically from that in "The Bear."

Sutpen, as has been pointed out, never learns anything; he remains innocent to the end. As Quentin sees the character: when Charles Bon first comes to his door, Sutpen does not call it "retribution, no sins of the father come home to roost; not even calling it bad luck, but just a mistake . . . just an old mistake in fact which a man of courage and shrewdness . . . could still combat if he could only find out what the mistake had been" (p. 267). I have remarked that Sutpen's innocence is peculiarly the innocence of modern man. For like modern man, Sutpen does not believe in Jehovah. He does not believe in the goddess Tyche. He is not the victim of bad luck. He has simply made a "mistake." He "had been too successful," Mr. Compson tells Quentin; his "was that solitude of contempt and distrust which success brings to him who gained it because he was strong instead of merely lucky" (p. 103).

Marshall McLuhan has somewhere pointed out that the more special feats of James Fenimore Cooper's woodsmen are always attributed to their skill, but those of William Gilmore Simms' woodsmen, to their luck. On this perhaps whimsical test of the sectional character, Sutpen turns out to be a Yankee, not a Southerner at all. At any rate, Sutpen resembles the modern American, whose character, as Arthur M. Schlesinger has put it, "is bottomed on the profound conviction that nothing in the world is beyond

[his] power to accomplish." Sutpen is a "planner" who works by blueprint and on a schedule. He is rationalistic and scientific, not traditional, not religious, not even superstitious.

We must be prepared to take such traits into account if we attempt to read the story of Sutpen's fall as a myth of the fall of the Old South. Unless we are content with some rather rough and ready analogies, the story of the fall of the house of Sutpen may prove less than parallel. The fall of the house of Compson as depicted in *The Sound and the Fury* is also sometimes regarded as a kind of exemplum of the fall of the old aristocratic order in the South, and perhaps in some sense it is. But the breakup of these two families comes from very different causes, and if we wish to use them to point a moral or illustrate a bit of social history, surely they point to different morals and illustrate different histories. Mr. Compson, whose father, General Compson, regarded Sutpen as a "little underbred," has failed through a kind of overrefinement. He has lost his grip on himself; he has ceased finally to believe in the values of the inherited tradition. He is a fatalist and something of an easy cynic. His vices are diametrically opposed to those of Thomas Sutpen, and so are his virtues.

One could even argue that Faulkner's most pertinent account of the fall of the Old South is set forth in his story of the rise of the Snopes clan. The latter-day Compsons and Sartorises and Benbows lack the requisite resolution and toughness to cope with the conditions of the modern world. The Snopeses, therefore, because they recognize no values but self-interest and have unlimited vitality, threaten to take over the modern South. But the story of Flem Snopes is a kind of success story, not a tragedy; and if Snopesism is destroying the older aristocracy, it is not Snopesism that destroys Sutpen. Indeed, Sutpen is at some points more nearly allied to Flem than he is to the Compsons and the Sartorises. Like Flem, he is a new man with no concern for the past and has a boundless energy with which to carry out his aggressive plans.

Yet to couple Sutpen with Flem calls for an immediate qualification. Granting that both men subsist outside the community and in one way or another prey upon the community, Sutpen is by contrast a heroic and tragic figure. He achieves a kind of grandeur. Even the obsessed Miss Rosa sees him as great, not as petty and sordid. His innocence resembles that of Oedipus (who, like him, had been corrupted by success and who put his confidence in his own shrewdness). His courage resembles that of Macbeth, and like Macbeth he is "resolute to try the last." Perhaps the most praiseworthy aspect of Faulkner is his ability to create a character of heroic proportions and to invest his downfall with something like tragic dignity. The feat is, in our times, sufficiently rare.

Faulkner's concern with innocence runs through all the novels. One of General Compson's impressions of Sutpen is that he spoke "with that frank innocence which we call 'of a child' except that a human child is the only living creature that is never either frank or innocent" (p. 246). Nor, as we have seen, are Faulkner's women innocent. The only people in Faulkner who are "innocent" are adult males; and their innocence amounts finally to a trust in rationality—an overweening confidence that plans work out, that life is simpler than it is.

But though Faulkner criticizes rationalism, he never glorifies irrationality. Even Uncle Isaac in "The Bear" does not merely accept nature, content to contemplate its richness and perennial vitality. He does not argue that because the spoliation of the wilderness is a rape that brings its own curse, man ought to cut no trees. He does not believe that it is possible for man to go back to Adam's existence in the happy Garden. Uncle Isaac acts; he helps kill the bear; he goes on the hunt to the end of his days. But he knows that efficiency as an end in itself is self-defeating. It is man's fate to struggle against nature; yet it is wisdom to learn that the fight cannot finally be won, and that the contest has to be conducted with love and humility and in accordance with a code of honor. Man realizes himself in the struggle; but the ultimate to be gained in the struggle is wisdom. Sutpen never really acquires wisdom, for he never loses his innocence. He will never learn. The figure of Time with his scythe never received a more grim embodiment than it does in the grizzled Wash Jones raising his rusty implement to strike Sutpen down.

Sutpen belongs to the company of Conrad's Kurtz (though perhaps Kurtz did learn something at the very end; Marlow thinks that he did). But it is not difficult to find his compeers closer to home. I have already suggested that we might search for them with good hope of success among the brownstone mansions of post–Civil-War New York. But it is easy to locate them in recent fiction. As was remarked in an earlier chapter, the Southern novelists of our time have been fascinated by this kind of character, perhaps because for them he still has some aura of the monstrous, and is still not quite to be taken for granted.

Up to this point we have been concerned with the character of Thomas Sutpen, especially in his relation to the claims of the family and the community. We have treated him as if he were a historical figure, but of course he is not. More than most characters in literature, Thomas Sutpen is an imaginative construct, a set of inferences—an hypothesis put forward to account for several peculiar events. For the novel *Absalom, Absalom!* does not merely tell the story of Thomas Sutpen, but dramatizes the process by which two young men of the twentieth century construct the character Thomas Sutpen. Fascinated by the few known events of his life and death, they try, through inference and conjecture and guesswork, to ascertain what manner of man he was. The novel then has to do not merely with the meaning of Sutpen's career but with the nature of historical truth and with the problem of how we can "know" the past. The importance of this latter theme determines the very special way in which the story of Sutpen is mediated to us through a series of partial disclosures, informed guesses, and constantly revised deductions and hypotheses.

Young Quentin Compson, just on the eve of leaving Mississippi for his first year at Harvard, is summoned by Miss Rosa Coldfield and made to listen to the story of her wicked brother-in-law, Thomas Sutpen. Sutpen had been a friend of Quentin's grandfather, General Compson, and as Quentin waits to drive Miss Rosa out to Sutpen's Hundred after dark, as she has requested, Quentin's father tells him what he knows about the Sutpen story.

Nobody had really understood the strange events that had occurred at Sutpen's Hundred—the quarrel between Thomas Sutpen and Henry, the disappearance of Henry with his friend Charles Bon, the forbidding of the marriage between Judith and Bon, and later, and most sensational of all, Henry's shooting of his friend Charles Bon at the very gates of Sutpen's Hundred in 1865. Mr. Compson makes a valiant effort to account for what happened. What evidently sticks in his mind is the fact that Charles Bon had an octoroon mistress in New Orleans. Presumably Judith had told General Compson or his wife about finding the octoroon's picture on Charles Bon's dead body. But in any case the visit, at Judith's invitation, of the woman to Charles Bon's grave would have impressed the whole relationship upon General Compson and upon his son, Mr. Compson. Mr. Compson thinks that it was the fact of the mistress that made Thomas Sutpen oppose Bon's marriage to his daughter, but that Henry was so deeply committed to his friend that he refused to believe what his father told him about Bon's mistress, chose to go away with Charles, and only at the very end, when Charles Bon was actually standing before his father's house, used the gun to prevent the match.

It is not a very plausible theory. For though it could account for Sutpen's opposition to Bon, it hardly explains Henry's violent action, taken so late in the day. Mr. Compson does the best that he can with this aspect of the story and says (p. 97): "[Henry] loved grieved and killed, still grieving and, I believe, still loving Bon, the man to whom he gave four years of probation, four years in which to renounce and dissolve the other marriage, knowing that the four years of hoping and waiting would be in vain." But Mr. Compson has to concede that, after all, "it's just incredible. It just does not explain. . . . something is missing" (p. 100).

Quentin's other informant about the Sutpens is Miss Rosa Coldfield, Sutpen's sister-in-law. Miss Rosa clearly does not understand what happened. She exclaims that "Judith's marriage [was] forbidden without rhyme or reason" (p. 18), and her only theory for accounting for the murder is that Sutpen was a demon, and as a demon, dowered his children with a curse which made them destroy themselves. Even Judith evidently did not know why her marriage was forbidden nor did she know why her brother killed Charles Bon. After the murder and Henry's flight, Judith tells Mrs. Compson, the General's wife, that the war will soon be over now because "they [the Confederate soldiers] have begun to shoot one another" (p. 128). The remark indicates her bafflement as well as her despair.

By the time we have reached the end of section 5—that is, half way through the book—we have been given most of the basic facts of the Sutpen story but no satisfactory interpretation of it. We know the story of Sutpen's life in the Mississippi community pretty much as the community itself knew it, but the events do not make sense. The second half of the book may be called an attempt at interpretation. When section 6 opens, we are in Quentin's room at Harvard and Quentin is reading a letter from his father telling about the death of Miss Rosa Coldfield. From this time on until past midnight, Quentin and Shreve discuss the story of Sutpen and make their own conjectures as to what actually happened. In this second half of the book there are, to be sure, further disclosures about Sutpen, especially with reference to his early life before he came to Mississippi. Sutpen, it turns out, had once told the story of his early life to General Compson, and his information had been passed on to Quentin through Mr. Compson. As Shreve and Quentin talk, Quentin feeds into the conversation from time to time more material from his father's and grandfather's memory of events, and one very brilliant scene which he himself remembers: how, hunting quail on a gray autumn day, he and his father came upon the graves in the Sutpen family graveyard and his father told him the touching story of Judith's later life. But as the last four sections of the book make plain, we are dealing with an intricate imaginative reconstruction of events leading up to the murder of Charles Bon—a plausible account of what may have happened, not what necessarily did happen.

If the reader reminds himself how little hard fact there is to go on—how much of the most important information about the motivation of the central characters comes late and is, at best, vague and ambiguous—he will appreciate how much of the story of Sutpen and especially of Sutpen's children has been spun out of the imaginations of Quentin and Shreve.

Absalom, Absalom! is indeed from one point of view a wonderful detective story—by far the best of Faulkner's several flirtations with this particular genre. It may also be considered to yield a nice instance of how the novelist works, for Shreve and Quentin both show a good deal of the insights of the novelist and his imaginative capacity for constructing plausible motivations around a few given facts. This theme would obviously be one dear to Faulkner's heart. Most important of all, however, *Absalom, Absalom!*

is a persuasive commentary upon the thesis that much of "history" is really a kind of imaginative construction. The past always remains at some level a mystery, but if we are to hope to understand it in any wise, we must enter into it and project ourselves imaginatively into the attitudes and emotions of the historical figures. Both of the boys make this sort of projection, though one would expect it to be easy for Quentin and difficult for Shreve. Actually, it does not work out in this way, for Shreve enters into the reconstruction of the past with ardor. He finds it, in his lack of any serious emotional commitment, a fascinating game—in fact, he consistently treats it as a game, saying "Let me play now." The novelty of fitting actual human beings into roles that he had earlier connected only with the stage intrigues him. At one point he teases Quentin by saying "Jesus, the South is fine, isn't it. It's better than the theatre, isn't it. It's better than Ben Hur, isn't it" (p. 217). Quentin, on the other hand, is too much involved—too fully committed to the problems and the issue—actually to enjoy the reconstruction. He feels a compulsion to do so, of course, the same compulsion that had caused him, against his better judgment, to go up into the bedroom at Sutpen's Hundred and look upon the wasted face of Henry Sutpen.

To note that the account of the Sutpens which Shreve and Quentin concoct is largely an imaginative construct is not to maintain that it is necessarily untrue. Their version of events is plausible, and the author himself—for whatever that may be worth—suggests that some of the scenes which they palpably invented were probably true: e.g. "the slight dowdy woman . . . whom Shreve and Quentin had . . . invented" and who was probably "true enough" (p. 335). But it is worth remarking that we do not "know," apart from the Quentin–Shreve semifictional process, many events which a casual reader assumes actually happened.

To provide some illustrations: Charles Bon's telling Henry "So it's the miscegenation, not the incest, which you cant bear" (p. 356) is a remark that rests upon no known fact. It is a conjecture, though a plausible one. Again, Bon's agonized waiting for his father to give him the merest hint of a father's recognition and Bon's comment that this was all that Sutpen needed to do to stop his courtship of Judith are both surmises made by Quentin and Shreve. So too is the scene in which the boys imagine the visit of Bon and Henry to New Orleans and hear Bon's mother's bitter question, "So she [Judith] has fallen in love with him" (p. 335), and listen to her harsh laughter as she looks at Henry. The wonderfully touching scene in which Judith asks Charles Bon's son to call her "Aunt Judith" is presumably an imaginative construction made by Quentin.

One ought to observe in passing that in allowing the boys to make their guesses about what went on, Faulkner plays perfectly fair. Some of their guesses have the clear ring of truth. They are obviously right. On the other hand, some are justified by the flimsiest possible reasoning. For example, notice Shreve's argument (p. 344) that it was Henry, not Bon, who was wounded at the battle of Shiloh.

One of the most important devices used in the novel is the placing of Shreve in it as a kind of sounding board and mouthpiece. By doing so, Faulkner has in effect acknowledged the attitude of the modern "liberal," twentieth-century reader, who is basically rational, skeptical, without any special concern for history, and pretty well emancipated from the ties of family, race; or section. In fact, Shreve sounds very much like certain literary critics who have written on Faulkner. It was a stroke of genius on Faulkner's part to put such a mentality squarely inside the novel, for this is a way of facing criticism from that quarter and putting it into its proper perspective.

Shreve teases Quentin playfully and even affectionately, but it is not mere teasing. When Shreve strikes a pose and in his best theatrical manner assigns a dramatic speech to Wash, Faulkner, in one of his few intrusions as author, observes: "This was not flippancy. . . . It too was just that protective coloring of levity behind which the youthful shame of being moved hid itself." The author remarks on Quentin's "sullen bemusement" but also on the "flipness, the strained clowning" (p. 280) on the part of both.

It is curious that Shreve, all of whose facts have been given him by or through Quentin, is allowed in the latter chapters to do most of the imaginative work—far more, I should say, than is allowed to Quentin. This is the more interesting since Quentin has met three of the participants in the tragedy face to face and is filled with vivid impressions of the scene. Perhaps the fact that Quentin is so involved makes it difficult or distasteful for him to talk. At any rate, it is the "outsider" who does most of the imaginative reconstruction. Quentin's role at times becomes merely that of a check or brake upon Shreve's fertile imagination.

The last sections of the novel tell us a great deal about Shreve's and Quentin's differing attitudes toward history and of their own relation to history. Shreve has been genuinely moved by the story of Sutpen. For all of his teasing, he is concerned to understand, and late in the evening he says to Quentin: "Listen. I'm not trying to be funny, smart. I just want to understand it if I can and I dont know how to say it better. Because it's something my people haven't got" (p. 361). And though he cannot suppress his bantering tone in alluding to the Southern heritage—it is "a kind of entailed birthright . . . of never forgiving General Sherman, so that forevermore as long as your children's children produce children you wont be anything but a descendant of a long line of colonels killed in Pickett's charge"—Shreve's question is seriously put. What is it that Quentin as a Southerner has that Shreve does not have? It is a sense of the presence of the past, and with it, and through it, a personal access to a tragic vision. For the South has experienced defeat and guilt, and has an ingrained sense of the stubbornness of human error and of the complexity of history. The matter has been recently put very well in C. Vann Woodward's *The Burden of Southern History*: "The experience of evil and the experience of tragedy," he writes, "are parts of the Southern heritage that are as difficult to reconcile with the American legend of innocence and social felicity as the experience of poverty and defeat are to reconcile with the legends of abundance and success."

In remarking on how little of hard fact one has to go on, we should bear in mind particularly the question of Bon's Negro blood and of his kinship to Henry. Quentin says flatly (p. 269) that "nobody ever did know if Bon ever knew Sutpen was his father or not." Did anyone ever know whether Bon knew that he was part Negro? In their reconstruction of the story, Shreve and Quentin assume (p. 356) that Bon was aware that he was Henry's part-Negro half-brother (though on page 327 Quentin and Shreve assume that Bon did not know that he had Negro blood). If in fact Bon did have Negro blood, how did Shreve and Quentin come by that knowledge? As we have seen, neither Judith nor Miss Rosa had any inkling of it. Nor did Mr. Compson. Early in the novel he refers to Bon's "sixteenth part negro son." Since Bon's mistress was an octoroon, his son could be one-sixteenth Negro only on the assumption that Charles Bon was of pure white blood—and this is evidently what Mr. Compson does assume. Mr. Compson, furthermore, knows nothing about Bon's kinship to Henry.

The conjectures made by Shreve and Quentin—even if taken merely as conjectures—render the story of Sutpen plausible. They make much more convincing sense of the story than Mr. Compson's notions were able to make. And that very fact suggests their probable truth. But are they more than plausible theories? Is there any real evidence to support the view that Bon was Sutpen's son by a part-Negro wife? There is, and the way in which this evidence is discovered constitutes another, and the most decisive, justification for regarding *Absalom, Absalom!* as a magnificent detective story. Precisely what was revealed and how it was revealed are worth a rather careful review.

In the course of his conversation with Quentin, Shreve objects that Mr. Compson "seems to have got an awful lot of delayed information awful quick, after having waited forty-five years" (p. 266). Quentin confirms the fact that his father *had* got delayed information—had got it from Quentin himself—had got it indeed the day after "we" (that is, Quentin and Miss Rosa) had gone out to Sutpen's Hundred. A little later (p. 274), when Quentin tells Shreve of Sutpen's long conversation with General Compson about his "design" and about the "mistake" that Sutpen had made in trying to carry it out, Shreve asks Quentin whether General Compson had then really known what Sutpen was talking about. Quentin answers that General Compson had not known; and Shreve, pressing the point, makes Quentin admit that he himself "wouldn't have known what anybody was talking about" if he "hadn't been out there and seen Clytie." The secret of Bon's birth, then, was revealed to Quentin on that particular visit. Shreve's way of phrasing it implies that it was from Clytie that Quentin had got his information, but, as we shall see, it is unlikely that Clytie was Quentin's informant. In any case, when Shreve puts his question about seeing Clytie, he did not know that another person besides Clytie and her nephew was living at Sutpen's Hundred.

Miss Rosa has sensed that "something"—she does not say *someone*—was "living hidden in that house." When she and Quentin visit Sutpen's Hundred, her intuition is confirmed. The hidden something turns out to be Henry Sutpen, now come home to die. Presumably, it was from Henry Sutpen that Quentin learned the crucial facts. Or did he? Here again Faulkner may seem to the reader either teasingly reticent or, upon reflection, brilliantly skillful.

We know from the last section of the book that after Miss Rosa had come down from the upstairs room with her "eyes wide and unseeing like a sleepwalker's" (p. 370), Quentin felt compelled to go up to that room and see what was there. He does go, though Faulkner does not take us with him into the room. He descends the stairs, walks out of the house, overtakes Miss Rosa, and drives her home. Later that night, however, after he has returned to his own home and is lying sleepless, he cannot—even by clenching his eyelids—shut out his vision of the bed with its yellowed sheets and its yellowed pillow and the wasted yellow face lying upon it, a face with closed "almost transparent eyelids" (p. 373). As Quentin tosses, unable to erase the picture from his eyes, we are vouchsafed one tiny scrap of his conversation with Henry, a conversation that amounts to no more than Quentin's question "And you are—?" and Henry's answer that he is indeed Henry Sutpen, that he has been there four years, and that he has come home to die. How extended was the conversation? How long did it last? Would Henry Sutpen have volunteered to a stranger his reason for having killed Charles Bon? Or would Quentin Compson, awed and aghast at what he saw, put such questions as these to the wasted figure upon the bed? We do not know and Faulkner—probably wisely—has not undertaken to reconstruct this interview for us. (It is possible, of course, that Henry did tell Miss Rosa why he had killed Bon and that Miss Rosa told Quentin in the course of their long ride back to Jefferson.)

At all events, the whole logic of *Absalom, Absalom!* argues that only through the presence of Henry in the house was it possible for Quentin—and through Quentin his father and Shreve and those of us who read the book—to be made privy to the dark secret that underlay the Sutpen tragedy.

At the end of the novel Shreve is able to shrug off the tragic implications and resume the tone of easy banter. His last comment abounds with the usual semi-sociological cliché the Negroes "will bleach out again like the rabbits and the birds. . . . In a few thousand years, I who regard you will also have sprung from the loins of African kings" (p. 578). Though the spell of the story has been powerful enough to fire his imagination and involve all his sympathies, he is not personally committed, and we can see him drawing back from the tragic problem and becoming again the cheery, cynical, common-sense man of the present day. In the long perspective of history, how few issues really matter! The long perspective is antihistorical: make it long enough and any "sense of history" evaporates. Lengthen it further still and the human dimension itself evaporates.

From his stance of detachment, Shreve suddenly, and apropos of nothing, puts to Quentin the question "Why do you hate the South?" And Quentin's passionate denial that he hates it tells its own story of personal involvement and distress. The more naïve reader may insist on having an answer: "Well, does he hate it?" And the response would have to be, I suppose, another question: "Does Stephen Daedalus hate Dublin?" Or, addressing the question to Stephen's creator, "Did James Joyce hate Ireland?" The answer here would surely have to be yes and no. In any case, Joyce was so obsessed with Ireland and so deeply involved in it that he spent his life writing about it.

At this point, however, it may be more profitable to put a different question. What did the story of Sutpen mean to Quentin? Did it mean to him what it has apparently meant to most of the critics who have written on this novel—the story of the curse of slavery and how it involved Sutpen and his children in ruin? Surely this is to fit the story to a neat, oversimple formula. Slavery was an evil. But other slaveholders avoided Sutpen's kind of defeat and were exempt from his special kind of moral blindness.

What ought to be plain, in any event, is that it is Henry's part in the tragic tale that affects Quentin the most. Quentin had seen Henry with his own eyes and Henry's involvement in slavery was only indirect. Even Henry's dread of miscegenation was fearfully complicated with other issues, including the problem of incest. In view of what we learn of Quentin in *The Sound and the Fury*, the problem of incest would have fascinated him and made him peculiarly sensitive to Henry's torment. Aside from his personal problem, however, Sutpen's story had for Quentin a special meaning that it did not have for Shreve.

The story embodied the problem of evil and of the irrational: Henry was beset by conflicting claims; he was forced to make intolerably hard choices—between opposed goods or between conflicting evils. Had Henry cared much less for Bon, or else much less for Judith, he might have promoted the happiness of one without feeling that he was sacrificing that of the other. Or had he cared much less for either and much more for himself, he might have won a cool and rational detachment, a coign of vantage from which even objections to miscegenation and incest would appear to be irrational prejudices, and honor itself a quaint affectation whose saving was never worth the price of a bullet. Had Henry been not necessarily wiser but simply more cynical or more gross or more selfish, there would have been no tragedy.

To say that Quentin was peculiarly susceptible to this meaning of Henry's story is not to make of Shreve a monster of inhumanly cool irrationality. But Shreve is measurably closer to the skepticism and detachment that allow modern man to dismiss the irrational claims from which Quentin cannot free himself and which he honors to his own cost.

The reader of *Absalom, Absalom!* might well follow Quentin's example. If he must find in the story of the House of Sutpen something that has special pertinence to the tragic dilemmas of the South, the aspect of the story to stress is not the downfall of Thomas Sutpen, a man who is finally optimistic, rationalistic, and afflicted with elephantiasis of the will. Instead, he ought to attend to the story of Sutpen's children.

The story of Judith, though muted and played down in terms of the whole novel, is one of the most moving that Faulkner has ever written. She has in her the best of her father's traits. She is the stout-hearted little girl who witnesses without flinching scenes which force poor Henry to grow sick and vomit. She is the young woman who falls in love with a fascinating stranger, the friend of her brother, who means to marry him in spite of her father's silent opposition, and who matches her father's strength of will with a quiet strength of her own. She endures the horror of her fiancé's murder and buries his body. She refuses to commit suicide; she keeps the place going for her father's return. Years later it is Judith who sees to it that Bon's mistress has an opportunity to visit his grave, who brings Bon's child to live with her after his mother's death and, at least in Quentin's reconstruction of events, tries to get the little boy to recognize her as his aunt and to set him free, pushing him on past the barriers of color. When she fails to do so, she still tries to protect him. She nurses him when he sickens of yellow fever, and she dies with him in the epidemic. She is one of Faulkner's finest characters of endurance—and not merely through numb, bleak Stoicism but also through compassion and love. Judith is doomed by misfortunes not of her making, but she is not warped and twisted by them. Her humanity survives them.

Because Henry knew what presumably Judith did not know, the secret of Bon's birth, his struggle—granted the circumstances of his breeding, education, and environment—was more difficult than Judith's. He had not merely to endure but to act, and yet any action that he could take would be cruelly painful. He was compelled to an agonizing decision. One element that rendered tragic any choice he might make is revealed in Henry's last action, his coming home to die. One might have thought that after some forty years, Henry would have stayed in Mexico or California or New York or wherever he was, but the claims of locality and family are too strong and he returns to Sutpen's Hundred.

Absalom, Absalom! is the most memorable of Faulkner's novels—and memorable in a very special way. Though even the intelligent reader may feel at times some frustration with the powerful but darkly involved story, with its patches of murkiness and its almost willful complications of plot, he will find himself haunted by individual scenes and episodes, rendered with almost compulsive force. He will probably remember vividly such a scene as Henry's confrontation of his sister Judith after four years of absence at war—the boy in his "patched and faded gray tunic," crashing into the room in which his sister stands clutching against her partially clothed nakedness the yellowed wedding dress, and shouting to her: "Now you cant marry him . . . because he's dead . . . I killed him" (p. 172). Or there is Miss Rosa's recollection of the burial of Charles Bon. As she talks to Quentin she relives the scene: the "slow, maddening rasp, rasp, rasp, of the saw" and "the flat deliberate hammer blows" as Wash and another white man work at the coffin through the "slow and sunny afternoon," with Judith in her faded dress and "faded gingham sun-bonnet . . . giving them directions about making it." Miss Rosa, who has never seen Bon alive and for whom he is therefore a fabulous creature, a mere dream, recalls that she "tried to take the full weight of the coffin" as they carried it down the stairs in order "to prove to myself that he was really in it" (p. 151).

There is the wonderful scene of Thomas Sutpen's return to Sutpen's Hundred, the iron man dismounting from his "gaunt and jaded horse," saying to Judith, "Well, daughter," and touching his bearded lips to her forehead. There follows an exchange that is as laconically resonant as any in Greek tragedy: "'Henry's not—?' 'No. He's not here.'—'Ah. And—?' 'Yes. Henry killed him'" (p. 159). With the last sentence Judith bursts into tears, but it is the only outburst of which Judith is ever guilty.

The reader will remember also the scenes of Sutpen's boyhood and young manhood—perhaps most vivid of all of them, that in which the puzzled boy is turned away from the plantation door by the liveried servant. Sometimes the haunting passage is one of mere physical description: the desolate Sutpen burial ground with the "flat slabs . . . cracked across the middle by their own weight (and vanishing into the hole where the brick coping of one vault had fallen in was a smooth faint path worn by some small animal—possum probably—by generations of some small animal since there could have been nothing to eat in the grave for a long time) though the lettering was quite legible: *Ellen Coldfield Sutpen. Born October 9, 1817. Died January 23, 1863*" (p. 188). One remembers also the account of something that had taken place earlier in this same graveyard, when Bon's octoroon mistress, a "magnolia-faced woman a little plumper now, a woman created of by and for darkness whom the artist Beardsley might have dressed, in a soft flowing gown designed not to infer bereavement or widowhood ... knelt beside the grave and arranged her skirts and wept," while beside her stood her "thin delicate child" with its "smooth ivory sexless face" (p. 193).

There is, too, the ride out to Sutpen's Hundred in the "furnace-breathed" Mississippi night in which Quentin shares his buggy with the frail and fanatical Miss Rosa, and smells her "fusty camphor-reeking shawl" and even her "airless black cotton umbrella." On this journey, as Miss Rosa clutches to her a flashlight and a hatchet, the implements of her search, it seems to Quentin that he can hear "the single profound suspiration of the parched earth's agony rising toward the imponderable and aloof stars" (p. 362). Most vivid of all is the great concluding scene in which Clytie, seeing the ambulance approaching to bear Henry away, fires "the monstrous tinder-dry rotten shell" (p. 375) of a house, and from an upper window defies the intruders, her "tragic gnome's face beneath the clean headrag, against a red background of fire, seen for a moment between two swirls of smoke, looking down at them, perhaps not even now with triumph and no more of despair than it had ever worn, possibly even serene above the melting clapboards" (p. 376).

These brilliantly realized scenes reward the reader and sustain him as he struggles with the novel; but it ought to be remembered that they are given their power by the way in which the novel is structured and thus constitute a justification of that peculiar structure. For example, consider Henry's confrontation of Judith with the word that he has killed her lover. The incident is alluded to in remarks made to Quentin by Miss Rosa (section 1), and later by Mr. Compson as he talks to Quentin on the porch of their home in the fading daylight (section 2). But the first major preparation for this scene does not occur until the end of section 3 with Wash's riding up to Miss Rosa's house on a saddleless mule and shouting "Hello, hello" at intervals until she comes to the door. Whereupon, "he lowered his voice somewhat, though not much. 'Air you Rosie Coldfield?' he said" (p. 133). But what he had to tell her is not stated. The reader may very well guess what it was, but if he wants to hear the rest of Wash's speech, he must read on all the way through section 4 to find, at the very end: "'Air you Rosie Coldfield? Then you better come on out yon. Henry has done shot that durn French feller. Kilt him dead as a beef.'" But the postponement of what Wash had to impart is, of course, no mere teasing of the reader. Because of what we learn in section 4, the episode becomes invested with tremendously increased power. The repetition with added and altered detail functions somewhat like the folk-ballad device of incremental repetition.

The conclusion of section 5 brings us up to the confrontation scene itself. For this scene, the sequel to the murder so tersely reported by Wash, is now visualized for us through Quentin's imagination: our own imaginations have been prepared for the presentation, and we are likely to hear the brother and sister, as Quentin does, speaking to one another in "brief staccato sentences like slaps, as if they stood breast to breast striking one another in turn neither making any attempt to guard against the blows" (p. 172).

The ending of section 5, however, does something more than bring to climactic focus the meeting of Henry and Judith: it generates a new line of suspense. For Quentin is jerked out of his abstracted reverie by suddenly apprehending the significance of something Miss Rosa has been saying. He asks her to repeat, and section 5 closes with her words: "There's something in that house. . . . Something living in it. Hidden in it. It has been out there for four years, living hidden in that house" (p. 172).

Section 6 resumes other narrative lines of the story and describes the decaying mansion at Sutpen's Hundred as Quentin had seen it a few years earlier on a hunt. But at the end of the section Shreve recurs to the possibility of something hidden at Sutpen's Hundred and of the journey that Quentin made with Rosa to test her intuition that this was so. The section ends with Shreve's excited query: "and so you went out there, drove the twelve miles at night in a buggy and you found Clytie and Jim Bond both in it and you said You see? and she (the Aunt Rosa) still said No and so you went on: and there was?" "Yes." "Wait then. . . . For God's sake wait" (p. 216).

Shreve is here the proper surrogate for the reader. The reader too wants to know the secret, but he does not want (or ought not to want) to know too quickly. Shreve, who is in some sense the perfect audience, yearns to know the secret, but only at the proper time when the revelation can come with full significance. Scattered through sections 7 and 8 there are a number of references to what Quentin's journey to Sutpen's Hundred revealed, though each of these sections ends with another and less important disclosure. The account of Quentin's journey is reserved for the last pages of the book. Indeed, though Quentin must have at some point during the evening told Shreve what he found at Sutpen's Hundred, his recounting it to Shreve is in fact never presented in this book. Instead, there is a compulsive re-enactment of the episode as Quentin lies in his bed, unable to sleep, feeling, even with the "chill pure weight of the snow-breathed New England air on his face" the dust of that "breathless . . . Mississippi September night" (p. 362).

Absalom, Absalom! is in many respects the most brilliantly written of all Faulkner's novels, whether one considers its writing line by line and paragraph by paragraph, or its structure, in which we are moved up from one suspended note to a higher suspended note and on up further still to an almost intolerable climax. The intensity of the book is a function of the structure. The deferred and suspended resolutions are necessary if the great scenes are to have their full vigor and significance. Admittedly, the novel is a difficult one, but the difficulty is not forced and factitious. It is the price that has to be paid by the reader for the novel's power and significance. There are actually few instances in modern fiction of a more perfect adaptation of form to matter and of an intricacy that justifies itself at every point through the significance and intensity which it makes possible. . . .

MICHAEL MILLGATE

The Hamlet

Faulkner said at the University of Virginia that he wrote *The Hamlet* "in the late twenties," mostly in the form of short stories, and that in 1940 he "got it pulled together."[1] Writing to Malcolm Cowley in 1945, he had given a fuller account of the book's history

> THE HAMLET was incepted as a novel. When I began it, it produced Spotted Horses, went no further. About two years later suddenly I had THE HOUND, then JAMSHYD'S COURTYARD, mainly because SPOTTED HORSES had created a character I fell in love with: the itinerant sewing-machine agent named Suratt. Later a man of that name turned up at home, so I changed my man to Ratliff for the reason thag [*sic*] my whole town spent much of its time trying to decide just what living man I was writing about, the one literary criticism of the town being 'How in the hell did he remember all that and when did that happen anyway?' Meanwhile, my book had created Snopes and his clan, who produced stories in their saga which are to fall in later volume: MULE IN THE YARD, BRASS, etc. This over about ten years, until one day I decided I had better start on the first volume or I'd never get any of it down. So I wrote an

---

From *The Achievement of William Faulkner*, pp. 180–200, 325–327, New York: Random House. © 1966 by Michael Millgate.

induction toward the spotted horse story, which included BARN BURNING, AND [*sic*] WASH, which I discovered had no place in that book at all. Spotted Horses became a longer story, picked up the HOUND (rewritten and much longer and with the character's name changed from Cotton to Snopes), and went on with JAMSHYD'S COURTYARD.[2]

There is no doubt that Faulkner began writing a Snopes novel some time in late 1926 or early 1927. In a newspaper article written at about that time Phil Stone spoke of two novels on which Faulkner was working: one was the book we now know as *Sartoris*, the other "something of a saga of an extensive family connection of typical 'poor white trash.'"[3] Meriwether, quoting this article, also quotes from a letter which Stone wrote to him in 1957: "Bill once wrote fifteen or twenty pages on the idea of the Snopes trilogy which he entitled 'Father Abraham'. . . ."[4] These comments substantiate Faulkner's own statements about the composition of the book, and help to date the 25-page manuscript of "Father Abraham" now in the Arents Collection of the New York Public Library.

This manuscript opens with an extended description of Flem as a symbolic and legendary figure, a by-product of the democratic principle in action and successor to the Southern gentleman as the representative figure of his region and his time. There follows an account of the Old Frenchman place and its legend, and of the inhabitants of Frenchman's Bend, which bears a direct and sometimes a close relationship to the opening pages of *The Hamlet*. Once the setting has been established the "Father Abraham" manuscript goes on to describe a number of characters, notably Uncle Billy Varner and his daughter Eula, and continues with a telling of the "spotted horses" story, from the standpoint of the omniscient author, that is similar in essentials to the version which appears in Chapter I of "The Peasants", the fourth book of *The Hamlet*. A typescript of "Father Abraham," now in the Alderman Library, introduces a number of features that are absent from the manuscript and develops in particular Mrs. Littlejohn's function as a silent commentator on the follies of the male world of horse-trading. It is apparently later than the manuscript and is certainly still closer to the version used in *The Hamlet*, although it seems to have gone no further than a point shortly following the moment when the injured Henry Armstid has been carried into Mrs. Littlejohn's boarding house.[5]

The "Father Abraham" manuscript gives a more or less complete account of the whole "spotted horses" episode, but its last page, written on different paper and in different ink from the preceding pages, suddenly breaks off, as though Faulkner had abruptly abandoned an attempt to extend the material further and to develop it into the Snopes novel that he apparently had in mind. The "Father Abraham" typescript may have been completed shortly afterwards; on the other hand, it may have been a product of that later stage in the history of *The Hamlet* to which Faulkner referred in his letter to Cowley: "About two years later suddenly I had THE HOUND, then JAMSHYD'S COURTYARD." "The Hound" was first published in *Harper's* in August 1931, "Lizards in Jamshyd's Courtyard" in the *Saturday Evening Post* for February 27, 1932, but it is clear from the sending schedule which Faulkner kept for his early stories that they existed in completed form by November 17, 1930, and May 27, 1930.[6] The short story *Spotted Horses* was published in *Scribner's* in June 1931, but a version may have been finished by August 25, 1930.[7] "Centaur in Brass," a Snopes story first published in the *American Mercury* (February 1932) and later incorporated in *The Town*, also existed by August 1931.[8] All of these stories, of course, may have been written at a somewhat earlier date. Faulkner says that his first attempt to write a Snopes novel did not go any further than "Spotted Horses" (i.e. "Father Abraham"), but there is no doubt that he had already worked up a great variety of Snopes material and already had in mind the general pattern of Flem's career.

Many years later he spoke of the moment when "I thought of the whole story at once like a bolt of lightning lights up a landscape and you see everything . . ."[9] The comprehensiveness of this conception is apparent from the various references to the Snopes family in *Sartoris*—brief references, to be sure, but sufficient to delineate the ground-plan of almost the whole Snopes saga:

[Montgomery Ward] Snopes was a young man, member of a seemingly inexhaustible family which for the last ten years had been moving to town in driblets from a small settlement known as Frenchman's Bend. Flem, the first Snopes, had appeared unheralded one day behind the counter of a small restaurant on a side street, patronized by country folk. With this foothold and like Abraham of old, he brought his blood and legal kin household by household, individual by individual, into town, and established them where they could gain money. Flem himself was presently manager of the city light and water plant, and for the following few years he was a sort of handy man to the municipal government; and three years ago, to old Bayard's profane astonishment and unconcealed annoyance, he became vice-president of the Sartoris bank, where already a relation of his was a bookkeeper. (*Sartoris*, p. 172)

It is presumably to *Sartoris* that Faulkner is referring when he speaks of "my book [which] had created Snopes and his clan." The novel had also created Suratt, the sewing machine agent, whose name, as Faulkner explains, he later changed to Ratliff, and it is conceivable that Faulkner—having first abandoned "Father Abraham" in order to work on *Sartoris*—returned to the Snopes material in the latter part of 1927, after the completion of the *Sartoris* typescript at the end of September. The final typescript of *The Sound and the Fury* was completed by October 1928, however, and it seems probable that the writing of this immensely ambitious work must have engrossed most if not all of Faulkner's energies during the intervening year. By the early summer of 1930, at all events, Faulkner had taken a fresh look at the Snopes material and had begun quarrying it for short stories. From the evidence of Faulkner's letter to Cowley, and in the absence of earlier manuscripts or typescripts, it would seem that "Spotted Horses," "The Hound," "Lizards in Jamshyd's Courtyard," and "Centaur in Brass" were written at this stage. The last three may have been written virtually from scratch, although Faulkner no doubt conceived of their essential features in that original vision of the whole Snopes sequence, but there is ample evidence to show that the writing of "Spotted Horses" and the subsequent incorporation of the episode in *The Hamlet* was by no means a simple process.

When composing the version of the Texas ponies anecdote which subsequently appeared in *Scribner's* as the story "Spotted Horses", Faulkner had a body of earlier material, including "Father Abraham," on which to draw, and in adapting this material he changed it radically. There is some evidence that at one stage—probably an early one—Faulkner may have experimented with a version of the story in which the "spotted horses" incident was divorced from any detailed account of Frenchman's Bend and its inhabitants;[10] in the Scribner's version actually published Faulkner did not omit this scene-setting, but he greatly reduced it in length. The most important change was in the narrative point of view, for the story is told, not in the third-person of "Father Abraham" and the novel, but in the first-person, from the point of view of a man who, although not specifically identified, is clearly the sewing-machine agent, Suratt/Ratliff. The narrator tells the story as though to a group of friends—"You-all mind the moon was nigh full that night," he says at one point—and in vigorously colloquial language: "They was colored like parrots and they was quiet as doves, and ere a one of them would kill you quick as a rattle-snake."[11] It is, in fact, essentially what the editor of Scribner's described it as being, "a tall tale with implications of tragedy";[12] but the point immediately to be made is that it is a by-product of the original Snopes conception, a story carved out of the material at a time when Faulkner, for whatever reason, felt unable or unwilling to work it up into a novel, and that the line of development between the original conception and *The Hamlet* does not pass through "Spotted Horses" as published in *Scribner's* but goes directly from "Father Abraham" to the novel. At the time when he was writing the version of the "spotted horses" episode which appears in the final section of *The Hamlet*, and also at the time when he was writing the present opening pages of the novel, Faulkner must certainly have had in front of him some version of the "Father Abraham" material; if he also had a copy of the Scribner's story he referred to it much less frequently. When adapting for incorporation into *The Hamlet* the tale of Pat Stamper's horse-trading activities which had previously been told in the Scribner's story, "Fool About a Horse," Faulkner again seems to have worked primarily from an earlier typescript rather than from the published story,[13] though no doubt he also had a copy of the story readily to hand.

Earlier in the letter to Cowley from which we have already quoted, Faulkner says that the *Scribner's* version of "Spotted Horses" was in the nature of a condensation of several chapters of *The Hamlet*, and it is entirely possible that Faulkner had actually got some way towards completing a Snopes novel at the time when "Spotted Horses" was written. Some day, indeed, firm evidence of this in the form of further manuscript or typescript material may become available, and in the meantime it is worth noting that Aubrey Starke, in his important article on Faulkner published in 1934, makes reference to the "the long promised, and eagerly awaited 'Snopes saga',—chief title on Mr. Faulkner's list of unpublished work."[14] Starke's further remarks on the Snopeses make clear how much material dealing with them Faulkner had already published by this time, and show that, to an intelligent reader, the whole trend of his treatment of them was already plain:

> And even if *The Snopes Saga* were not already promised we could safely predict that Mr. Faulkner would continue for some time to come the story of the Snopeses, for the rise of the class to which the Snopeses belong and the decay and disintegration of the class to which Sartorises and Compsons belong is surely the central, symbolic theme of Mr. Faulkner's comedy, as it—more than the traditional color problem—is the central problem of that part of the world in which Mr. Faulkner lives.[15]

In fact, it was not until several years later that Faulkner "pulled together" the various segments of Snopes material, although even at this stage he got no further than *The Hamlet*. It was to be another seventeen years before the publication of a further volume, *The Town*, despite the fact that the conclusion of *The Hamlet* clearly invites a sequel—the final page of the typescript setting copy actually bears the deleted words, "end Volume One."

The final composition of *The Hamlet* apparently began some time late in 1938, and a considerable amount of manuscript and typescript material has survived from this stage, including a manuscript which is practically complete up to a point corresponding to the end of the second section of

Book Three, Chapter II, of the published book, a complete typescript setting copy, and many miscellaneous pages of both manuscript and typescript.[16] In the process of working towards the final version of the novel Faulkner made a great many minor additions and improvements, and the typescript setting copy is especially of interest for the evidence it provides of the many rearrangements which Faulkner made in the material of the book before eventually deciding on its final form. To take one example of many, it is clear that at one time the opening of the first new paragraph on page 128 of the published book appeared not in the first chapter of the "Eula" section but as the beginning of a proposed third chapter.[17]

The most interesting features of manuscript and typescript alike, however, are the vestiges of Faulkner's experimentation with different opening chapters. Faulkner mentions to Cowley that when he began pulling *The Hamlet* together he wrote an "induction toward the spotted horse story"; he adds that the induction included "Barn Burning" and "Wash"— "which I discovered had no place in that book at all." It seems remarkable that Faulkner should ever have thought that "Wash", much of which he had already incorporated into *Absalom, Absalom!*, might find a place in the "Snopes Saga," and one can only surmise that he may have thought of giving an historical dimension to his largely economic study of the rise of the "poor white" Flem Snopes:[18] is he later used "Was" to add such a dimension to his treatment of white–Negro relationships in *Go Down, Moses*. At all events, there appears to be no clear evidence to show that "Wash" was incorporated into any of the later versions of *The Hamlet*: there is no such evidence, at least, in the manuscript and typescript versions at the University of Virginia.

The case of "Barn Burning" is different. The 17-page manuscript of the story in the Alderman Library bears the heading "BOOK ONE/ Chapter I" in addition to the deleted title "Barn Burning," while the 32-page typescript bears no title at all but simply the heading "Chapter One."[19] Deleted pagination in the typescript setting copy of *The Hamlet* shows that 32 pages have at some stage been removed and very clearly suggests that "Barn Burning" was until a fairly late stage incorporated into the novel as its opening chapter, with a version of the present first chapter as Chapter II. Sometime during the winter of 1938–1939, however, Faulkner must have changed his mind about the way the novel should open: among a group of rejected typescript pages in the Alderman Library there is a version of page 1, close to the first page (p. 3) of the published book, which bears the pencilled editorial note "Rec'd 3/20/39," while "Barn Burning" itself was published as an independent entity, and with only minor alterations from the typescript version headed "Chapter One," in *Harper's Monthly* for June 1939. Faulkner seems to have experimented with a number of other possible openings to the novel, including one which began with the first encounter between Jody

Varner and Ab Snopes which now appears on page 8 of the published book. It is hard to think that this would have made a satisfactory opening, but there is no doubt that the deeply moving story of "Barn Burning" would have been in many ways an extremely effective introduction.[20] We do not know why Faulkner finally decided to take it out, but it may have been in some measure the result of a decision not to use Colonel Sartoris Snopes, the boy of "Barn Burning," as a character elsewhere in the novel, or of some feeling that the episode gave too favourable an impression of the Snopes family to serve satisfactorily as a prologue to the history of Flem. The boy is certainly absent, apart from Ratliff's reference to another little Snopes whom he remembers having once seen, from the summary of the narrative events of "Barn Burning" which appears in the present opening chapter.

The long history of *The Hamlet* reveals it clearly as a novel conceived as a single whole but written over a period of many years, with many interruptions, much revision and reworking, and a continually enriching accretion of observation, anecdote and imagery; the finished book, far from being a series of loosely connected incidents,[21] demands consideration as a carefully organised and wholly organic structure. An example of the care and deliberate artistry which went into the composition of *The Hamlet* is provided by Faulkner's extremely skilful incorporation of the "Fool About a Horse" and "Spotted Horses" episodes. As short stories "Fool About a Horse" and "Spotted Horses" are fairly straightforward and very funny tall tales of men being successfully and outrageously tricked in horse-trades.[22] The stories remain firmly within the tall tale convention, with no wider implications. When these episodes appear in the wider context of the novel, however, the characters who in the short stories are little more than conventional counters become fully known to us as individuals, as human beings capable of suffering. In these circumstances Faulkner deliberately adapts and manipulates the tall-tale convention so that while it does not control and delimit the action, as it does in the short stories, it remains as an ironic background against which the events of the novel are played out, its restricted outlines providing an implicit contrast to the more fully realised characters and actions of the novel and at the same time offering one possible way of viewing these events. In a sense it is another example of that multiple point of view which is fundamental to so much of Faulkner's work. The "Spotted Horses" episode as we have it in *The Hamlet* is a brilliant variation on the traditional horse-trade theme, but it also tells us a great deal about the economic and social relationships operating within the world of Frenchman's Bend and brings out with painful clarity the suffering implicit for the losers in a horse-trade and for their wives and families—something which lies wholly beyond the limits of the tall tale. The episode also places Flem Snopes among his fellows, the other traders of genius, but at the same time distinguishes him from them: he appears as absolutely predatory and unpitying in his treatment of Mrs. Armstid, he employs an agent, and we see that he never treads the same path twice, his victims being not merely fresh scalps as they would be for Pat Stamper, but further upward steps on the ladder leading to the banker's mansion in Jefferson.

The "Spotted Horses" and "Fool About a Horse" episodes thus fall into place in the total pattern of the novel as versions of the tall tale, itself an essential feature of the novel's mode, and as stages in the central narrative of the rise of Snopesism. They have an even more important function, however, as variations on the theme of greed, one of the two major themes running throughout the book. The other principal theme is that of love, and the parallel and often inter-reflecting investigations of love and greed, of men dominated by the desire for sexual or economic possession, are pursued in terms of various episodes of love and marriage, on the one hand, and of trading and barter on the other. The view that this thematic pattern provides the chief unifying factor in *The Hamlet* seems first to have been clearly propounded by Robert Penn Warren,[23] and it is now so firmly established that there is some danger of the novel's unity being thought of as exclusively thematic. It is true that the linear progression of the novel is constantly interrupted and diversified by a series of stories and episodes which are chiefly significant in terms of their relationship to the central themes. But such apparent diversions all possess strong narrative links with the main action, and in view of the criticisms which have often been made of *The Hamlet*'s "episodic" structure it seems necessary to emphasise the strong element of straightforward narrative continuity which runs throughout.

The theme which is the more closely tied to the narrative continuity of the book is that of greed and self-interest, and it is perhaps worth noting that it was this theme which seems to have dominated, almost exclusively, the Snopes material which Faulkner wrote during the early stages of his extended work on *The Hamlet* and its successors; the counterpointed theme of love seems to have been added during that final "pulling together" of *The Hamlet* in the late 1930's. In Book One of the novel, "Flew," as we follow the rise of Flem Snopes to the point where he is able to supplant Will Varner in his favourite flour-barrel chair at the Old Frenchman place, it is the theme of greed which predominates, although Book One also creates most of the characters who are to play major roles later in the novel as well as many of the situations through which Faulkner later develops the theme of love. The shift of interest to this latter theme in Book Two is heralded by its title, "Eula," but after the stories of the implacable passivity of Eula and the passionate fury of Labove have been told, Faulkner skilfully involves them in the theme of self-interested greed and swings the whole section into line with the central narrative by means of Eula's marriage to Flem and Ratliff's vision of Flem taking over Hell.

Book Three, "The Long Summer," is taken up with the stories of Ike Snopes, Houston, and Mink Snopes, each story merging smoothly into its successor: Ike's beloved cow belongs at first to Houston, Houston himself is murdered by Mink. These episodes relate primarily to the theme of love, but the theme of greed irresistibly enters, generally with tragic or ironic effects. It would be ridiculous to speak of Ike's passion for the cow as being endorsed by Faulkner, but the heightened language, the mythological allusions, and the sensitive evocation of nature all work to persuade us at least of its absolute sincerity and generosity; what finally appear as more grotesque and perverted than Ike's own role are the attempts of his relatives to exploit his love and, Ratliff suspects, to turn it to profit. The episode closes, however, with a shift of mood entirely characteristic of this immensely diversified novel, and we are given the almost unqualified humour of I.O.'s successful trickery of Eck, who finds himself paying far more than his fair share of the cost of buying the cow for slaughter and so protecting the Snopes name:

> "But I still dont see why I got to pay fifteen dollars, when all you got to pay is—?"
>
> "Because you got four children. And you make five. And five times three is fifteen."
>
> "I aint got but three yet," Eck said.
>
> "Aint that just what I said? five times three? If that other one was already here, it would make four, and five times four is twenty dollars, and then I wouldn't have to pay anything."
>
> "Except that somebody would owe Eck three dollars and twenty cents change," Ratliff said.
>
> "What?" I.O. said. But he immediately turned back to his cousin or nephew. "And you got the meat and the hide," he said. "Cant you even try to keep from forgetting that?" (p. 234)[24]

Flem, absent throughout "The Long Summer," returns to Frenchman's Bend at the beginning of Book Four, "The Peasants"; his wife, Eula, has returned at the end of the previous book, bringing with her, Persephone-like, the end of that bitter winter "from which the people as they became older were to establish time and date events" (p. 296). The economic motif now again becomes dominant, first in the sale of the spotted Texas horses and finally in the defeat of Ratliff himself partly betrayed by cupidity, in the affair of the salted treasure hoard, and as Flem moves off on the last page we see that in linear terms *The Hamlet* can be simply and accurately described as the story of Flem's upward progress from near-rags to near-

riches, from a dirt-farm to the ownership of a substantial bank-balance, a
superbly handsome wife, and a half-share in a Jefferson restaurant. It is in
the later novels of the trilogy that Faulkner completes what he must have
recognised as being, among many other things, an ironic version of the
American "success" myth.

Of the various episodes of the novel, it can be argued that the story
of Labove is somewhat tenuously connected with the other events and
characters; the others, however, are strongly bound to the central narrative
line. All the episodes, including Labove's, are related in a multiplicity of ways
both to the major themes of the novel and to each other. The various tales
of barter and trading all throw light upon one another, and upon the whole
economic and social situation of Frenchman's Bend at this particular moment
in time. Similarly interrelated are the various marriages and love stories,
and we can see that although the action of the novel tends to focus on the
male world epitomised by the horse-swap, Faulkner also offers through his
presentation of such characters as Ab's wife, Mink's wife, and Mrs. Armstid
a series of comments on the role of women in this society, and especially
on their capacity for sheer endurance. If we compare the short story, "The
Hound," with the Mink Snopes portion of "The Long Summer," in which
the same narrative material appears, we can see that although the short story
is extremely powerful in its own right, the novel version has many additional
qualities which it can accommodate simply because it is not a separate entity
but a constituent part of a larger and intricately interrelated whole. The short
story, for example, has no counterpart to the following passage in the novel:

> [Mink] watched the night emerge from the bottom and mount
> through the bitten corn, taking corn, taking the house itself at
> last and, still rising, become as two up-opening palms releasing
> the westward-flying ultimate bird of evening. Below him,
> beyond the corn, the fireflies winked and drifted against the
> breast of darkness; beyond, within it, the steady booming of the
> frogs was the steady pulse and beat of the dark heart of night, so
> that at last when the unvarying moment came—that moment
> as unvarying from one dusk to the next as the afternoon's
> instant when he would awake—the beat of that heart seemed
> to fall still too, emptying silence for the first deep cry of strong
> and invincible grief. He reached his hand backward and took
> up the gun. (p. 263)

In the limited framework of the short story such a passage would be wholly
out of proportion. In the context of the novel, however, this description of
the swamp lands near Mink's farm serves, at the simplest level, to extend a

little further the overall description of the countryside around Frenchman's Bend, and, as such, it falls naturally into place in a larger pattern. But nature imagery is also being used here, as throughout the novel, to evoke and define the particular quality of the experiential moment and at the same time, as with a kind of visual rhetoric, to elevate moments and events to a higher, more general level of significance, and this is something of a quite different and more ambitious order. Throughout the novel Faulkner insists on the closeness to nature of the world of Frenchman's Bend, and his presentation of that world makes it possible for him to invoke nature imagery without any sense of arbitrariness or strain. This is especially, and most remarkably, true of the account of Ike Snopes's love for the cow, in which the rapturous evocation of the beauty and fecundity of nature is still further heightened by extravagant effects of rhetorical language and mythological allusion.

Stylistically, indeed, *The Hamlet* is one of Faulkner's greatest triumphs. Throughout the novel he exercises the utmost flexibility of style and language, ranging from direct and simple narrative to the colloquial vigour of Ratliff's telling of the "Barn Burning" and "Fool About a Horse" materials, to the baroque elevation of many of the passages describing Eula and, especially, Ike's idyll with the cow. Each episode is treated in a manner which brings out its individual quality but which also establishes its place in the structural and thematic patterns of the novel as a whole, and, where necessary, its relationship to more universal frames of reference: thus the mythological allusions in passages about Ike and Eula serve to suggest the degree to which their stories resemble those epitomisations of human experience embodied in ancient myth. This stylistic virtuosity is early established as an essential aspect of the novel's technique, and by the time Book Three has been reached it has clearly become irrelevant to wonder whether Mink himself, in the passage quoted, would have regarded the approach of darkness in quite this way. No more than in *As I Lay Dying* is Faulkner restricted to the vocabulary and manner of the characters whose attitudes and feelings he is describing: from the beginning of the novel he has established a mode which permits him to match rhetoric not so much to individuals as to emotional states and moments of crisis—of joy, agony, discovery, awareness of beauty—or, rather, to the significance of those states and moments in relation to the overall meaning of the novel.

That Faulkner is clearly aware of writing in a language foreign to his characters is evident from those moments when he skilfully plays off the richness of his formal language against the juxtaposed simplicity of colloquial speech. As Ratliff and his companions walk back to Mrs. Littlejohn's with Will Varner, who is to attend the injured Henry Armstid, we are given a description of the moonlit night:

The moon was now high overhead, a pearled and mazy yawn in the soft sky, the ultimate ends of which rolled onward, whorl on whorl, beyond the pale stars and by pale stars surrounded. They walked in a close clump, tramping their shadows into the road's mild dust, blotting the shadows of the burgeoning trees which soared, trunk branch and twig against the pale sky, delicate and finely thinned. They passed the dark store. Then the pear tree came in sight. It rose in mazed and silver immobility like exploding snow; the mockingbird still sang in it. "Look at that tree," Varner said. "It ought to make this year, she."

"Corn'll make this year too," one said.

"A moon like this is good for every growing thing outen earth," Varner said. (pp. 350–351)

Here the simple remark, "Corn'll make this year," stands in a mutually enriching relationship to the elevated description of the "burgeoning" life of the spring landscape seen by moonlight; the characters themselves are clearly incapable of speaking of nature in the terms which Faulkner employs, but by placing the countryman's ostensibly practical observation in the context of the description he suggests that the men, for all their simplicity, are not unaffected by the beauty of what they see.

In the larger context of the novel the passage just quoted is also closely related to Faulkner's presentation of Eula Varner, as her father continues his remarks on the fecundating properties of the moon with an account of how Mrs. Varner lay in the moonlight after Eula had been conceived in order to ensure that the child would be a girl. Throughout the novel Eula is associated with fertility and the forces of nature and evoked in terms of repeated allusions to the pagan deities, to Helen and Venus and Persephone, and her marriage with Flem Snopes, that forced and grotesque union of fecundity and sterility, provides *The Hamlet* with its most disturbing, most affronting, symbol. Labove, the schoolmaster, whose own love for Eula takes on almost the nature of demonic possession, foresees the marriage of this Venus, this supreme embodiment of fertility and the sexual principle, to some "crippled Vulcan . . . who would not possess her but merely own her by the single strength which power gave, the dead power of money, wealth, gewgaws, baubles, as he might own, not a picture, statue: a field, say" (p. 135). Flem is the eventual Vulcan to Eula's Venus, marrying her not from love or even desire but in exchange for a cheque and the deed to the Old Frenchman place. This coincidence of Labove's vision with subsequent narrative events serves to illustrate once again how constantly and how intricately the thematic materials of the novel interact and coalesce in terms of the narrative line: for what is significant in both the vision and its realisation

is the way in which possession of Eula is linked with the ownership and
exploitation of land, effecting a conjunction of the themes of love and greed
and setting both against the background of the land, which with its history,
and its permanence transcending history and all human concerns, constitutes
one of Faulkner's major preoccupations throughout his work.

At one stage in the writing of *The Hamlet* Faulkner apparently intended
to apply to the whole book the title, "The Peasants,"[25] which he eventually
used for the fourth and final section. One of Balzac's novels is called *Les
Paysans*, and *The Hamlet* itself opens in almost Balzacian fashion with a
precise and detailed description of the historical, geographical, social, and
economic setting of the novel's subsequent events. Later in the book this
basic framework is extended outwards by additional descriptions of places
nearby, as, for example, when Faulkner supplies vivid and often precisely
detailed impressions of Mink Snopes's farm and the land round about, and
of the countryside through which Ike walks with the cow. An extract will
suggest the degree of Faulkner's concern, in this novel, with the historical
forces, both natural and man-made, which have shaped the landscape, and
especially with the sad results of man's exploitation:

> A mile back he had left the rich, broad, flat river-bottom
> country and entered the hills—a region which topographically
> was the final blue and dying echo of the Appalachian mountains.
> Chickasaw Indians had owned it, but after the Indians it had
> been cleared where possible for cultivation, and after the Civil
> War, forgotten save by small peripatetic sawmills which had
> vanished too now, their sites marked only by the mounds of
> rotting sawdust which were not only their gravestones but the
> monuments of a people's heedless greed. Now it was a region
> of scrubby second-growth pine and oak among which dogwood
> bloomed until it too was cut to make cotton spindles, and
> old fields where not even a trace of furrow showed any more,
> gutted and gullied by forty years of rain and frost and heat into
> plateaus choked with rank sedge and briers loved of rabbits and
> quail coveys, and crumbling ravines striated red and white with
> alternate sand and clay. (p. 196)

But such passages do not stand isolated in the novel as mere historical
footnotes loosely incorporated into the text. Faulkner is concerned to
establish an image of a particular society in a particular place at a particular
time; but the image is evoked primarily in terms of characters and their
interaction, and the descriptive passages function also in terms of the human
situation. The description of Mink's house, for instance, is important for its

own sake, as an additional facet of the analytical portrait of the area, but it is also crucial to our understanding of Mink himself and of the reasons why he murders Houston. Thus there is obvious dramatic point in the utter poverty of the place being evoked through the eyes of Mink himself as he returns from the murder:

> It was dusk. He emerged from the bottom and looked up the slope of his meagre and sorry corn and saw it—the paintless two-room cabin with an open hallway between and a lean-to kitchen, which was not his, on which he paid rent but not taxes, paying almost as much in rent in one year as the house had cost to build; not old, yet the roof of which already leaked and the weather-stripping had already begun to rot away from the wall planks and which was just like the one he had been born in which had not belonged to his father either. . . . (p. 251)

Later, when Mink goes to the Negro's cabin to find his axe, his poverty is re-emphasised in the concrete terms of a comparison with the economic position of a Negro whose cabin is "shabbier than his" but whose surrounding corn is "better than his" (p. 286). Later still, as Mink is being taken to the jail in Jefferson, his own background is implicitly evoked in terms of his awareness of "the long broad rich flatlands lush with the fine harvest" (p. 293) around Whiteleaf store and of the trim and prosperous world of Jefferson itself:

> the surrey moving now beneath an ordered overarch of sunshot trees, between the clipped and tended lawns where children shrieked and played in bright small garments in the sunset and the ladies sat rocking in the fresh dresses of afternoon and the men coming home from work turned into the neat painted gates, toward plates of food and cups of coffee in the long beginning of twilight. (p. 295)

This is a world completely alien to Mink, as to the other inhabitants of Frenchman's Bend and its environs. The description at once extends, by contrast, the definition of these people's lives, and projects forward an image of the richer economic pastures to which Flem Snopes moves at the end of the novel. Nothing is wasted here. Instead of "clipped and tended lawns" the properties on which the poor whites like Mink, Ab Snopes, and Henry Armstid live have yards that are "weed-choked and grass-grown" and give an overall appearance of "cluttered desolation" (pp. 53–54); they have no "neat painted gates," for both Ab's and Mink's gates are broken and even their cabins paintless; their womenfolk wear "gray shapeless" (p. 331) garments, not "the fresh dresses of afternoon"; while their children, who are never presented as playing, have no "bright small garments" and are lucky, indeed, if they have a single pair of shoes between them.

In its sheer sociological richness *The Hamlet* recalls *Sartoris* rather than any other of Faulkner's earlier books, and it was *Sartoris* which first created in print many of the characters whose potentialities Faulkner here for the first time develops to the full. *The Hamlet* also demonstrates that sense of the slow inevitable procession of the seasons which provides an especially powerful undercurrent in *Sartoris*, but which figures to some degree in almost all of Faulkner's books from *The Marble Faun* and *Soldiers' Pay* onwards. The advance which *The Hamlet* marks over earlier novels, however, is in its wholly organic incorporation of themes and materials which had often appeared either sporadically, in set pieces, or in direct and usually ironic juxtaposition or counterpoint to the main action. One of the features of the novel which stays longest in the mind is the grouping, usually the pairing, of characters which emerges from Faulkner's thematic method. The opposition of Eula and Flem is one obvious example, but Flem's coldness and impotence is implicitly commented upon by Ike's yearning love for his cow, while the anti- or non-Snopesism of Ike is itself contrasted with the quintessential Snopesism of the other family idiot, St. Elmo. It is easy, too, to see intricate cross-references, particularly in view of Faulkner's early insistence on Eula's somewhat bovine placidity, between the Labove–Eula and Ike–cow situations. In a more direct confrontation, that between Houston and Mink Snopes, his murderer, we come to see that in large measure the very things they have in common—their fierce pride, their bitter isolation, their absolute capitulation to the women they marry—are those which most inflame their antagonism, although it should be added that Mink's principal motive for the murder seems to have been his fundamental anger at his ill-luck, especially in comparison with that of a relative like Flem or a neighbour like Houston. Even the greater attractiveness of Will Varner as compared with his son Jody—it is significant, in terms of the novel's particular scale of values, that Will Varner's sexual lustiness is not matched by his son—is also to some extent paralleled by the far greater condemnation which is reserved for Flem Snopes in comparison with his father. It has already been suggested that Faulkner may have abandoned "Barn Burning" as an opening chapter because of the extent to which it might generate undue sympathy for the Snopes family; even so, considerable sympathy for Ab's desperate economic plight is aroused in the present first chapter both by the version of the barn burning episode which Ratliff relates to Jody and by Jody's own mean calculations of how the maximum profit may be extorted from Ab's situation, while Ratliff's further recital of the Pat Stamper episode, in a version of the material first used in published form in the story, "Fool About a Horse," also evokes an Ab Snopes who is by no means a wholly unattractive figure, although Ratliff repeatedly stresses that these events date from a period before Ab "soured" (p. 30).

The most important paired opposition in the novel, and the one upon which the action as well as the morality of the book largely turns, is that between Flem and Ratliff. The whole pattern of Flem's action is set by the early episode in which Jody, as the result of his own greed and overconfidence, has put himself in the position of having to bribe Flem with a job in the store in return for a protection against Ab's barn-burning tendencies which Flem does not even promise to provide:

> Once more Varner expelled his breath through his nose. This time it was a sigh. "All right," he said. "Next week then. You'll give me that long, wont you? But you got to guarantee it." The other spat.
>   "Guarantee what?" he said. (p. 27)

It is characteristic of Flem that he puts nothing into words, that the blackmail is never stated, only implied, and that he exchanges nothing of value in return for the position which is to give him his first foothold in Frenchman's Bend. Throughout the novel Flem's silence is scarcely broken: his longest speech consists of 25 words, and he speaks only 244 words in all, with a further 33 in the Hell scene created in Ratliff's imagination. For long portions of the novel he is out of sight. He is never long out of mind, however, and usually another Snopes is present to remind us of his influence. In the second chapter of "The Long Summer," for instance, Flem is represented by one of his chief henchmen, Lump Snopes, his successor as the clerk in Varner's store. In his attempts to get his hands on the money which Houston carried, and in his complete disregard for all considerations of loyalty, humanity, or simple decency, Lump offers a concrete exemplification of greed in action which is simply a crude outward manifestation of qualities embodied more subtly but not less firmly by Flem himself. Here, as elsewhere in the novel, Faulkner uses Lump to demonstrate quite clearly the evil which Snopesism represents without needing to compromise his consistent presentation of Flem himself as a silent tactician and master strategist. The account of the sale of the spotted Texas horses which occupied most of the first chapter of "The Peasants" again shows Flem operating through substitutes, himself a silent witness or—during most of the auction and the whole of the subsequent court hearings—actually absent. Lump acts as his representative on this occasion, but not even Lump, it seems, is present to lend comfort to Mink Snopes at his trial in the County Courthouse in Jefferson.

It is Ratliff, in a passage of bitter understatement, who links Mink's situation with that of Mrs. Armstid, the chief victim in the affair of the spotted horses. After describing the dreary round of Mrs. Armstid's life as she waits for her husband's leg to heal and for Flem Snopes to return the money paid for the horse, Ratliff continues:

> And after that, not nothing to do until morning except to stay close enough where Henry can call her until it's light enough to chop the wood to cook breakfast and then help Mrs Littlejohn wash the dishes and make the beds and sweep while watching the road. Because likely any time now Flem Snopes will get back from wherever he has been since the auction, which of course is to town naturally to see about his cousin that's got into a little legal trouble, and so get that five dollars. (p. 359)

This linking of the two people who are vainly waiting for Flem to rescue them reveals in miniature the pattern of the whole novel, its establishment of a composite picture of Flem, his activities, their effect, and their significance. The heavily ironic diminutive, "a little legal trouble," as a description of the brutal murder for which Mink is to be tried, precisely catches the note of Ratliff's strenuous efforts to maintain that detachment which at this point still distinguishes him from the other actual and potential victims of Flem's machinations.

The final accolade of Flem's success in *The Hamlet* is a comment spoken by an unidentified local inhabitant, representative in his anonymity of the whole world of Frenchman's Bend:

> "Couldn't no other man have done it. Anybody might have fooled Henry Armstid. But couldn't nobody but Flem Snopes have fooled Ratliff." (p. 420)

It is characteristic of the ironies implicit in Faulkner's working out of the book's thematic patterns that it should be Ratliff, the chief and most redoubtable opponent of Snopesism, who sells Flem the share in the restaurant which gives him his first foothold in Jefferson, just as it should have been Jody, who had most to lose from his coming, who had supplied Flem with his original opening in Frenchman's Bend. Ratliff had clearly recognised Jody's folly in the opening chapter of the novel, and throughout the book he remains almost entirely uninvolved in the activities of Flem and his relations: there is no danger of his buying one of the spotted horses, and in his one direct exchange with Flem, over the contract for the goats and the signed notes he accepts from Mink, he emerges with a clear, though not unqualified, victory. He is thus presented as a worthy opponent of Flem, and it is this which makes his final downfall so triumphant a conclusion to Flem's career in Frenchman's Bend. At the same time, the fact that one of Ratliff's motives is greed, and the cause of his defeat his overconfidence in his own reading of the situation and in his own understanding of Flem's character, fits precisely into the overall pattern of greed and self-delusion established by Jody Varner at the beginning of the novel.

Ratliff was clearly a character whom Faulkner regarded as being especially important, both for what he did and for what he represented. In the early short stories in which the sewing-machine agent appears—in "Lizards in Jamshyd's Courtyard," for example, in which he is still called Suratt—he remains essentially the same loquacious, dialect-speaking character with the "shrewd plausible face" whom Faulkner first presented in *Sartoris*. In *The Hamlet* the dialect element in Ratliff's speech has been greatly reduced, and he himself is no longer simply an engaging teller of tall tales. In an interview in 1955 Faulkner named Dilsey and Ratliff as his favourite characters in his own work: "Ratliff is wonderful," he said. "He's done more things than any man I know."[26] In one of the discussions at Charlottesville in 1957 Faulkner developed his belief that man will prevail in terms of the human instinct to fight against Snopesism: "When the battle comes it always produces a Roland. It doesn't mean that they will get rid of Snopes or the impulse which produces Snopes, but always there's something in man that don't like Snopes and objects to Snopes and if necessary will step in to keep Snopes from doing some irreparable harm."[27]

That Faulkner saw Ratliff as occupying a central and representative position in the battle against Snopesism, itself a microcosm of mankind's determined struggle to prevail, is clear from *The Hamlet* itself. Both as a character and as a representative figure, however, Ratliff is more complex than has generally been realised. He is, in the first place, very similar to Flem in many ways. He is a trader, making his living by buying and selling, and he has done well: starting from exactly the same background as Flem himself—"My pap and Ab were both renting from Old Man Anse Holland then" (p. 34), says Ratliff of the "Fool About a Horse" episode—he has, while still a comparatively young man, gained a steady economic position, a house in Jefferson, and a half-share in a restaurant there. In so far as Ratliff and Flem are both traders, there is a natural economic rivalry between them; on the moral plane it is Ratliff's practised skill at Flem's economic game which gives him at once the confidence and the capacity to challenge Flem on his own ground. Although he seems voluble where Flem is silent, we are specifically told that Ratliff always did "a good deal more listening than anybody believed until afterward" (p. 15). He is also like Flem in being something of an outsider to the world of Frenchman's Bend, different from its inhabitants in a way of which they themselves are a little antagonistically aware: "I thought something was wrong all day," says one of them when Ratliff appears after the finish of the horse auction. "Ratliff wasn't there to give nobody advice" (p. 342).

Ratliff, as he appears in *The Hamlet*, is in the world of Frenchman's Bend but by no means entirely of it. His detachment is insisted on throughout, and like Flem, though for different reasons, he tends to be absent from the scene at crucial moments, and especially when the local farmers are being cheated of what little money they have. The reasons for Ratliff's apparent withdrawal are worth examining in some detail. His detachment from Frenchman's Bend must be related to his powers of inner detachment, his gift for viewing himself and his own actions with the disenchanted eye of reason. Nowhere does this gift appear more clearly than in the exchange with Mrs. Littlejohn in which Ratliff plainly acknowledges the puritanical streak in himself which is urging him to stop the exploitation of Ike's love for the cow, and then as firmly declares his determination to act nonetheless, not ignoring what self-knowledge has told him, but embracing that awareness as part of the personal price to be paid:

> "I aint never disputed I'm a pharisee," he said. "You dont need to tell me he aint got nothing else. I know that. Or that I can sholy leave him have at least this much. I know that too. Or that besides, it aint any of my business. I know that too, just as I know that the reason I aint going to leave him have what he does have is simply because I am strong enough to keep him from it. I am stronger than him. Not righter. Not any better, maybe. But just stronger.
>
> "How are you going to stop it?"
>
> "I dont know. Maybe I even cant. Maybe I dont even want to. Maybe all I want is just to have been righteouser, so I can tell myself I done the right thing and my conscience is clear now and at least I can go to sleep tonight." (p. 227)

This intellectual quality of Ratliff's, which marks him off from the inhabitants of Frenchman's Bend, is both his strength and his weakness. As a trader, making his living by barter, Ratliff must operate within the established trading conventions as they are understood in the world of Frenchman's Bend. But his intelligence and his humanity will not allow him to remain blind to the implications of privation and suffering which the processes of trade, especially in their quintessential form of the horse-swap, may often carry for the defeated, and especially for their womenfolk. Ratliff is well aware of the traditional limits of the code, and especially of its principles of respect for the most skilful, of unconcern for the defeated, and, at all times, of noninterference in other men's trading: "He done all he could to warn me," thinks Ratliff of Bookwright early in the novel. "He went as far and even further than a man can let his self go in another man's trade" (p. 94). The crucial question for Ratliff is whether he shall go outside the limits of the convention in order to try and combat Snopesism.

The clearest statement of Ratliff's position comes in answer to Bookwright's query as to whether he gave Henry Armstid the five dollars he lost to Flem in trading for one of the spotted horses:

> "I could have," he said. "But I didn't. I might have if I could just been sho he would buy something this time that would sho enough kill him, like Mrs Littlejohn said. Besides, I wasn't protecting a Snopes from Snopeses; I wasn't even protecting a people from a Snopes. I was protecting something that wasn't even a people, that wasn't nothing but something that dont want nothing but to walk and feel the sun and wouldn't know how to hurt no man even if it would and wouldn't want to even if it could, just like I wouldn't stand by and see you steal a meat-bone from a dog. I never made them Snopeses and I never made the folks that cant wait to bare their backsides to them. I could do more, but I wont. I wont, I tell you!" (p. 367)

The final cry recalls the agony of Quentin Compson at the end of *Absalom, Absalom!* when Shreve asks him why he hates the South "*I dont. I dont! I dont hate it! I dont hate it!*" (p. 378). Ratliff longs for a continuation of the detachment he has practised, with only minor deviations, up to this point: he has, it is true, pitted his wits against Flem's over the matter of the goats, but this was a direct test of skill in the game of barter, with nothing seriously at issue. He knows that to intervene in "another man's trade," and especially to enquire what that trading means for the man's dependents, for women like Mrs. Armstid, inevitably brings pain to a man of his intelligence and humanity. He knows, in short, that involvement hurts, and that in detachment lies not merely discretion but self-protection. Yet he knows, too, that he must take action, become involved, and his "I wont. I wont, I tell you!" evokes the agony of his dilemma. Ratliff's hesitation, his reluctance to act, is presented as the inevitable concomitant of his personal intelligence and self-awareness, and, hence, as essential to Faulkner's conception of him. Equally essential, of course, is the courage, the moral commitment, which Ratliff displays when he decides nevertheless—again, not ignoring but accepting without self-deception what self-knowledge tells him—to abandon detachment and actively challenge Flem in a bid to stop his progress by the infliction of a resounding economic defeat.

In the event, of course, it is Ratliff who is defeated—partly because of the impetuousness which overcomes him in his eagerness to act, partly because of his disabling unfamiliarity with the nature and magnitude of the operation on which he embarks, and partly, it seems, because he too has been self-betrayed by some measure of that greed and overconfidence which had earlier brought defeat to Jody Varner and to so many others who thought themselves smarter than Flem. Once Ratliff acts, abandoning his customary devices of self-protection and stepping outside the accustomed bounds of his trader's experience to do so, it becomes inevitable not only that he should be defeated by Flem, but that he should be defeated on a scale exceeding any of Flem's previous conquests. It is essential to realise, however, that Ratliff's economic defeat is not accompanied by any defeat in human terms. The strength of Ratliff appears in the very moment of his realisation of Flem's victory, as he lingers luxuriously over his breakfast before resuming the digging which he already knows to be fruitless—"We even got a new place to dig" (p. 412), he thinks, with a humour which is not destroyed by its own wryness—and, a little later, as he bets Bookwright that he himself will have in his sack the oldest of the coins by which they have both been deluded. Once again, it is this capacity for combining decency and moral solicitude with clear-eyed intellectual detachment which gives Ratliff the ability to survive defeat and to continue, not merely the struggle against Snopesism, but the perpetual affirmation of life. Ratliff's opposition to Flem Snopes is obviously of great importance, but still more important is what he represents in himself, irrespective of the particular demands of the anti-Snopes campaign. It is extremely significant that Ratliff should be able to challenge Flem at his own game, but it is even more significant that Ratliff should continually demonstrate his aptitude for another and finer game than Flem's and thus affirm the persistence, whatever triumphs Snopesism may achieve, of those qualities by which, Faulkner believed, man will ultimately prevail. As Faulkner wrote to Warren Beck in 1941:

I have been writing all the time about honor, truth, pity, consideration, the capacity to endure well grief and misfortune and injustice and then endure again, in terms of individuals who observed and adhered to them not for reward but for virtue's own sake, not even merely because they are admirable in themselves, but in order to live with oneself and die peacefully with oneself when the time comes. I don't mean that the devil will snatch every liar and rogue and hypocrite shrieking from his deathbed. I think liars and hypocrites and rogues die peacefully every day in the odor of what he calls sanctity. I'm not talking about him. I'm not writing for him. But I believe there are some, not necessarily many, who do and will continue to read Faulkner and say, "Yes. It's all right. I'd rather be Ratliff than Flem Snopes. And I'd still rather be Ratliff without any Snopes to measure by even."[28]

Notes

1. *Faulkner in the University*, pp. 14–15.

2. Faulkner to Cowley, 7.

3. Meriwether, "Sartoris and Snopes: an Early Notice," p. 37; see above, p. 24.

4. Ibid., p. 38.

5. This point corresponds to the top of p. 19 of the Arents Collection manuscript and to p. 348 of the published book. The second page of the manuscript is reproduced as Fig. 18 of *Literary Career*.

6. *Literary Career*, p. 173.

7. *Literary Career*, p. 174 (see under "Peasants").

8. *Literary Career*, p. 171.

9. *Faulkner in the University*, p. 90.

10. In the Alderman Library are two pages, numbered 18 and 19, of a typescript entitled "Abraham's Children" (see *Literary Career*, Fig. 19, for a reproduction of p. 18); a third page, numbered 29, has been grouped with these but should perhaps be better described as belonging to a version of "Father Abraham." Both this page and p. 19 of "Abraham's Children" are almost identical with p. 29 of the "Father Abraham" typescript also in the Alderman Library, and it seems possible to suggest that "Abraham's Children" may represent an abbreviated version of "Father Abraham" produced by a single drastic deletion of the long opening descriptions of Flem, Eula, and Frenchman's Bend. These descriptions occupy approximately 11½ pages of "Father Abraham" typescript; allowing for the introductory material necessary to establish the situation for short-story purposes (as in the Scribner's version of "Spotted Horses"), this would account for the pagination of "Abraham's Children" running about ten pages behind. It is necessary to emphasise, however, that these speculations are extremely tentative (more of this early Snopes material may yet come to light) and that in any case the fact that "Abraham's Children" is narrated in the third-person makes it unlikely to have been an immediate source for the published "Spotted Horses."

11. *Scribner's*, LXXXIX (June 1931), 587, 586.

12. Ibid., p. 585.

13. Evidence for this conclusion can be obtained from comparison of the various versions of the material available in the Alderman Library: see *Literary Career*, pp. 69–70, and Figs. 20 and 21.

14. Starke, "An American Comedy: An Introduction to a Bibliography of William Faulkner," *The Colophon*, XIX (1934), [15].

15. Ibid., p. [16].

16. This material is all in the Alderman Library: see *Literary Career*, pp. 70–73.

17. Typescript setting copy, Alderman Library, p. 179.

18. Professor Meriwether has suggested to me that Faulkner may have seen "Wash" as related, with the Mink Snopes material, to an exposition of the desperate plight of such men and of their capacity for a kind of dignity; the Wash Jones episode might then have balanced the Mink episode at the end of *The Mansion* and emphasised even more strongly that Flem was not necessarily typical of his class. Cf. Robert Penn Warren, "William Faulkner," in *Three Decades*, p. 120.

19. The first page of the manuscript is reproduced as Fig. 15 of *Literary Career*, for the typescript, also in the Alderman Library, see *Literary Career*, p. 70.

20. The evocation of the De Spain mansion and of its significance for the boy would also have looked forward to Flem's purchase and occupation of the building in the later books of the trilogy.

21. Cf. two of the most recent books on Faulkner: Peter Swiggart, *The Art of Faulkner's Novels* (Austin, Texas, 1962), p. 195, repeats the familiar view that *The Hamlet* is "based upon a number of short stories published originally in the early thirties," and Lawrance Thompson, *William Faulkner: An Introduction and Interpretation* (New York, 1963), p. 135, speaks of Faulkner "choosing to perform a scissors-and-paste job, patching together pieces or wholes of six short stories [Thompson includes "Afternoon of a Cow," which has only incidental similarities with the Ike Snopes episodes and nothing textually in common with them] which had previously existed as unrelated units"—a job, Thompson adds, which seems to have been done with "a cavalier laziness." The inadequacy of such views has been evident for some time from Faulkner's own remarks recorded in *Faulkner at the University* and from the information collected by James B. Meriwether in *Literary Career*.

22. See Burton Rascoe's analysis of the climax of the "Fool About a Horse" episode recounted by Ratliff and his comment that "Mr. Faulkner never even suspects that New York reviewers can be so ignorant of physiology that they accept such a tale literally and don't know yod can't pump up a horse with a bicycle pump" (Rascoe, "Faulkner's New York Critics," *American Mercury*, L [June 1940], 246).

23. *Three Decades*, p. 123.

24. This passage in the novel (part of a section omitted from the English edition) has been revised, and greatly improved, from the version which appears on p. 146 of the manuscript:

> "But I still dont see why I got to pay $15.00—"
> "Because you got 4 children and you make 5, and 5 times 3 is 15.["]
> "I aint got but 3 yet," Eck said.
> "But you got the meat and hide." I.O. said. "Cant you even try to keep from forgetting that?"

25. The rejected typescript version of p. 1 which bears the pencilled note "Rec'd 3/20/39" (see p. 185, above) also bears the title "THE PEASANTS/BOOK ONE/Chapter I".

26. Grenier, "The Art of Fiction," p. 174.

27. *Faulkner in the University*, p. 34.

28. Warren Beck, "Faulkner: a Preface and a Letter," *Yale Review*, LII (October 1962), 159.

DAVID MINTER

The Self's Own Lamp

During the early months of 1928, Faulkner mixed spasmodic efforts to revise *Flags in the Dust* with other activities. He began several new stories and accepted occasional odd jobs, usually as a painter. At one time or another, he painted everything from the domes of large buildings to houses and signs; once or twice he even lacquered brass horns. During these months, he also made a second gift copy of *The Wishing Tree* "as a gesture of pity and compassion for a doomed child."[1] He had told his fairy tale to Margaret Brown many times; she was the youngest child in a family he had known for years. Now she was dying of cancer, and he wanted her parents to be able to read the story to her as often as she wished to hear it. Yet nothing seemed to help Faulkner, neither writing nor odd jobs nor acts of kindness. Failure was not new to him: he had gone along experiencing some of it and anticipating more, trying to prepare defenses that would mute its pain. But the disappointment he felt now was intense, and there was no one with whom he could share it. Although he remained close to his mother, he knew that her tolerance had never extended to complaints, let alone to failure. Relations with his father had eased over the years; by now he felt less shame about being the son of a failure, while his father felt less outrage about being the father of "a bum."[2] But Murry Falkner had never shared his disappointments with others or invited them to share theirs with him.

From *William Faulkner: His Life and Work*, pp. 91–112, 282–285. © 1980 by The Johns Hopkins University Press.

For different reasons, Faulkner also found it difficult to talk freely with Phil Stone or Estelle Franklin. Pride had always made it hard for him to express his need for tenderness, and now his relations with both Phil and Estelle had become strained. During the writing of *Flags in the Dust*, he had considered breaking with Phil altogether, apparently because he felt that Phil was trying to dictate what he should write. With *Flags* finished, he had enjoyed sharing his high expectations with Phil, and so the tension between them had eased.[3] But he was not ready to share disappointment and failure with Phil, and he had never felt more uncertain about his relations with Estelle. Her divorce would soon be final, and he knew that she was counting on him to marry her. He had continued seeing her so regularly that people in Oxford were gossiping. Yet he felt that he might be in love with someone else. In early 1928 he wrote a letter to his Aunt Bama in which he describes his efforts to revise *Flags* and mentions reviews of *Mosquitoes*. He also refers to a woman he does not name: "We all wish you would [come down]. I have something—someone, I mean—to show you, if you only would. Of course it's a woman. I would like to see you taken with her utter charm, and intrigued by her utter shallowness. Like a lovely vase. . . . She gets the days past for me, though. Thank God I've no money, or I'd marry her. So you see, even Poverty looks after its own."[4] Since Faulkner's lovely vase remained nameless, it is impossible to know whom he meant. But since Aunt Bama had long since met Estelle, it is clear whom he did not mean. Also unspecified in the letter are the barriers other than poverty that stood between him and his new love. If infatuation with his lovely vase kept him from confiding freely in Estelle, his sense of responsibility to Estelle probably made it difficult for him to confide in another woman. Feeling cut off, finding no one to help dispel his disappointment and doubt, he turned inward. Simply getting through the days became a problem. At odd moments he found himself singing morbid songs, thinking about how he might die, or wondering where he might be buried. "You know, after all," he said to a friend, "they put you in a pine box and in a few days the worms have you. Someone might cry for a day or two and after that they've forgotten all about you."[5]

Soon he was writing stories about some children named Compson. Taking a line from W. C. Handy's "St. Louis Blues," he called one of the stories "That Evening Sun Go Down." Another he called "A Justice."[6] Both were based on memories out of his own childhood, and both concern children who face dark, foreboding experiences without adequate support or adequate sponsors. At the end of "A Justice" he depicts the children moving through a "strange, faintly sinister suspension of twilight."[7] As his imagination played with the Compson children, he began to see them quite clearly, poised at the end of childhood and the beginning of awareness—a moment that possessed particular poignancy for him, as scattered comments suggest, and as both the deep resonance and the making of the Compson stories confirm. "Art reminds us of our youth," Fairchild says in *Mosquitoes*, "of that age when life don't need to have her face lifted every so often for you to consider her beautiful." "It's over very soon," Faulkner later remarked as he observed his daughter moving toward adolescence. "This is the end of it. She'll grow into a woman."[8] At every turn the Compson children see things they cannot understand, feel things they cannot express. In "A Justice," as twilight descends around them and their world begins to fade, loss, consternation, and bafflement become almost all they know.

In early spring, Faulkner began a third story about the Compsons. Calling it "Twilight," he thought to make it an exploration of the moment "That Evening Sun" and "A Justice" had made the Compsons' inclusive moment. By the time he finished it, this third story had become *The Sound and the Fury*, his first great novel. Faulkner was capable, as he once remarked, of saying almost anything in an interview; on some subjects, he enjoyed contradicting himself.[9] In discussing *The Sound and the Fury*, he displayed remarkable consistency for thirty years. His statements vary, of course, in the quality of emotion they express and the quantity of information they convey, but they show that his fourth novel occupied a secure place in his memory, and they suggest that it occupied a special place in his experience. From his statements several facts emerge, all intimating that he wrote *The Sound and the Fury* in the midst of a crisis that was both personal and professional.

The professional dimension to that crisis is clear: Faulkner's high expectations for *Flags in the Dust* prepared for it, Liveright's harsh rejection initiated it, and Faulkner's response intensified it. More and more baffled as well as hurt, Faulkner soon found himself wondering again about his vocation. He probably knew that the threat to sell his typewriter and surrender his vocation was empty, but he apparently believed that he could alter his intentions and expectations—that he could teach himself to live without hope of recognition and reward. For several years he had written in order to publish. After publication of *Soldiers' Pay*, that had meant writing with Horace Liveright in mind. As his work became more satisfying to him personally, it had become less acceptable to his publisher. Refusing to go back to writing books as youthfully glamorous as *Soldiers' Pay* or as trashily smart as *Mosquitoes*, he decided to relinquish a part of his dream.[10] "One day I seemed to shut a door between me and all publishers' addresses and book lists. I said to myself, Now I can write"—by which he meant that he could write for himself alone. Almost immediately, he felt free. Writing "without any accompanying feeling of drive or effort, or any following feeling of exhaustion or relief or distaste," he began with no plan at all. He did not even think of his manuscript as a book. "I was thinking of books, publication, only in . . . reverse, in saying to myself, I won't have to worry about publishers liking or not liking this at all."[11]

But Faulkner was also grappling with personal problems. Protecting his privacy, he remained vague as to what they were. To Maurice Coindreau he spoke of the "severe strain" imposed by "difficulties of an intimate kind" ("des difficultés d'ordre intime").[12] Though his problems probably had something to do with Estelle and his "lovely vase," and almost certainly had something to do with his loneliness and despair, they remained unspecified. About them, we know only that they ran deep and that they became intimately involved in the writing of *The Sound and the Fury*. About the writing, we know that it brought Faulkner great joy, that it produced great fiction, and that it was carried on with unusual secretiveness. Apparently no one, not even Estelle and Phil, knew anything about *The Sound and the Fury* until it was virtually finished.[13]

Like *Flags in the Dust*, *The Sound and the Fury* is set in Jefferson and recalls family history. The Compson family, like the Sartoris family, mirrors Faulkner's sense of his family's story as a story of declension. But *The Sound and the Fury* is bleaker, more personal, and more compelling. Despite its pathos, *Flags* remained almost exuberant; and despite its use of family legends, it remained open, accessible. Faulkner's changed mood, his new attitude and needs, altered not only his way of working but his way of writing. If writing for himself implied freedom to recover more personal materials, writing without concern for publishers' addresses implied freedom to become more experimental. The novel accordingly represented a move back toward Faulkner's childhood and the family configuration of his earliest years—a move into the past and into the interior. At the same time, through the fictional techniques and strategies that Faulkner used to discover, displace, and transfigure the memories he found waiting for him, his novel represented an astonishing breakthrough. A moving story of four children and their inadequate parents, *The Sound and the Fury* is thematically regressive, stylistically and formally innovative.

Of the several corollaries implicit in its regressive principle, at least two are crucial: first, the presence of the three Compson brothers, who recall Faulkner's own family configuration; and second, memory and repetition as formal principles.[14] Faulkner possessed the three Compson brothers, as he later put it, almost before he put pen to paper. To anchor them in time and place, he took a central event and several images from his memory of the death of the grandmother he and his brothers called Damuddy, after whose lingering illness and funeral they were sent away from home so that the house could be fumigated. For Faulkner as for Gertrude Stein, memory is always repetition, being and living never repetition. *The Sound and the Fury*, he was fond of remarking, was a single story several times told. But since he used the remembered as he used the actual—less to denominate lived events, relationships, and configurations, with their attendant attributes and emotions, than to objectify them and so be free to analyze and play with them—the remembered was never for him simple repetition. To place the past under the aspect of the present, the present under the aspect of the past, was to start from the regressive and move toward the innovative. Like the novel's regressive principle, its innovative principle possessed several corollaries, including its gradual evocation of Caddy, the sister Faulkner added to memory, and its slow move from private worlds toward a more public world.[15]

The parental generation, which exists in *Flags in the Dust* only for the sake of family continuity, is crucial in *The Sound and the Fury*. Jason is aggressive in expressing the contempt he feels for his mother and especially his father. Attached to them, he nonetheless resents and hates them. Although Benjy feels neither resentment nor hatred, he does feel the vacancies his parents have left in his life. Although Quentin disguises his hostility, it surfaces. Like Benjy's and Quentin's obsessive attachments to Caddy, Jason's hatred of her originates in wounds inflicted by Mr. and Mrs. Compson. In short, each brother's discontent finds its focus in Caddy, as we see in their various evocations of her.

To the end of his life, Faulkner spoke of Caddy with deep devotion. She was, he suggested, both the sister of his imagination and "the daughter of his mind." Born of his own discontent, she was for him "the beautiful one," his "heart's darling." It was Caddy, or more precisely, Faulkner's feelings for Caddy, that turned a story called "Twilight" into a novel called *The Sound and the Fury*: "I loved her so much," he said, that "I couldn't decide to give her life just for the duration of a short story. She deserved more than that. So my novel was created, almost in spite of myself."[16]

In the same discussions in which Faulkner stressed the quality of his love for Caddy, he emphasized the extent to which his novel grew as he worked on it. One source of that growth was technical. The novel, he was fond of remarking, was a story that required four tellings. Having presented Benjy's experience, he found that it was so "incomprehensible, even I could not have told what was going on then, so I had to write another chapter." The second section accordingly became both a clarification and a counterpoint to the first, just as the third became both of these to the second.[17] The story moves from the remote and strange world of Benjy's idiocy and innocence, where sensations and basic responses are all we have; through the intensely subjective as well as private world of Quentin's bizarre idealism, where thought shapes sensation and feeling into a kind of decadent poetic prose full of idiosyncratic allusions and patterns; to the more familiar, even commonsensical meanness of Jason's materialism, where rage and self-pity find expression in colloquialisms and clichés. Because it is more conventional, Jason's section is more accessible, even more public. Yet it too describes a circle of its own.[18] Wanting to move from three peculiar and private worlds toward a more public and social one, Faulkner adopted a more detached voice. The fourth section comes to us as though from "an outsider." The story, as it finally emerged, tells not only of four children and their family, but of a larger world at twilight. "And that's how that book grew. That is, I wrote that same story four times. . . . That was not a deliberate *tour de force* at all, the book just grew that way. . . . I was still trying to tell one story which moved me very much and each time I failed."[19]

Given the novel's technical brilliance, it is easy to forget how simple and moving its basic story is. In it we observe four children come of age amid the decay and dissolution of their family. His sense of it began, Faulkner recalled, with "a brother and a sister splashing one another in the brook" where they have been sent to play during the funeral of a grandmother they call Damuddy. From this scene came one of the central images of the novel—Caddy's muddy drawers. As she clambers up a tree outside the Compson home to observe the funeral inside, we and her brothers see her drawers from below. From this sequence, Faulkner got several things: his sense of the brook as "the dark, harsh flowing of time" that was sweeping Caddy away from her brothers; his sense that the girl who had the courage to climb the tree would also find the courage to face change and loss; and his sense that her brothers, who had waited below, would respond very differently—that Benjy would fail to understand his loss; that Quentin would seek oblivion rather than face his; and that Jason would meet his with terrible rage and ambition.[20] The novel thus focuses not only on the three brothers Faulkner possessed when he began but also on Caddy, the figure he added to memory—which is to say, on the only child whose story he never directly told as well as on those whose stories he directly tells. His decision to approach Caddy only by indirection, through the eyes and needs and demands of her brothers, was in part technical; by the time he came to the fourth telling, he wanted a more public voice. In addition, he thought indirection more "passionate." It was, he said, more moving to present "the shadow of the branch, and let the mind create the tree."[21]

But in fact Caddy grew as she is presented, by indirection—in response to needs and strategies shared by Faulkner and his characters. Having discovered Benjy, in whom he saw "the blind, self-centeredness of innocence, typified by children," Faulkner became "interested in the relationship of the idiot to the world that he was in but would never be able to cope with." What particularly agitated him was whether and where such a one as Benjy could "get the tenderness, the help, to shield him."[22] The answer he hit upon had nothing to do with Mr. and Mrs. Compson, and only a little to do with Dilsey.

Mr. Compson is a weak, nihilistic alcoholic who toys with the emotions and needs of his children. Even when he feels sympathy and compassion, he fails to show it effectively. Mrs. Compson is a cold, self-involved woman who expends her energies worrying about her ailments, complaining about her life, and clinging to her notions of respectability. "If I could say Mother. Mother," Quentin says to himself. Dilsey, who recalls Mammy Callie, epitomizes the kind of Christian Faulkner most admired. She is saved by a minimum of theology. Though her understanding is small, her wisdom and love are large. Living in the world of the Compsons, she commits herself to the immediate; she "does de bes" she can to fill the vacancies left in the lives of the children around her by their loveless and faithless parents. Since by virtue of her faith she is part of a larger world, she is able "to stand above the fallen ruins of the family."[23] She has seen, she says, the first and the last. But Dilsey's life combines a measure of effective action with a measure of pathetic resignation. Most of Benjy's needs for tenderness and comfort, if not help and protection, he takes to his sister. And it was thus, Faulkner said, that "the character of his sister began to emerge."[24] Like Benjy, Quentin and Jason also turn toward Caddy, seeking to find in her some way of meeting needs frustrated by their parents. Treasuring some concept of family honor his parents seem to him to have forfeited, Quentin seeks to turn his fair and beautiful sister into a fair, unravished, and unravishable maiden. Believing that his parents have sold his birthright when they sold their land, yet still lusting after an inheritance, Jason tries to use Caddy's marriage to secure a substitute fortune.

The parental generation thus plays a crucial, destructive role in *The Sound and the Fury*. Several readers have felt that Faulkner's sympathies as a fictionist lie more with men than with women.[25] But his fathers, at least, rarely fare better than his mothers, the decisive direction of his sympathy being toward children, as we see not only in *The Sound and the Fury* but also in works that followed it. Jewel Bundren must live without a visible father, while Darl discovers that in some fundamental sense he "never had a mother." Thomas and Ellen Sutpen's children live and die without having either an adequate father or an adequate mother. Rosa Coldfield lives a long life only to discover that she had lost childhood before she possessed it. Held fast yet held without gentleness, these characters find repetition easy, independence and innovation almost impossible.

Although he is aggressive in expressing the hostility he feels for his parents, Jason is never able satisfactorily to avenge himself on them. Accordingly, he takes his victims where he finds them, his preference being for those who are most helpless, like Benjy and Luster, or most desperate, like Caddy. Enlarged, the contempt he feels for his family enables him to reject the past and embrace the New South, which he does without

recognizing in himself vulgar versions of the materialism and self-pity that
we associate with his mother. Left without sufficient tenderness and love,
Quentin, Caddy, and Benjy turn toward Dilsey and each other. Without
becoming aggressive, Benjy feels the vacancies his parents create in his life,
and so tries to hold fast to those moments in which Caddy has met his need
for tenderness. In Quentin we observe a very different desire: repulsed by the
world around him, he determines to possess moments only in idealized form.
Like the hero of Pound's *Cantos*, he lives wondering whether any sight can
be worth the beauty of his thought. His dis-ease with the immediate, which
becomes a desire to escape time itself, accounts for the strange convolutions
of his mind and the strange transformations of his emotions. In the end it
leads him to a still harbor where he fastidiously completes the logic of his
father's life. Unlike her brothers, Caddy establishes her independence and
achieves freedom. But her flight severs ties, making it impossible for her
to help Quentin, comfort Benjy, or protect her daughter. Finally, freedom
sweeps "her into dishonor and shame."[26] Deserted by her mother, Miss
Quentin is left no one with whom to learn love, and so repeats her mother's
dishonor and flight without knowing her tenderness. If in the story of Jason
we observe the near-triumph of all that is repugnant, in the stories of Caddy
and Miss Quentin we observe the degradation of all that is beautiful. No
modern story has done more than theirs to explore Yeats's terrible vision
of modernity in "The Second Coming," where the "best lack all conviction"
while the "worst are full of passionate intensity."

Faulkner thus seems to have discovered Caddy in essentially the way
he presents her—through the felt needs of her brothers. Only later did he
realize that he had also been trying to meet needs of his own: that in Caddy
he had created the sister he had wanted but never had and the daughter he
was fated to lose, "though the former might have been apparent," he added,
"from the fact that Caddy had three brothers almost before I wrote her name
on paper." Taken together, then, the Compson brothers may be seen as
manifesting the needs Faulkner expressed through his creation of Caddy.
In Benjy's need for tenderness we see signs of the emotional confluence
that preceded the writing of *The Sound and the Fury*. The ecstasy and relief
Faulkner associated with the writing of the novel as a whole, he associated
particularly with "the writing of Benjy's section."[27] In Jason's preoccupation
with making a fortune, we see a vulgar version of the hope Faulkner was
trying to relinquish. In Quentin's almost Manichaean revulsion toward
all things material and physical, we see both a version of the imagination
Allen Tate has called "angelic" and a version of the moral sensibility that
Faulkner associated with the fastidious aesthete.[28] It is more than accident
of imagery that Quentin, another of Faulkner's poets manqués, seeks refuge,
first, in the frail "vessel" he calls Caddy, and then, in something very like the

"still harbor" in which Faulkner had imagined Hergesheimer submerging himself—"where the age cannot hurt him and where rumor of the world reaches him only as a far faint sound of rain."[29]

In one of his more elaborate as well as more suggestive descriptions of what the creation of Caddy meant to him, Faulkner associated her with one of his favorite images. "I said to myself, Now I can write. Now I can make myself a vase like that which the old Roman kept at his bedside and wore the rim slowly away with kissing it. So I, who had never had a sister and was fated to lose my daughter in infancy, set out to make myself a beautiful and tragic little girl."[30] The image of the urn or vase had turned up in the Hergesheimer review, "Elmer," *Mosquitoes*, and *Flags in the Dust*; it had appeared recently in the letter to Aunt Bama describing his new love; and it would make several later appearances. It was an image, we may fairly assume, that possessed special force for Faulkner, and several connotations, including at least three of crucial significance.

The simplest of these connotations—stressing a desire for escape— Faulkner had earlier associated with Hergesheimer's "still harbor" and later associated with "the classic and serene vase" that shelters Gail Hightower "from the harsh gale of living."[31] In *The Sound and the Fury* Benjy comes to us as a wholly dependent creature seeking shelter. Sentenced to a truncated life of pain—"like something eyeless and voiceless which . . . existed merely because of its ability to suffer"[32]—he is all need and all helplessness. What loss of Caddy means to him is a life of unrelieved and meaningless suffering. For Quentin, on the other hand, loss of Caddy means despair. In him we observe a desire, first for relief and shelter, then for escape. In one of the New Orleans sketches, Faulkner introduces a girl who presents herself to her lover as "Little Sister Death." In the allegory he wrote for Helen Baird, a maiden of the same name turns up in the company of a courtly knight and lover—which is, of course, the role Quentin seeks to play.[33] At first all Quentin's desire seems to focus on Caddy as the maiden of his dreams. But as his desire becomes associated with "night and unrest," Caddy begins to merge with "Little Sister Death"—that is, with an incestuous love forbidden on threat of death. Rendered impotent by that threat, Quentin comes to love, not the body of his sister, nor even some concept of Compson honor, but death itself. In the end, he ceremoniously gives himself, not to Caddy but to the river. "The saddest thing about love," says a character in *Soldiers' Pay*, "is that not only the love cannot last forever, but even the heartbreak is soon forgotten."[34] Quentin kills himself in part as punishment for his forbidden desires; in part because Caddy proves corruptible; in part, perhaps, because he decides "that even she was not quite worth despair." But he also kills himself because he fears his own inconstancy. What he discovers in himself is deep psychological impotence that manifests itself in his inability to play either of the heroic roles—seducer or avenger—that he deems appropriate to his fiction of himself as a gallant, chivalric lover. But beyond the failure he experiences lies the failure he anticipates, a moment when Caddy's corruption no longer matters to him. Suicide thus completes his commitment to the only role left him, that of the despairing lover.

Never before had Faulkner expressed anxiety so deep and diverse. In Quentin it is not only immediate failure that we observe; it is the prospect of ultimate failure. Later, Faulkner associated the writing of *The Sound and the Fury* with anxiety about a moment "when not only the ecstasy of writing would be gone, but the unreluctance and the something worth saying too." In Quentin we see clearly Faulkner's sense that the desire to escape such anxiety was potentially destructive. If he wrote *The Sound and the Fury* in part to find shelter, he also wrote knowing that he would have to emerge from it. "I had made myself a vase," he said, though "I suppose I knew all the time that I could not live forever inside of it."[35] Having finished *The Sound and the Fury*, he found emergence traumatic. Still, it is probably fair to say that he knew all along that he would make that move. Certainly his novel possessed other possibilities for him, just as the image through which he sought to convey his sense of, it possessed other connotations, including one that is clearly erotic and one that is clearly aesthetic.

We can begin untangling the erotic by examining the relation between the old Roman who kept the vase at his bedside so that he could kiss it and the withered cuckold husband who "took the Decameron to bed with him every night."[36] Both of these figures are committed to a kind of substitution, and practice a kind of autoeroticism. The old Roman is superior only if we assume that he is the maker of his vase—in which case he resembles Horace Benbow, maker of his own "almost perfect vase." With Horace and his vase we might seem to have come full circle, back to Faulkner and his "heart's darling."[37] For Horace not only keeps his vase by his bedside; he also calls it by his sister's name. In *The Sound and the Fury* affection of brother and sister replaces affection of parents and children as an archetype of love; and with Caddy and Quentin, the incestuous potential of that love clearly surfaces—as it had in "Elmer," *Mosquitoes*, and *Flags in the Dust*, and as it would in *Absalom, Absalom!*.

The circle, however, is less perfect than it might at first appear, since at least one difference between Horace Benbow and William Faulkner is crucial. Whereas Horace's amber vase is a substitute for a sister he has but is forbidden to possess, Faulkner's is a substitute for the sister he never had. In this regard Horace is closer to Elmer, Faulkner to Gordon in *Mosquitoes*. Elmer is in fact a more timid version of Horace. Working with his paints— "thick-bodied and female and at the same time phallic: hermaphroditic"— Elmer creates figures he associates with something "that he dreaded yet longed for." The thing he both seeks and shuns is a "vague shape" he holds in his mind; its origins are his mother and a sister named Jo-Addie. His art, like Horace's, is devoted to imaginative possession of figures he is forbidden and fears sexually to possess. When Horace calls his amber vase by his sister's name, he articulates what Elmer only feels. Like Elmer, however, Horace finds in indirect or imaginative possession a means of avoiding the fate Quentin enacts. Through their art, Elmer and Horace are able to achieve satisfaction that soothes one kind of despair without arousing guilt that might lead to another.

In *Mosquitoes* the origins of Gordon's "feminine ideal" remain obscure, though his art is clearly devoted to creating and possessing it. For Gordon as for Elmer and Horace, the erotic and the aesthetic are inseparable. A man is always writing, Dawson Fairchild remarks, "for some woman"; if she is not "a flesh and blood creature," she is at least "the symbol of a desire," and "she is feminine."[38] Elmer and Horace work in their art toward a figure that is actual; they make art a substitute for love of a real woman. Gordon, on the other hand, makes art a way of approaching an ideal whose identity remains vague. About it we know two things: that it is feminine and that it represents what Henry James called the beautiful circuit and subterfuge of thought and desire. Horace expresses his love for a real woman through his art, whereas Gordon expresses his devotion to his sculpted ideal by temporarily pursuing a woman who happens to resemble it.[39] Horace is a failed and minor artist, Gordon a consecrated one—the difference being that Gordon devotes his life as well as his art to a figure that exists perfectly only in thought and imagination.

On his way to Europe, shortly after finishing *Soldiers' Pay* and before beginning "Elmer" and *Mosquitoes*, Faulkner told William Spratling that he thought love and death the "only two basic compulsions on earth."[40] What engaged his imagination as much as either of these, however, was his sense of the relation of each to the other and of both to art. The amber vase Horace calls Narcissa, he also addresses "Thou still unravished bride of quietude." "There is a story somewhere," Faulkner said,

> about an old Roman who kept at his bedside a Tyrrhenian vase which he loved and the rim of which he wore slowly away with kissing it. I had made myself a vase, but I suppose I knew all the time that I could not live forever inside of it, that perhaps to have it so that I too could lie in bed and look at it would be better; surely so when that day should come when not only the ecstasy of writing would be gone, but the unreluctance and the something worth saying too. It's fine to think that you will leave something behind you when you die, but it's better to have made something you can die with.[41]

In this brief statement the vase becomes both Caddy and *The Sound and the Fury*, both "the beautiful one" for whom he created the novel as a commodious space and the novel in which she found protection and privacy as well as expression. In its basic doubleness the vase is many things: a haven or shelter into which the artist may retreat; a feminine ideal to which he can give his devotion; a work of art that he can leave behind when he is dead; and a burial urn that will contain at least one expression of his self as an artist. If it is a mouth he may freely kiss, it its also a world in which he may find shelter; if it is a womb he may enter, it is also an urn in which his troubled spirit now finds temporary shelter and hopes to find lasting expression.[42]

Of all his novels, it was for *The Sound and the Fury* that Faulkner felt "the most tenderness." Writing it not only renewed his sense of purpose ("something to get up to tomorrow morning") and hope (a task he could "believe is valid"),[43] it also gave him an "emotion definite and physical and yet nebulous to describe." Working on it, he experienced a kind of ecstasy, particularly in the "eager and joyous faith and anticipation of surprise which the yet unmarred sheets beneath my hand held inviolate and unfailing."[44] Since, as Faulkner once noted, *The Sound and the Fury* is a "dark story of madness and hatred," and since writing it cost him dearly,[45] such statements may seem surprising. But he had discovered in *The Sound and the Fury* the kind of work he had anticipated in *Mosquitoes*: one "in which the hackneyed accidents which make up this world—love and life and death and sex and sorrow—brought together by chance in perfect proportions, take on a kind of splendid and timeless beauty."[46] In the years to come he continued to describe his fourth novel as a grand failure. Imperfect success would always be his ideal. To continue his effort to match his "dream of perfection," he needed dissatisfaction as well as hope. If failure might drive him to despair, success might deprive him of purpose: "It takes only one book to do it. It's not the sum of a lot of scribbling, it's one perfect book, you see. It's one single urn or shape that you want."[47]

In a letter to Malcolm Cowley, Faulkner once said that he wanted "to be, as a private individual, abolished and voided from history"; it was his aim to make his books the sole remaining sign of his life. Informing such statements was both a desire for privacy and a tacit conception of his relation to his art. Faulkner assumed that his authentic self was the self variously and nebulously yet definitely bodied forth by his fictions.[48] And it is in this slightly unusual sense that his fiction is deeply autobiographical. "I have never known anyone," a brother wrote, "who identified with his writings more than Bill did. . . . Sometimes it was hard to tell, which was which, which one Bill was, himself or the one in the story. And yet you knew somehow that the two of them were the same, they were one and inseparable."[49] Faulkner knew that characters, "those shady but ingenious shapes," were indirect ways of exploring, projecting, and reaffirming both the life he lived and the tacit, secret life underlying it. At least once he was moved to wonder if he "had invented the world" of his fiction "or if it had invented me."[50]

Like imperfect success, however, indirect knowledge and indirect expression imply partial completion and carry several connotations. Both Faulkner's need to approach Caddy only by indirection and his need to describe his novel as a series of imperfect acts only partially completed ally it with the complex. His descriptions of *The Sound and the Fury* are in part a tribute to epistemological problems and in part an acknowledgement that beauty is difficult—that those things most worth seeing, knowing, and saying can never be directly or fully seen, known, and said. But the indirection and incompletion that his descriptions stress are also useful strategies for approaching forbidden scenes, uttering forbidden words, committing dangerous acts. For Elmer Hodge, both his sister Jo-Addie and behind her "the dark woman. The dark mother" are associated with a "vogue shape somewhere back in his mind"—the core for him of everything he dreads and desires. Since attainment, the only satisfying act, is not only dangerous but forbidden, and therefore both cannot and must be his aim, Elmer's life and art become crude strategies of approximation. The opposite of crude, the art of *The Sound and the Fury* is nonetheless an art of concealment as well as disclosure—of delay, avoidance, and evasion— particularly where Caddy is concerned. For the work that provides her expression also grants her shelter and even privacy. Beyond Faulkner's sense that indirection was more passionate lay his awareness that it was more permissive. For him both desire and hesitation touched almost everything, making his imagination as illusive as it is allusive, and his art preeminently an art of surmise and conjecture. In *Flags in the Dust* Faulkner had taken ingenious possession of a heritage that he proceeded both to dismember and to reconstruct. In *The Sound and the Fury* he took possession of the pain and muted love of his childhood—its dislocations and vacancies, its forbidden needs and desires. The loss we observe in *The Sound and the Fury* is associated with parental weakness and inadequacy, with parental frigidity, judgment, and rejection. In the figure of Dilsey Faulkner recreated a haven of love he had learned early to count on; in the figure of Caddy he created one he had learned to long for. If the first of these figures is all maternal, the second is curiously mixed. In the figure of the sister he had never had, we see not only a sister but a mother (the role she most clearly plays for Benjy) and a lover (the possibility most clearly forbidden). Like the emotion Faulkner experienced in writing it, the novel's central figure comes to us as one "definite and physical and yet nebulous." Forced to avoid her even as he approached her, to conceal her even as he disclosed her, Faulkner created in Caddy a heroine who perfectly corresponds to her world: like *The Sound and the Fury*, she was born of regression and evasion, and like it, she transcends them.

By September 1928 Faulkner had finished the manuscript of *The Sound and the Fury* and had begun a typescript. Believing that he "would never be published again," he had no plan for submitting it to a publisher.[51] He wanted something he could bind for himself. Late in September, however, he received in the mail a contract for *Sartoris*. Harcourt, Brace was going to publish at least part of the novel Liveright had rejected. Almost immediately Faulkner decided to pack his manuscript and partial typescript and go to New York. He had a new three hundred dollar advance to live on; he had friends like Lyle Saxon, Bill Spratling, and Ben Wasson to visit; and he could revise and type as well in New York as in Oxford.

For a few days he stayed in Lyle Saxon's apartment; then, wanting a place to work, he found a room of his own. While Ben Wasson cut *Flags in the Dust*, Faulkner revised *The Sound and the Fury*. Although he had always revised with care, he worked now with deep intensity; sometimes his friends did not see him for several days at a time. In part his revisions reflect continuing commitment and affection: "I worked so hard at that book," he later asserted, "that I doubt if there's anything in it that didn't belong there."[52] But they also reflect growing hope that his book might be published. To himself and his friends, he still voiced doubt. He had no intention of building expectations only to see them dashed. It is "the damndest book I ever read," he wrote Aunt Bama. "I dont believe anyone will publish it for 10 years." Yet his revisions reflect a clear effort to enhance the novel's accessibility, to make it less exclusively his own. He increased the number of italicized passages indicating jumps in time; he added passages that clarified episodes; he made links and associations more explicit.[53]

Having finished the revision, Faulkner dated his typescript—"New York, N.Y./October 1928"—and gave it to Ben Wasson. It had been a long, intense, and satisfying labor. "I had just written my guts into *The Sound and the Fury*," he said later.[54] At first he felt exultant. "Read this, Bud," he said to Ben Wasson. "It's a real son-of-a-bitch."[55] But he had learned years before that for him the sense of completion often triggered depression and lifelessness, regret and guilt; that tomorrow he was likely to "wake up feeling rotten."[56] Writing *The Sound and the Fury* had been a deep excursion not only into his imaginative kingdom but into his own interior. Reversing direction proved almost impossible. The end he had labored hard to reach, he had dreaded, as though he dared not "risk cutting off the supply, destroying the source." Perhaps, like Proust and Rilke, he knew that "the gratitude of the completed" implied silence.[57] Perhaps it was not only silence but rejection and punishment that he anticipated. Certainly what he did in the days that followed both imposed silence and inflicted punishment.

Accustomed to the way he worked, his friends scarcely noticed his absence. One night two of them, Jim Devine and Leon Scales, happened by his flat, where they found him alone, unconscious, and lying on the floor, with empty bottles scattered around him. Seeing that he was ill and badly debilitated, they took him with them and nursed him back to health.[58] In later years there were several repetitions of this episode. Sometimes they came with little apparent reason, sometimes in response to painful tasks or unpleasant situations, often after prolonged, intensive writing. In *Mosquitoes* a character suggests that people not only seek but find moments of "timeless beatitude . . . through an outside agency like alcohol."[59] Although Faulkner's journeys into alcoholic twilight may not always have yielded such visions, they were clearly necessary for him. Sensing in the end of a novel the end of a world, and in the end of a world a final judgment, he often needed and sought an interface.

Able to write again, he stayed briefly with Devine and Scales in the apartment they shared with another friend, then moved in with an artist named Leon Crump. He had had enough of solitude for a time. Both he and Crump worked in the flat, and both worked hard, one painting while the other wrote. Faulkner remained skeptical about the future of *The Sound and the Fury*, but since Horace Liveright had released him from his contract, he was more hopeful. Harcourt, Brace had announced publication of *Sartoris*. In Ben Wasson, he had a loyal friend, in Hal Smith an editor who admired his work.

Wanting to publish and needing to make money, Faulkner began writing stories. He had finished *The Sound and the Fury* before reading any of it to anyone. Now he spent his evenings telling friends versions of the stories he worked on during the day. The war figured in some of them, his trip to Europe in others. In one, called "As I Lay Dying," he reworked material from "Father Abraham." Separately, both the material and the title would become famous; now, together, they found no publisher. Hoping to sell stories before he left New York, Faulkner asked Wasson to introduce him to some editors. Several gave him advice, and at least one, Alfred Dashiell of *Scribner's*, offered encouragement. For a time Faulkner thought he might stay in New York until after the January publication of *Sartoris*. But as Christmas drew near and money ran short, he changed his mind. No one was accepting his stories, and New York was beginning to irritate him. Having jotted down a few addresses, he packed his clothes and manuscripts and caught a train."[60]

Back in Oxford, he continued writing, hoping for some kind of breakthrough. At first his luck held steady; no one wanted anything. Then shortly after publication of *Sartoris*, 31 January 1929, he received a contract for *The Sound and the Fury*. He had been right about Harcourt, Brace. Having kept the manuscript for several weeks, Alfred Harcourt decided to let Hal

Smith take it with him when he left to form the firm of Jonathan Cape & Harrison Smith."[61] It was, therefore, with a new publisher, his third, that Faulkner signed a contract for his fourth novel.

The Sound and the Fury was an ambitious undertaking for a new firm: it was a strange book, and it presented special printing problems. But Hal Smith was eager, and he had hired Ben Wasson as an editor. When the proofs arrived in July, Faulkner found changes everywhere. Wasson had removed all the italics and inserted spaces to indicate shifts in time; and he had made a few scattered additions to the text. Although Faulkner knew Wasson meant well, he was angry. Revising carefully, he restored the italics and removed the additions. Writing Wasson, he argued that italics worked as effectively as spacing, and that spacing was unsightly. And he insisted that his text not be tampered with: "Dont make any more additions to the script, bud," he added; "I know you mean well, but so do I. I effaced the 2 or 3 you made."[62] In October the novel was published with italics and without Wasson's additions. Almost immediately it began attracting attention. Even reviewers who found it baffling recognized that it was not simply another novel. But two weeks after its release the economy of the United States collapsed, discouraging sales. In 1931 two small printings followed the first. A total of about three thousand copies would last until 1946.

Between February, when he signed the contract for *The Sound and the Fury*, and July, when he read proof for it, Faulkner made two remarkable moves: he wrote a novel designed to make money, and he married Estelle Franklin. Writing *The Sound and the Fury* had redoubled his old uneasiness about writing for money and recognition. Working without any ulterior motive—not for fame, certainly not for profit—he had "discovered that there is actually something to which the shabby term Art not only can, but must, be applied."[63] Because it was free of ulterior, contaminating motives, *The Sound and the Fury* would always epitomize what he thought art should be. But he had never stopped needing recognition and money, and with publication of *Sartoris* his hope of them had revived: once again he was thinking of himself "as a printed object" and "of books in terms of possible money."[64] Such thoughts might seem base; one part of him, despising them, would always advocate repression.[65] But with *The Sound and the Fury* behind him, he had gone back to writing stories he thought of as public and commercial. Telling them to friends at night, he wrote and hawked them during the day.

His first weeks back in Oxford, he continued writing and pushing stories. At times Alfred Dashiell in particular seemed on the verge of accepting one. But as the mail continued to mix vague encouragement with clear rejections, Faulkner became angry. Internal resistance did nothing so much as redouble the humiliation of failure. It was bad enough to abuse one's talents; it was worse to find no buyers for the products of the abuse.

For several years he had worked hard without ever making enough money to live on. Within a few months Estelle's divorce would be final. However uncertain he was about wanting to marry her, he knew that he did not want to do it on borrowed money. Yet he had a publisher for novels that made little or no money and a stack of stories that no one would publish.

As his frustration and anger deepened, Faulkner decided to write a novel that would make money when Hal Smith published it. In late January he began it; in late May he finished it.[66] He called it *Sanctuary*. Disturbed by his motives in writing it, he later disparaged the novel, confusing public response to it. It was, he said, "basely conceived. . . . I thought of the most horrific idea I could think of and wrote it" in order to make money.[67] Suggesting that the work itself must necessarily be contaminated, Faulkner did his novel a disservice. Many readers have followed his lead: assuming that it was basely conceived, they have concluded that it must be base. The disservice aside, however, it is probably fair to say that *Sanctuary* was written less out of injury than anger, and more for money than for itself; and it is certainly fair to say that it is one of Faulkner's bleakest, bitterest, and most brutal novels.

Faulkner began *The Sound and the Fury* knowing little about the direction it would take; he began *Sanctuary* knowing a great deal. Although writing it took several times the "three weeks" he allowed it in retrospect, it was in fact written quickly.[68] In part the speed suggests what the manuscript shows—that Faulkner wrote and revised it with less care than he had lavished on its predecessor. But Faulkner often played with the elements of a story for months, sometimes working them out in detail in his mind before writing a word, and several elements in *Sanctuary* had almost certainly undergone extended gestation. One element was the underworld of rural Mississippi, which revolved around the manufacture and sale of illegal whiskey. Faulkner had been doing business with small, independent "moonshiners" for years, and he admired their courage and resourcefulness, and even shared some of their contempt for "respectable" society. A second element was the gangster milieu of Memphis, where organized gangs battled for control not only of illegal whiskey but of gambling and prostitution. On excursions with Phil Stone, Faulkner had been visiting roadhouses and clubs controlled by Memphis gangs for years. Although he usually watched while Phil gambled, he enjoyed frequenting places like Reno De Vaux's. If most of the customers seemed ordinary, many of the gangsters seemed exotic. From his knowledge of the rural underworld, Faulkner created several crucial figures, including Lee Goodwin and Ruby Lamar, whom he clearly respects. From his knowledge of Memphis he created characters ranging from the comic Miss Reba to the grotesque Popeye. Miss Reba, who would reappear in the last of his novels, *The Reivers*, was based on a well-known Memphis "madam"; Popeye, who had turned up in an early unpublished story, "The Big Shot," was based on a notorious Memphis gangster named Popeye Pumphrey.[69]

Wanting his novel to be popular, Faulkner drew on two kinds of fiction, gangster stories and detective stories, which were read even in Mississippi. He had been reading as well as writing detective fiction for years, and he would continue to experiment with it. Despite the clear and relatively simple models that he had in mind, however, problems pertaining to plot persisted. He needed to find some way of joining the more sensational elements of the underworld to the more familiar social elements of Jefferson; even after several false starts, he continued to revise and shift. He also needed to find some way of controlling his discontent, which included society and men but focused on women. *Sanctuary* displays contempt for the male politicians who control society as well as for the middle-aged matrons who epitomize its hypocrisies. But its action centers on Popeye's brutal victimization of Temple Drake, who is young as well as female; and it reflects deep bitterness toward women. Whether or not this bitterness owes something to the shallow woman Faulkner described to Aunt Bama, or something to old wounds inflicted by Estelle and Helen, or something to the intimate difficulties Faulkner described to Maurice Coindreau, its focus and its depth are clear: as much as any work Faulkner wrote, *Sanctuary* suggests what Albert Guerard has termed a "persistent misogyny."[70] The scenes featuring Temple are so taut, spare, and detached as to seem almost clinical. In the sense that they center on action rather than thought and emotion, they are dramatic. Clearly they were conceived in part as a means of making *Sanctuary* more sensational and more remunerative. But these scenes are curious on other grounds, primarily because the depravity in them is overwhelming. During the course of the novel we meet several familiar forms of corruption, from dishonest politicians and cynical socialites to murderers and prostitutes. But both the amoral impotence of Popeye and the corruption of Temple move far beyond usual bounds.

Through most of his life Faulkner felt a "rather strong distrust of women."[71] The move of a young girl through puberty to sexuality seemed to him almost to epitomize the Fall. "It's over very soon," he said later, as his daughter neared that fateful moment. "This is the end of it. She'll grow into a woman."[72] Temple enters *Sanctuary* as a young woman who, having already made this crucial move, is curious to discover its consequences. She loves parties; merely walking, she almost dances. Without fully understanding why, she is playful, flirtatious, provocative. Yet even to readers inclined to censure her curiosity and eagerness, her punishment must seem excessive.

"I am now writing a book," Faulkner told Ben Wasson, "about a girl who gets raped with a corn cob."[73] Having raped Temple, the impotent Popeye takes her to a room at Miss Reba's, where he watches while a surrogate lover named Red so thoroughly corrupts Temple that she becomes both willing and, finally, insatiable. In this curious triangle no character shows any tenderness or affection for another. They are all fascinated by violence and lust. Experiencing this fascination, Temple discovers evil within as well as around her. Because Popeye has introduced her to evil, she is drawn to him as well as repulsed by him. Soon after her rape she passes up a clear opportunity to escape, in part because she is already divided within herself. But her inaction also reflects the influence of her society. Escape, and perhaps survival, interest her less than keeping her refined and respectable friends from knowing what has happened to her because she knows that her society would rather condone evil than acknowledge it. Near the end of the novel, when she returns to the society from which she has been taken, she cynically cooperates in convicting Lee Goodwin of a murder she knows Popeye has committed. She thus comes to us as one who is both instinctually depraved and socially corrupt. Having found lust and violence magical, she becomes totally cynical. Flanked by her powerful father ("My father's a judge; my father's a judge") and four stalwart brothers, she calmly lies.

It may be that Faulkner fails to work out Temple's motivation in committing perjury and convicting an innocent man. But Temple's action presents fewer problems than many readers have suggested.[74] Even before she returns to society, others have begun conspiring to convict Lee Goodwin. The Memphis underworld wants Popeye protected; the district attorney of Jefferson, Eustace Graham, wants a conviction that will enhance his record and help him win election to Congress; Clarence Snopes wants to make a profit and curry influential friends; and Narcissa Benbow Sartoris wants to protect her good name by terminating a sensational trial in which her brother is defending a disreputable man. Although none of these characters commits perjury, none of them shows much interest in truth. Graham is far more interested in his career than in justice; and Narcissa is far less offended by the death of an innocent man than by the scandal of his common-law wife. In Jefferson the law is controlled by men who are interested in power and profit, and the church is controlled by "church ladies" who are interested in convenience and respectability.

Allied against these forces are Lee Goodwin, who knows that Jefferson is indifferent to truth; Ruby Lamar, his wife, who tries to help her husband without incensing the town; and Horace Benbow, Faulkner's improbable knight-errant. Part detective and part trial lawyer, Benbow insists that someone must care enough about truth and justice to pursue them. At times he is resourceful, even energetic and shrewd, and he experiences several fine moments. But in the end, he is overmatched, partly because he is too academic and timid, and partly because the forces allied against him possess great power. "Perhaps it is upon the instant that we realize, admit, that there is a logical pattern to evil, that we die," he thinks at one point. More than defeat, it is the totality of his capitulation that marks him with failure. If Temple's encounter with evil leaves her cynical, Horace's leaves him spent and resigned.

Like "Father Abraham," *Sanctuary* is set in the twentieth century; and like "Father Abraham," it uses the Old Frenchman's Place to evoke the shadowy beginnings of Faulkner's imaginative kingdom. Like *Flags in the Dust*, it suffered a strangely complicated fate between its completion and its publication; and like *Flags*, it underwent substantial revision in the process. While writing it, Faulkner's spirits continued to rise and fall, as they had over the last several years. The more he labored, the more he wanted his new novel to be a work he could regard with pride. But there were times when he felt that whatever he did, he would fail. Shortly before he finished *Sanctuary* he told Phil Stone that he had finally resigned himself: "I think I not only won't ever make any money out of what I write," he said, "I won't ever get any recognition either."[75] Still he could not relinquish hope. In early May, while he was revising and typing his manuscript, he received a new contract and a new advance from Hal Smith. A few weeks later, shortly after mailing his manuscript, he received a largely unexpected response. "Good God," Hal Smith wrote, "I can't publish this. We'd both be in jail."[76] Since Smith's reservations had little to do with the quality of the manuscript, he said nothing to disparage Faulkner's development as a writer. He also refrained from asking that Faulkner return the advance. But he made clear the shock felt by readers at the press, and he said nothing to offer encouragement. Once again Faulkner accepted his failure and hid his disappointment, this time without protest or feigned confidence: he did not even ask his publisher to return his manuscript so that he could try it on someone else. "You're damned," he said to himself, "You'll have to work now and then for the rest of your life."[77]

With his career at yet another turning point, Faulkner began trying to sort out his personal life. The question before him was what to do about Estelle. Her divorce had been granted in April, and he knew that she was waiting. Eleven years before he had felt certain. Now he was less sure, and the signs around him were mixed. Estelle wanted to get married—her younger sister, Dorothy, had called him to say that he should stop stalling. But Estelle's father remained adamant. Faulkner might be interesting, even likeable, but he seemed without prospects at an age when most men had established themselves. Faulkner's own family was scarcely less blunt. His father and brothers said he should get a job and earn some money before thinking about marriage. His mother did not want him marrying anyone, certainly not a divorced woman who was known to drink whiskey.[78] Given more advice than he had sought or wanted, Faulkner decided to ignore it.

Some of it seemed to him irrelevant, and some of it presumptuous. He could borrow money to meet immediate expenses; later, if it became necessary, he could get a job. Even with the Depression deepening, he believed that he could earn enough money to support a family.

The larger problem was one of timing. The moment of which he and Estelle had dreamed was gone, and he knew that they could never go back. He may even have known that the residual bitterness within him ran deeper than time's power to heal. Certainly some of it had recently found expression in *Sanctuary*, where Temple's degradation reaches its culmination in scenes that put old preoccupations to new uses. Shortly after she arrives at Miss Reba's, Temple lies in bed remembering the dances she has loved. Later her tireless love of dancing leads directly to uncontrollable desire for fornication. "Call yourself a man, a bold, bad man, and let a girl dance you off your feet," she chides; and then, "Give it to me, daddy." In between these scenes, Popeye watches, "hanging over the foot of the bed," a pale slobbering Mephistopheles, while Red and Temple, "nekkid as two snakes," fornicate. But there was no reason to believe that further delay would soothe problems delay had exacerbated. And despite everything, marriage to Estelle seemed to him inevitable. The first time the Old Colonel had seen Lizzie Vance he had announced his intention to come back and marry her. Several years, one wife, and one child later, he had done just that. The first time Estelle had seen Faulkner, she had made a similar declaration. Now, several years, one husband, and two children later, she was going to do it.[79] There was reversal as well as repetition in the pattern, but both appealed to Faulkner. On 19 June 1929 he and Estelle drove to the courthouse in Oxford and got a marriage license. The next day he went alone to see his mother and Estelle's father. But his mood was no longer interrogative. He and Estelle had listened and waited long enough. With Dorothy as an attendant and a minister's wife as a witness, they were married.

Notes

GENERAL NOTE: Blotner discusses this period in *Faulkner*, chaps. 29–31. See also Meriwether, *Literary Career*, pp. 16–17, 18–20, 59–60, 65; Millgate, "The Career," pp. 26–29; and especially *Selected Letters*, pp. 39–46. The best discussion of the early Compson stories is in Norman Holmes Pearson, "Faulkner's Three Evening Suns," *Yale University Library Gazette* (29 Oct. 1954), pp. 61–70. On the dating of these stories, see Millgate, *Achievement*, p. 90; and Blotner, *Faulkner*, pp. 565–67 and notes to vol. 1, p. 82. See also the discussion in note 6 to this chapter. On the writing of *The Sound and the Fury*, see Maurice Coindreau's preface to *Le bruit et la fureur* (Paris, 1938), which is available, translated by George M. Reeves, in "Preface to *The Sound and the Fury*," *Mississippi Quarterly*, 19 (Summer 1966), 107–15. Also helpful is Coindreau's "The Faulkner I Knew," *Shenandoah*, 16 (Winter 1965), 26–35, which makes clear not only the very special place *The Sound and the Fury* occupied in Faulkner's life but also the exactness of his memory of it. Describing a conversation that took place in June 1937, Coindreau remarks that Faulkner "seemed" to know *The Sound and the Fury* by heart, referring me to such and such a paragraph, to such and such a page, to find the key to some highly enigmatic obscurity" (p. 29). Also valuable is James B. Meriwether, "Notes on the Textual History of *The Sound and the Fury*," *Papers of the Bibliographical Society of America*, 56 (1962), 285–316. Both the shorter (1972) and longer (1973) versions of Faulkner's "An Introduction to *The Sound and the Fury*" are of deep interest.

On the origins of *Sanctuary*, see especially Carvel Collins, "A Note on *Sanctuary*," *Harvard Advocate*, 135 (Nov. 1951), 16. The most interesting discussion of *The Sound and the Fury* in relation to Faulkner's preoccupations as a writer is in Irwin, *Doubling & Incest*. In addition, Otto Rank, *The Double*, trans. and ed. Harry Tucker, Jr. (Chapel Hill, N.C., 1971), and Søren Kierkegaard, *Repetition*, trans. Walter Lowrie (New York, 1964), have been very useful to me. On Faulkner as misogynist and on *Sanctuary*, see Guerard, *Triumph of the Novel*, especially pp. 109–35. See also Sharon Smith Hult, "William Faulkner's 'The Brooch': The Journey to the Riolama," *Mississippi Quarterly*, 27 (Summer 1974), 291–305, for an interesting discussion of Faulkner's male protagonists as crippled by some "fantasy of an ideal female." In relation to this theme, see especially Faulkner's "Nympholepsy." On Faulkner's efforts to place his short fiction see James B. Meriwether, ed., "Faulkner's Correspondence with *Scribner's Magazine*" and "Faulkner's Correspondence with the *Saturday Evening Post*."

1. To Harold Ober, 4 Feb. 1959, *Selected Letters*, p. 421.

2. Introduction to *Sanctuary*, in *Essays, Speeches & Public Letters*, p. 176.

3. See Blotner, *Faulkner*, pp. 555–56; and [Phil Stone] to H. V. Kincannon, 29 Oct. 1927, in the Humanities Research Center, University of Texas, Austin.

4. This letter was probably written in the first half of 1928. It is in the William Faulkner Collections, Alderman Library, University of Virginia, Charlottesville, and is quoted with permission of Jill Faulkner Summers.

5. J. W. Harmon in *Faulkner of Oxford*, pp. 93–94.

6. On the dating of these stories see Pearson, Millgate, and Blotner as cited in the general note. "That Evening Sun Go Down" was first published in *The American Mercury* (Mar. 1931). It later appeared, slightly revised, as "That Evening Sun" in *These 13* (1931). For an earlier version, see "Never Done No Weeping When You Wanted to Laugh," a manuscript in the Beinecke Library, Yale University, New Haven, Conn. Although there is no conclusive evidence for dating the stories earlier than *The Sound and the Fury*, there is good circumstantial evidence—that Quentin is older in "That Evening Sun" than he lives to be in *The Sound and the Fury*, and that Benjy does not appear in the stories. On anticipations of the Compsons in earlier writings, see note 13 to chapter 4.

7. "A Justice," in *These 13*, p. 207.

8. See *Mosquitoes*, p. 319; and Faulkner as quoted in Blower, *Faulkner*, p. 1169.

9. See *Lion in the Garden*, p. 276.

10. To Horace Liveright [mid- or late Feb. 1928], *Selected Letters*, pp. 39–40.

11. See both versions of Faulkner's "An Introduction to *The Sound and the Fury*."

12. Maurice Coindreau, "Preface," *Le bruit et la fureur*, (1938), p. 14. See Meriwether, "Notes on the Textual History of *The Sound and the Fury*," especially p. 288; and the translation of Coindreau's preface, p. 114, as cited in the general note to this chapter.

13. See Meriwether, "Notes on the Textual History of *The Sound and the Fury*," p. 289; and Blotner, *Faulkner*, pp. 579–80.

14. Faulkner had three brothers, of course, but during the crucial years to which his memory turned in *The Sound and the Fury*, he had two. Leila Dean Swift, the grandmother Faulkner called Damuddy, died on 1 June 1907. Dean Swift Faulkner was born on 15 August 1907.

15. See Conrad Aiken, "William Faulkner: The Novel as Form," *Harvard Advocate*, 135 (Nov. 1951), 13, 24–26; Donald M. Kartiganer, "*The Sound and the Fury* and Faulkner's Quest for Form," *ELH* 37 (Dec. 1970), 613–39; and Isadore Traschen, "The Tragic Form of *The Sound and the Fury*," *Southern Review*, 12 (Autumn 1976), 798–813.

16. See Faulkner on Hergesheimer in *Early Prose and Poetry*, p. 102; *Faulkner in the University*, p. 6; and the translation of Coindreau's preface, p. 109.

17. *Faulkner at Nagano*, pp. 103–5.

18. See F. H. Bradley, *Appearance and Reality* (New York, 1908), p. 346; and compare T. S. Eliot's note to line 412 of *The Waste Land*.

19. *Faulkner at Nagano*, pp. 103–5.

20. See "An Introduction to *The Sound and the Fury*" [1973].

21. *Faulkner at Nagano*, p. 72. See *Lion in the Garden*, p. 128. Note the relation between Faulkner's defense of indirection and Mallarmé's assertion: "*Nommer* un object, c'est supprimer les trois-quarts de la jouissance du poeme." See also A. G. Lehmann, *The Symbolist Aesthetic in France, 1885–1895* (Oxford, 1950), particularly chaps. 1, 2, 6.

22. *Lion in the Garden*, p. 146. For an earlier version of Benjy, see "The Kingdom of God," *New Orleans Sketches*, pp. 55–60.

23. See Faulkner's "An Introduction to *The Sound and the Fury*" [1972].

24. *Lion in the Garden*, p. 146.

25. See Guerard, *Triumph of the Novel*, pp. 109–35.

26. See Faulkner's "An Introduction to *The Sound and the Fury*" [1973].

27. Ibid.

28. See Allen Tate, "The Angelic Imagination" in *The Man of Letters in the Modern World* (New York, 1955), pp. 113–31; and Robert M. Slabey, "The 'Romanticism' of *The Sound and the Fury*," *Mississippi Quarterly*, 16 (Summer 1963), 152–57.

29. See the piece on Hergesheimer in *Early Prose and Poetry*, p. 102.

30. See Faulkner's "An Introduction to *The Sound and the Fury*" [1972].

31. See my discussion of *Mosquitoes* in chapter 3.

32. See Faulkner's "An Introduction to *The Sound and the Fury*" [1973]. Compare my discussion of Donald Mahon and *Soldiers' Pay* in chapter 3.

33. See "The Kid Learns," *New Orleans Sketches*, p. 91; and *Mayday*, as discussed in chapter 3. See also the discussion in Collins, "Introduction," *New Orleans Sketches*, pp. xxix–xxx.

34. *Soldiers' Pay*, p. 318. Compare Marietta in *Marionettes*: "nothing save death is as beautiful as I am."

35. See Faulkner's "An Introduction to *The Sound and the Fury*" [1973].

36. *Mosquitoes*, p. 210.

37. Compare *Flags in the Dust*, pp. 162–63; and *Faulkner in the University*, p. 6.

38. *Mosquitoes*, p. 250.

39. See Irwin, *Doubling & Incest*, pp. 160–61.

40. William Spratling, "Chronicle of a Friendship: William Faulkner in New Orleans," *Texas Quarterly*, 9 (Spring 1966), 38.

41. See "An Introduction to *The Sound and the Fury*" [1973].

42. See Irwin, *Doubling & Incest*, pp. 162–63.

43. *Lion in the Garden*, p. 147; *Faulkner in the University*, p. 67.

44. See "An Introduction to *The Sound and the Fury*" [1973].

45. Quoted in Coindreau, preface to *The Sound and the Fury*, p. 109.

46. *Mosquitoes*, p. 339. Compare Faulkner to Mrs. M. C. Falkner [postmarked 6 Sept. 1925], *Selected Letters*, pp. 17–18, for an early description of his response to the sense of having written something beautiful and perfect.

47. *Faulkner in the University*, p. 65. Compare *Soldiers' Pay*, p. 283. For a sense of how far back Faulkner's preoccupation with imperfect success went, see the fragment "... [Th]is life you bear like an invulnerable shield....": "Would you possess a thing / You had not striven for, and failed, and striven again?" And later: "Know you not that when once you have wrought / The absolute, then you can only die?" Humanities Research Center, University of Texas, Austin. Quoted by permission of Jill Faulkner Summers.

48. To Malcolm Cowley, Friday [11 Feb. 1949], *Faulkner-Cowley File*, p. 126. Compare Irwin, *Doubling & Incest*, pp. 171–72.

49. *My Brother Bill*, p. 275.

50. This quote is from a manuscript fragment in the Beinecke Library, Yale University, New Haven, Conn. Quoted by permission of Jill Faulkner Summers.

51. See to Alfred Harcourt, 18 Feb. 1929, *Selected Letters*, pp. 42–43; and the introduction to *Sanctuary*, in *Essays, Speeches & Public Letters*, p. 177.

52. This statement is from an unpublished portion of one of the sessions at the University of Virginia, 5 June 1957. Quoted by permission of Jill Faulkner Summers. A portion of this session is in *Faulkner in the University*, pp. 201–8. The full text of the session is available in the William Faulkner Collections, Alderman Library, University of Virginia, Charlottesville.

53. To Mrs. Walter B. McLean, Wednesday [probably Oct. 1928], *Selected Letters*, p. 41. On Faulkner's revision of *The Sound and the Fury*, see Meriwether as cited in the general note, pp. 293–94.

54. See Faulkner's introduction to *Sanctuary*, in *Essays, Speeches & Public Letters*, pp. 176, 177.

55. Quoted in Meriwether, "Notes on the Textual History of *The Sound and the Fury*," p. 289.

56. To Mrs. Murry C. Falkner [postmarked 6 Sept. 1925], *Selected Letters*, pp. 17–18.

57. See W. H. Auden, sonnet XXIII, in "In Time of War," in W. H. Auden and Christopher Isherwood, *Journey to a War* (New York, 1944). Compare Auden, sonnet XIX, in "Sonnets from China," in *Collected Shorter Poems, 1927–1957* (New York, 1966). See also *Absalom, Absalom!*, pp. 373–74.

58. Blower, *Faulkner*, pp. 590–92.

59. *Mosquitoes*, p. 339.

60. See Blotner, *Faulkner*, pp. 591–98. See Faulkner to Alfred Dashiell [answered 22 Dec. 1928], *Selected Letters*, 41–42.

61. See Blotner, *Faulkner*, p. 603; and *Selected Letters*, pp. 42–45.

62. To Ben Wasson [early summer 1929], *Selected Letters*, pp. 44–45.

63. See "An Introduction to *The Sound and the Fury*" [1972].

64. Introduction to *Sanctuary*, in *Essays, Speeches & Public Letters*, p. 177.

65. Compare, for example, ibid; "Speech of Acceptance upon the Award of the Nobel Prize for Literature," in *Essays, Speeches & Public Letters*, pp. 119–21; and *Faulkner in the University*, pp. 90–91.

66. See the typescript of *Sanctuary* in the William Faulkner Collections, Alderman Library, University of Virginia, Charlottesville.

67. *Faulkner in the University*, pp. 90–91. Compare his introduction to *Sanctuary*, in *Essays, Speeches & Public Letters*, p. 177.

68. See the title page and p. 358 of the typescript of *Sanctuary*, William Faulkner Collections, Alderman Library, University of Virginia, Charlottesville. Faulkner began the manuscript in January and finished the typescript on 25 May 1929.

69. See Beatrice Lang, "An Unpublished Faulkner Story: 'The Big Shot," *Mississippi Quarterly*, 26 (Summer 1973), 312–24; Robert Cantwell, "Faulkner's Popeye," *Nation*, 1.86 (1958), 140–41; Collins, "A Note on *Sanctuary*," as cited in the general note to this chapter; and L. S. Kubie, "William Faulkner's *Sanctuary*," *Saturday Review of Literature*, 11 (1934), 218, 224–26. See also Phil Stone to Louis Cochran, 28 Dec. 1931, Faulkner Collections, Humanities Research Center, University of Texas, Austin.

70. Guerard, *Triumph of the Novel*, p. 8.

71. See Victoria Fielden Black, quoted in Evans Harrington and Ann J. Abadie eds., *The South and Faulkner's Yoknapatawpha* (Jackson, Miss., 1977), p. 151.

72. Quoted in Blotner, *Faulkner*, p. 1169.

73. Ibid., p. 613.

74. See the discussion in Brooks, *Yoknapatawpha Country*, pp. 121–27, 392.

75. Emily W. Stone, "Faulkner Gets Started," *Texas Quarterly*, 8 (Winter 1965), 144.

76. Quoted in Faulkner's introduction to *Sanctuary*, in *Essays, Speeches & Public Letters*, p. 177. Compare *Faulkner in the University*, pp. 90–91.

77. Introduction to *Sanctuary*, in *Essays, Speeches & Public Letters*, p. 177.

78. See Blower, *Faulkner*, pp. 618–20.

79. Ibid., pp. 10, 85.

ERIC J. SUNDQUIST

The Strange Career of Joe Christmas

The literature of passing had become relatively common by the publication of *Light in August*, most prominently in gothic romances such as Cable's *The Grandissimes* (1880) and Chesnutt's *The House behind the Cedars* (1900), but one of its most penetrating expressions had appeared in James Weldon Johnson's *The Autobiography of an Ex-Coloured Man* (1912). Johnson's protagonist, embodying the struggle with invisibility that Faulkner and Ellison would only be able to approach from their contrary positions of visibility, succinctly depicts his first thoughts on discovering that he is no longer white but black: "I did indeed pass into another world. From that time I looked out through other eyes, my thoughts were coloured, my words dictated, my actions limited by one dominating, all pervading idea which constantly increased in force and weight until I finally realized in it a great, tangible fact."[24] Although the novel is hardly Johnson's own autobiography, it acquires more force by posing as such and by offering testimony whose singular authority makes the frenzy of Faulkner's version all the more pointed and inevitable. The relevance of the *Autobiography*, whose hero more prosaically but certainly more convincingly passes back and forth between black and white, gains further power from the fact that Johnson once projected in his notebooks a novel to be entitled "The Sins of the Fathers," which was to involve unknowing incest between the white daughter and the

From *Faulkner: The House Divided*, pp. 71–95, 167–172. © 1983 by The Johns Hopkins University Press.

bastard Negro son of a Southern planter, culminating in the accidental death of the son and the suicide of the guilty father. Thomas Dixon had already used the title and a very similar theme, and Faulkner, familiar with Dixon if not with Johnson, would later write nearly the same novel—namely, *Absalom, Absalom!* To reach the novel he never wrote, Johnson, like Faulkner, was moving from the twentieth century to the nineteenth, from Jim Crow to the slumbering nightmare out of which he had sprung. He was moving, then, toward a more historical understanding of the entangling myths of race that only the passing of several generations could make wholly visible; and he was doing so, as Joseph Skerrett points out, by dramatizing in the *Autobiography* the tragic strategy of true irony, which Kenneth Burke rightly insists is based on "a sense of fundamental kinship with the enemy, as one needs him, is indebted to him, is not merely outside him as an observer but contains him *within*, being consubstantial with him."[25]

It is worth focusing all the attention we can on the irony Burke describes, for like Faulkner's metaphor of the photograph and its negative it elucidates a "kinship"—in the actuality of blood, in the legalities and illegalities of "separate but equal," in the embraces and denials of racial hysteria—whose generative power permeates Faulkner's major works. In *Absalom, Absalom!* and *Go Down, Moses* Faulkner would expose, in flashes of released cultural anxiety, the draining intimacy of that kinship; but in *Light in August*, where the stark sensuality of the sexual encounters between Joe Christmas and Joanna Burden is more shocking than intimate, kinship is continually denied. Although the entire novel strives prodigiously, in detail after detail, to connect its characters by merging their responsibilities and actions, and by embedding their lives within one another in almost ridiculous ways, the effect of such exertions is quite simply to render the endless analogous details superfluous and the embedded lives fruitless. No sooner are the stories of two or more characters brought together than they are torn away from one another, creating in the novel, as in the problem of race it maintains at an agonizing pitch, an energy of fusion and division in which opposites appear to be created neither by emotional merger nor by extreme alienation but rather by holding both in generative, ironic proximity. What Irving Howe says of the book's social, religious, and sexual levels—that they can be distinguished for the purpose of analysis but actually "work into one another as the materials of estrangement, the pressures that twist men apart"[26]—expresses this paradoxical tension well and defines, moreover, the true torment of Christmas's invisibility: the explosive pressure of containing the invisible in the visible and, more to the point, the visible in the invisible.

The circle of bondage that Joe Christmas at first seems to have broken in murdering Joanna Burden only leads him fatefully back to his place of birth.

In returning to Mottstown in the borrowed shoes of a Negro—"the black tide creeping up his legs, moving from his feet upward as death moves"—he has "made a circle and he is still inside of it." Having been carried by fate to what seems his last destination, Christmas is finally called by his true, schizophrenic name—the "white nigger"—and, as an anonymous narrator appropriately assuming the collective title of "they" tells us, he acts accordingly: "He never acted like either a nigger or a white man. That was it. That was what made folks so mad. For him to be a murderer and all dressed up and walking the town like he dared them to touch him, when he ought to have been skulking and hiding in the woods, muddy and dirty and, running. It was like he never even knew he was a murderer, let alone a nigger too."[27] Finally Christmas does "act like a nigger" and allows himself to be beaten and jailed, as though in brief anticipation of allowing himself to be shot and castrated, an act in which Gavin Stevens, we recall, would have us believe he "defied the black blood for the last time." The posture of Christmas in his seemingly insane passivity, fusing the contradictory tranquilities of Stowe's Uncle Tom and Nat Turner but in essence resembling neither, can be construed as a kind of psychological exhaustion motivated as much by the spent fury and defeat of his character in the novel's formal terms as in terms of any fully conscious (from his own point of view) or fully conceived (from Faulkner's point of view) ideological decision. This is not to say that his death—or its manner, or particularly its mode of presentation—is insignificant but, rather, that it must be viewed as representing a continuation of the formal crisis that Faulkner pursues frenetically throughout the book: the crisis of containing the dominant story of Joe Christmas *within* a book he threatens to tear into dispersed fragments and, consequently, of containing the novel's excessive physical and emotional violence *within* a meaningful and legitimately tragic structure.[28]

The extreme ambiguity of Christmas's behavior on the streets of Mottstown and in Hightower's kitchen (whether or not he acts like a "nigger," and why, is a point we must return to) can only be approached in abstract terms for the very good reason that the intense pressure of the novel, which resembles classical tragedy insofar as it leads Faulkner to a precarious invocation of Fate, appears to have grown out of the unexpected eruption, into "another" story, of the character Joe Christmas. To describe this eruption as a return of the repressed, the sudden casting over a story of the South of its long, peculiar shadow, is appropriate but, in formal terms, inadequate; aside from the special case of Joanna Burden and Joe Christmas there does not exist in the novel the kind of psychological union (and its inevitable inversion) between master and slave that compels *Pudd'nhead Wilson* and *Benito Cereno*. In terms of composition Twain's novel, because it began as a farce about Siamese twins and ended as a brilliantly botched

meditation on slavery and miscegenation, offers the best comparison, but it
is bound in contrast to appear, as it were, more psychologically integrated.
When Faulkner wrote to his editor, Ben Wasson, that *Light in August*
"seems topheavy" because "this one is a novel: not an anecdote,"[29] he not
only brought into perspective the work of his career up to that point but
also indicated an important formal development. Growing out of the violent
superficiality of *Sanctuary*, which had itself been reworked in terms of the
struggle in *As I Lay Dying* with loving, antagonistic analogous form, the
new novel represented a hybrid of the two in which Faulkner mastered the
realism of form by seeming to surrender to something beyond his control. The
many complaints voiced by readers that *Light in August* struggles desperately
but fails to bring the story of Christmas even into contact with the story of
Joanna Burden (and more notably the stories of Hightower and Hines, and
most notably those of Byron Bunch and Lena Grove) are perfectly justified:
perfectly, for how else can Christmas's strange career, as man and as symbol,
be characterized? The plunging, ravaging appropriation of larger and larger
blocks of historical material, the summoning of one after another approach
toward and withdrawal from the stranglehold of the past, leave Christmas
no less mysterious than when he is discovered on the steps of the orphanage
and christened with his blasphemous name.

It is not clear whether Faulkner thought the material devoted to
Christmas or that not devoted to him was responsible for making the novel
"topheavy," but it hardly matters. It is precisely these two bodies of material,
like the body of Christmas himself, that express in tangled and repulsive
contradiction the novel's precipitous achievement of the only union possible
between form and theme, between black and white, between the community
and its sacrificial object. The best critical comment on *Light in August* appears
almost incidentally in a 1945 letter to Faulkner from Malcolm Cowley, who
was then preparing *The Portable Faulkner*. Although he declared *Light in
August* "the best of your novels as novels," Cowley was frustrated because,
while it seemed to him at first that the novel "dissolved too much into the
three separate stories" of Lena, Hightower, and Christmas, he ultimately
found that they were "too closely interwoven" to be pulled apart. "It would be
easy for you to write Joe Christmas into a separate novel," Cowley remarked,
"but the anthologist can't pick him out without leaving bits of his flesh
hanging to Hightower and Lena."[30] The suggestive brutality of Cowley's
metaphor is no doubt equally incidental (surely more so than his decision,
with Faulkner's approval, to anthologize the story of Percy Grimm), but it
is nonetheless telling; for it describes, first, the wrenching physical union
between Christmas and his community that is violently longed for and
realized, and with more than equal violence rejected, in the novel; and
second, it describes the formal union that drives into fusion with others the

story of Christmas and yet leaves his story, like his self, isolated, naked, living nowhere and murdered everywhere.

The formal violence that is needed to include Christmas within the novel's plot (which is less a plot than a puzzle put together under the strain of forced analogy) is most evident in the single link between Christmas and Lena Grove, the character with whom the novel begins (as did Faulkner's composition) and ends, and whose story provides the frame and the filtered domestic warmth that makes Christmas's story all the more terribly ironic. The alienating contrast between Joe and Lena, who never meet except through the novel's relentless probing of mediated psychological union, has led Cleanth Brooks, with oxymoronic precision, to characterize *Light in August* as "a bloody and violent pastoral."[31] More immediately, it led Faulkner to what is at once the most improbable, haunting, and necessary scene in the book. When she mistakes Lena's baby for her grandson, "Joey . . . my Milly's little boy," Mrs. Hines brings the anguish of Joe [Hines]-McEachern-Christmas into a heightened relief that is only surpassed by Lena's consequent confusing of Christmas himself with the child's father, Lucas Brown-Burch: "She [Mrs. Hines] keeps on talking about him like his pa was that . . . the one in jail, that Mr Christmas. She keeps on, and then I get mixed up and it's like sometimes I can't—like I'm mixed up too and I think that his pa is that Mr—Mr Christmas too—".[32]

The union of Christmas and Lena exists only in—one might rather say, between—these two confusions about him as father and as son, a significant coupling because throughout the novel it is exactly the ambiguity of the filial relationship that determines the burden of his life. Moreover, and more importantly, it is also the relationship that is made to represent the trauma of the South in its acute sexual crisis—the threat that an invisible menace will become all too visible. Because the novel constantly raises the specter of miscegenation, that menace appears before us on every page, in nearly every line of Christmas's story with paradoxical clarity; but precisely for that reason—and even in spite of the vivid, lurid trysts of Joe and Joanna—we may forget, may want to forget what looms in the background of Christmas's life and his novel. Like the early illustrator of *Pudd'nhead Wilson* who either failed to read the book or was stricken by moral vertigo when he depicted the decidedly beautiful *white* Roxy as an Aunt Jemima figure, we may (certainly in the 1930s if not in the 1980s) simply not believe our eyes. The one doubtful and unverified fact of Christmas's existence that is responsible for Mrs. Hines's mad confusion (that he is the *son* of a "nigger") also sets in motion the menace unwittingly articulated in Lena's confusion (that the "nigger" will *father* a white woman's child) and compels Faulkner, on the verge of failing to bring his novel into any coherent focus, to risk a connection that is perfect to the very extent that it is the product of desperate fantasy. The power, as well as the necessity, of such a fantasy is the single feature that holds the fragmented, momentary crossings of plot in place and saves the novel from wasting every one of its passionate efforts at characterization. As he exists in this more extreme form of "passing" between worlds—from son of a "nigger" to "nigger" as white father—Christmas seems nearly a perverse caricature of white racial hysteria. Not so perverse, however, as the amendment to a typical "racial purity" bill introduced into the Virginia legislature in 1925 that would have required all citizens to register, with the state Bureau of Vital Statistics, all racial strains, however remote, that had ever entered their families; and not so hysterical as the climate of anxiety that led to the measure's rejection—because it was clear that many fine Virginians, living and dead, would be classed as Negroes.[33]

That hysteria in part determines the elegantly distorted shape of the novel, a shape determined (it might also be said) by the complementary pressure of containing Christmas, as character and as fantasy, who seems passively to bend the lives around him into a form capable of expressing his own, which in itself, if it is not nothing, is certainly left veiled and intangible. Irving Howe has noted that the "mulatto" excites in Faulkner "a pity so extreme as often to break past the limits of speech" and thus produces some of his "most intense, involuted and hysterical writing."[34] Simply at the level of syntax this observation applies more exactly to *Absalom, Absalom!* and parts of *Go Down, Moses*; but it is with respect to the form of *Light in August*, which may in the end pose more interesting formal problems, and which in any event appears to have made the later novels possible, that the importance of Howe's claim must be judged. In the novel that turned Faulkner's career toward its greatest materials and their most significant expression, the crisis of blood works jointly with the crisis of form, both turning Faulkner back toward the 1860s in search of a solution, however partial and fragile, to the continuing crisis of history in the South.

By way of passing to a more explicit consideration of the problem of the novel's form, let us note again that the intersection of the three crises—of form, of blood, of history—lies in the embracing crisis of sexuality, which compels the confusions that bring Christmas and Lena into their first, fantastic moment of contact and which generates a second, more oblique but more conclusive one, the contact made in the mediating presence of Hightower when Christmas is lynched. Although Brooks has rightly insisted that Christmas's death is a "murder" rather than a lynching,[35] I want to use the word with full deliberation in order to stress the climate of fantasy the book assumes and depends on for its power. In his 1929 study of lynching, dedicated to James Weldon Johnson, Walter White reported that the issue of sex "in the race problem and specifically in lynching is distorted by [a] conspiracy of semi-silence into an importance infinitely greater than the actual facts concerning it would justify." That conspiracy both results from and produces something of a willful blindness to what clearly exists (the historical fact of the rape of black women by white men during and after slavery) and a hallucinatory frenzy about what exists more in fantasy than in fact (the inexorable craving for and rape of white women by black men), thus making it nearly impossible, White noted, to elicit from many Southerners any kind of response on the subject but one of "berserk rage."[36]

There is no more need to point out that White's formulation is not intended to be definitive of an entire people than there is to add that it is true enough as an abstract representation, not of the South alone but of the entire nation that brought Jim Crow into visible existence, to warrant our attention. Before the character Christmas can bring these tensions and fears to their climactic expression in the outraged cry of his priestlike executioner, Percy Grimm—"Has every preacher and old maid in Jefferson taken their pants down to the yellowbellied son of a bitch?"[37]—he must himself be made to represent, to embody from both sides of the mask, the distortions of feeling and fate that the crisis of sexuality can release. He does so in the long, long plunge into his past that Faulkner requires seven chapters (almost exactly the middle third of the book) to negotiate. The flashback of Joe's earlier life centers him "within" a novel pervaded by frames, by memories of memories, by stories embedded within stories embedded within stories; that is, it brings him, as the novel does each of its major characters, out of the resonant darkness of the past and into the slight but explosive moments of contact before communion breaks in denial by rendering formally visible his unknown or unrecognized being already within them.

As Christmas exists as a fantasy of black within white, he comes in the novel's action to inhabit and create the critical moments of the lives of others—fortuitously in the case of Joanna Burden, fatefully in the case of Doc Hines, tragically in the case of Hightower, by the gamble of tenuous analogy in the case of Lena Grove, and with apparently preordained justice in the case of Percy Grimm. Faulkner's surging narrative dislocations of time have received more attention than any other aspect of the novel,[38] and rightly so, for they are all that can make dramatically plausible the lives of characters that are otherwise stunted by gorgeous but deadening obsessions. What is noticed less often is that the lives of those characters who most embody the life of Christmas as a racial fantasy (Joanna Burden, Hightower, Hines, Percy Grimm) are also the ones that Faulkner seems able to treat only by analogously disjointed plunges into the past. Once this is seen, however, we recognize as well that the shape of the novel is more distorted than ever. Aside from her functional act of childbearing, which reveals the potential contamination of Christmas as it appears and passes away in its most unnerving, because radically peripheral, form, Lena Grove serves simply and beautifully to frame and contain the violence of the novel;[39] and Byron Bunch, the displaced narrator on whom much of the burden of Faulkner's story falls, appears hardly more than the medium of Lena's containment of that violence, which centers in Christmas and reaches back toward chapter one and forth toward chapter twenty-one through the subsidiary frame of Hightower's life. The book's symmetry, of course, is not perfect, and there is no particular reason to wish it were; for though we may object to the narrative's chaotic detours and its forcing into probability coincidence upon coincidence, particularly in the aftermath of Joanna Burden's murder, the possibility ought also be entertained that it is only those diversions from a single line of action—into the extended recapitulative histories of Hines, Hightower, and Grimm—that can make visible the complete alienation of Christmas in formal terms. In order to eventuate in its appropriate sacrificial function, the story of Christmas must set in motion the stories that surround his not so much by merging, but rather by colliding, with them. Joe Christmas must be both central and marginal, sacred and profane, galvanizing and menacing: he must momentarily release into the public horror of revealed story those distorted passions of a community that are otherwise hidden and suppressed.

In recognizing that *Light in August*, like *As I Lay Dying* before it and *Go Down, Moses* after it, contains four or five incipient novels, we need to note that Faulkner's psychological chronology works toward an approximation of life rather than the seamless web of "fiction." As Byron Bunch realizes of his own increasingly perilous involvement with Lena, "*it was like me, and her, and all the other folks that I had to get mixed up in it, were just a lot of words that never stood for anything, were not even us, while all the time what was us was going on and going on without even missing the lack of words.*" This remark applies just as clearly and appropriately to Joe Christmas, who, like Addie in *As I Lay Dying*, almost willessly determines the shape of the stories that surround and impinge upon his own. The novel's expressed antagonisms between public and private, along with the attendant misunderstandings and hypocrisies they make possible, are realized in a narrative form whose rhetorical melodrama creates stories as they are needed, virtually at the moment they come into the action of being. Joanna Burden's story thus becomes "public" (as her life becomes meaningful) in the novel's terms by being expressively contained in Christmas's and released by her murder; the stories of Hines and Grimm, and the more significant depth of Hightower's, are similarly released by and into the public crisis precipitated by that murder and their own fated involvement in it. In an early scene that clarifies the degree to which *Light in August* represents an extension of the formal experiments of *As I Lay Dying*, the novel itself forecasts the form these expressions will take when Lena waits for a wagon that will take her to Jefferson. As the wagon approaches, "like already measured thread being rewound onto a spool . . . as though it were a ghost travelling a half a mile ahead of its own shape," Lena thinks to herself, "*it will be as if I were riding for a half mile before I even got into the wagon, before the wagon even got to where I was waiting, and . . . when the wagon is empty of me again it will go on for a half mile with me still in it.*"[40] There is no need to elaborate the way in which the novel, in story after story, in a recollective form that insists on the sudden and precarious violation of one life by others, gathers and rewinds the potentially random but critically connected threads of its lives. Any one of the characters might be compared to the wagon as a ghost traveling ahead of, and therefore determining, its own shape; they each "contain" already within themselves the lives that will be made manifest in strained momentary contact, and this containment, as well as the strain it expresses, is reflected in the visible, literal containment enacted by the novel's form.

In stressing that the issues of race and miscegenation are fully involved in the novel's form, there is no reason to suggest that this involvement is an explicitly causal one; *Light in August* might well have had a similar form without the ambiguity of Christmas's blood, without his being "Negro" at all. Obviously, though, it would not be the same novel, nor would it be capable of expressing with such haunting social and psychological complexity, with such power to contaminate and bring to crisis, the radical internalization of black within white. In this respect, the issue of blood, the epitome of the many spurious connections and analogies that fuse the novel's divergent lives, appears to be the only feature that rescues much of the narrative from a collapse into cascading, uncontrolled rhetoric. It does so by keeping that rhetoric at the tenuous edge of collapse and thereby measuring the fragility of the South's social and psychological order. Faulkner himself intimated the formal crisis the novel expresses when, in response to a question about the "style" of *Light in August*, he characteristically replied that he didn't "know much about style" but went on to speak vaguely of something "pushing inside him to get out."[41] Since Joe Christmas says almost exactly the same thing of his contaminated blood, there is nothing to prevent us from saying that this something, bluntly, is the "nigger in him"—"nigger" not as blood, as enslaving memory, as the simultaneously feared and needed *other*, but as all of these, as the formal and psychological embodiment of a crisis that became even more acute in the life of Jim Crow than it had been in the second generation of slaves and masters Cash speaks of. "Negro entered into white man as profoundly as white man entered into Negro—subtly influencing every gesture, every word, every emotion and idea, every attitude."[42]

The form of Joe Christmas's early life, released in a flashback constituting a third of the novel and framed by his murder of Joanna Burden, is itself pervaded by stories within stories that enact in further significant detail the interiorization of lives with which the remainder of the novel struggles. The most important of those stories, the story of Joanna Burden's heritage as it is placed within the context of her sexual ravishing, bears almost the entire moral weight of the issue of miscegenation. It ties together the different religious zealotries of Christmas's two surrogate fathers, McEachern and Hines, and it is forced into more explicit genealogical parallel with that of his last figurative father, Hightower, both in its antebellum depth and in the aroused suspicion of "nigger-loving." Like the corncob rape of Temple Drake in *Sanctuary*, what we remember most—are perhaps most meant to remember—about *Light in August* is the violent sexuality of Joe and Joanna, whose analogous expression is the ecstasy of religious fanaticism. This analogous relationship is amplified as soon as we notice in turn that the story of Hines, representing the obverse merger of the two, has a function similar to the psychobiography of Popeye that Faulkner appended in his revisions of *Sanctuary*. Although it is not the ironic joke that the story of Popeye's childhood seems to be, the story of Christmas's fated origin, placed within that of the maniacal Hines, represents an excursion into religious naturalism that expands, but cannot possibly explain, the horror that has already been revealed.

Extending the naturalistic tragedy of *Pudd'nhead Wilson* by enveloping it in an aura of Calvinistic damnation, Faulkner creates for Joe Christmas the prominent place in the classic American tradition many readers have sensed he has. He does so, however, in a way that has seldom been taken into full account, for Hines's obsession with the "bitchery" of original sin, raised to an extreme pitch by the specter of miscegenation, brings into view a very peculiar strain of Southern racist thought. Among the many bizarre and scandalous efforts to justify white supremacy by evicting the Negro altogether from the human species (and surely something of a highpoint in centuries of "scholarly" and "scientific" research into the subject), the most notorious at the turn of the century were those of Charles Carroll, who argued in *The Negro a Beast* (1900) and *The Tempter of Eve* (1902) that Eve was seduced by an apelike Negro, not a serpent, and that the whole history of man's long fall from grace therefore derived from this original sin of bestial miscegenation.[43] Such a distant tainting of white blood obviously raised questions answered only by a fanatical devotion that is more preposterous than its own germinal theory. It was a devotion the South was familiar with in less extravagant forms; and as we have seen in the case of *The Sound and the Fury*—and more particularly in the case of *Sanctuary*, where Popeye at several points is described with deliberate ambiguity as a "black man"—Faulkner had already begun developing a psychology of American original sin that would include its most troublesome, because undeniably "real," form—the mixing of white masters and black slaves. Faulkner invokes the hysteria of miscegenation as original sin only tangentially in *Light in August* (without further clarifying its broader historical import, as he would in *Absalom, Absalom!* and *Go Down, Moses*), but it is important to note that it, too, determines the form of Christmas's life by determining the form that the dependent crises of blood and sexuality take.

In the long act of narrative memory devoted to Christmas's life as he consciously knows it, both the resonant sexual terror of Joe and Joanna, which the whole novel strives to encompass and contain, and the "womansinning and bitchery" of Hines into which Faulkner's fascination with this terror eventually dissolves, are prefigured by an act of formal interiorization enveloping what may be the book's most preposterous and penetrating scene. In chapter eight, approximately in the middle of Christmas's story, his affair with Bobbie moves toward its violent climax—the apparent killing of McEachern—by moving first into the recent past. The chapter begins with Joe "passing swift as a shadow" down the rope he uses to escape his bedroom, and the next chapter begins with McEachern, the full power of his "bigotry and clairvoyance" turned on, recognizing Joe's shadow and following him to the dance. In between, we are carried back into a recollected account of Joe's affair with Bobbie, and in the middle of that account we are carried back to a peculiar moment earlier in Joe's life that is also framed on the one hand by his first surreptitious meeting with Bobbie and on the other by his physical attack on her when she reveals on that occasion that she is having her period and cannot make love. The brief flashback that interrupts the larger flashback, which interrupts yet larger flashbacks, is nothing less than a primitive act of sacrifice. Horrified by one of his adolescent friend's description of menstruation—"the temporary and abject helplessness of that which tantalised and frustrated desire; the smooth and superior shape in which volition dwelled doomed to be at stated and inescapable intervals victims of periodical filth"—Joe slaughters a sheep and kneels to it, "his hands in the yet warm blood of the dying beast, trembling, drymouthed, backglaring. Then he got over it, recovered." He does not forget what he has been told, but simply finds that he can "live with it, side by side with it." This strange act of purification, which is presented with little irony but which seems nonetheless flagrantly absurd, thematically recapitulates Joe's earliest memory (the parodic primal scene between the doctor and the dietician); it refers more immediately back to his refusal of a sexual encounter with a black girl ("enclosed by the womanshenegro," he is overcome by "something in him trying to get out, like when he had used to think of toothpaste"); and it points forward to his future sexual exploits—in which he will insist to lovers and whores alike that he is a Negro, through which the twisted passion of Joanna Burden will be released, and for which he will in the end be killed and castrated.[44]

The scene of the sheep slaughter is not particularly well conceived, and it is typical of Faulkner's lapses into obfuscation at critical moments in his plotting of symbolic action. It has little of the sacrificial significance of the hunt in *Go Down, Moses* and cannot carry the burden Faulkner apparently wants it to unless we recognize the figurative function of the blood sacrifice. We should emphasize, in this regard, that the novel's focus on sexuality at its climactic moments represents both a furthering and a containing of the form of violence it continually refers to more obliquely—the violence of slavery and racial hysteria, which either immediately or more remotely is dependent upon sexuality; that is, on "blood." The importance of this sacrificial scene thus lies in part in the fact, as René Girard has pointed out in a different context, that menstrual blood may easily be taken "as a physical representation of sexual violence," a representation whose "very fluidity gives form to the contagious nature of violence."[45] It is precisely such contagion that is rendered doubly powerful in the specter of miscegenation, the specter yoking violence with sexuality under whose aegis Joe Christmas is sacrificed in a violent denial of sexuality. The nature of that sacrifice requires further examination; but to see it clearly we must first see clearly the one union between two characters in *Light in August* that determines the warped shape of all the others: the relationship of Joe Christmas and Joanna Burden.

Their union is, of course, the book's center. It is a union of two masks, of mirror images (even in their names), that also parodies the possibility of real, loving union by reducing it to violent sex between a spinster living in "an old colonial mansion house" and a small-time hood living in its deserted "negro cabin." The enervating compulsion of their relationship arises as Faulkner, apparently striving to counter one myth, creates another that necessarily includes, extends, and makes more terrifying the first. For in countering the violent sexual desires of Christmas with the ever more frantic desire for violation he arouses in Joanna, Faulkner produces a psychological amalgamation that responds to the menace of physical amalgamation by internalizing it as a brutal struggle between conscious repression and unconscious eruption. As they exist in a bizarre replica of slave and master, enacting and passing between the South's own version of original sin and the contemporary threat it makes credible, Christmas and Joanna represent at a psychological level the tangle between *repression* and its failure that corresponds to the tangle between *oppression* and its failure at a social and political level. The fact that Joanna is a "nigger-loving" descendant of New Englanders is important to the extent that it reflects Southern accusations both before and after the war that the North endorsed miscegenation, and manifests in the mind of the South exactly that emancipation, in fact and in fantasy, which makes Christmas a monstrous figure; but this in turn is only fully dramatized when, once Joanna has been murdered, the community's antiabolitionist sentiments are forgotten and completely engulfed by racial hysteria. As the narrative puts it, she is killed "not by a negro but by Negro"; and when the community, hoping "that she had been ravished too," begins to "canvass about for someone to crucify,"[46] Joanna becomes more than anything else a "white woman," archetypically embodying Southern gynealotry and its concomitant "rape complex."

That complex, the result of an intense confusion between guilt and self-justification, has been analyzed by a number of social historians,[47] but prior to Faulkner it achieved its most popularly significant (though far less interesting and complicated) expression in the racist novels of Thomas Dixon, which had a prominent place among the racist sociological literature that quickened the rebirth of Jim Crow. The climactic scene of *The Clansman: An Historical Romance of the Ku Klux Klan* (1905), for example, involves the rape of a white heroine by a black "animal": "A single tiger-spring, and the black claws of the beast sank into the soft white throat and she was still." In the wake of such moral horror and degradation, the girl and her mother commit suicide rather than face the public humiliation it entails.[48] When Dixon's novel became *The Birth of a Nation* in 1915, the image of "the Negro as beast," long a stock figure in the South and elsewhere, was visibly fixed as the icon to which almost any justification of Jim Crow could ultimately be referred. Although the climate of hysteria that existed probably did not require it, the iconography received ample support, not just from obvious lunatics like Charles Carroll, but also from more respected commentators like William Hannibal Thomas, who dedicated *The American Negro: What He Was, What He Is, What He May Become* (1901) to "all American men and women of Negroid ancestry who have grown to the full stature of manhood and womanhood" but maintained, among other things, that "negro nature" is so "thoroughly imbruted with lascivious instincts" and "so craven and sensuous in every fibre of its being that a negro manhood with respect for chaste womanhood does not exist."[49] After endorsing Thomas's views, the novelist Thomas Nelson Page added that, although the actions of lynch mobs are indeed shocking, there is a deeper shock "at the bottom of their ferocious rage—the shock which comes from the ravishing and butchering of their women and children." The problem arises, Page observed in a characteristic mixture of frenzy and delicacy, because the teaching of equality means but one thing "to the ignorant and brutal young Negro"—"the opportunity to enjoy, equally with white men, the privilege of cohabiting with white women."[50]

Although there was considerable disagreement as to whether the "pure black" or the "mulatto" was most degenerate, and therefore most likely to violate white women, miscegenation was, at the height of Jim Crow, hardly seen as a serious solution. The point was nearly moot, however, since in the wake of *Plessy v. Ferguson* the "one-drop" rule prevailed in fact if not in every courtroom: as Thomas remarked, "a mass of white negroes would . . . merely add to an already dangerous social element," because "the variegated freedman would still be a negro in mind, soul, and body."[51] This, of course, is Joe Christmas's problem. And in *Can the White Race Survive?*—like White's *Rope and Faggot*, also published in 1929, the year in which *Light in August* appears to be set—James D. Sayers picked up the old and still predominant argument that civilization would eventually be destroyed unless the "frightful cancer" of miscegenation was eradicated with a surgeon's knife wielded "vigorously and with a steady hand . . . before it gets so spread into [our] vitals that it cannot be rooted out."[52] This, of course, is Percy Grimm's theory—not an uncommon one, either, even though the statistics on lynching, such as they were, showed that between 1900 and 1930 fewer than one sixth of the blacks lynched could actually be accused of rape.[53] But "those who believe in the visibility of ghosts," wrote Frederick Douglass, "can easily see them," for race prejudice "creates the conditions necessary to its own existence" and "paints a hateful picture according to its own diseased imagination."[54]

This is nearly the language of Hawthorne, and as such it clarifies one aspect of the "romance" of race in the South and in the nation, clarifies it even more brutally when we recall that Dixon's white supremacy novels were subtitled *Romances*. No more appropriate term can be imagined, however, for *Romance* in this case brings together in the "diseased imagination" Douglass invoked a virulent nostalgia, the menace of sexual violation, and a twisted utopian vision, which, to say the least, make the Southern penchant for Walter Scott pale in comparison. Such a characterization perfectly describes Dixon's *The Leopard's Spots: A Romance of the White Man's Burden, 1865–1900 (1902)*, the language of whose preface is calculated to arouse fantasy—"It will be a century yet before people outside the South can be made to believe a literal statement of the history of these times. I have tried to write this book with the utmost restraint"—and whose abiding message is the threat of the "mongrel breed" articulated most vividly by the Reverend John Durham: "*In a Democracy you cannot build a nation inside a nation of two antagonistic races; and therefore the future American must be either an Anglo-Saxon or a Mulatto.*" The test of a man's belief in equality, Durham later asserts, is "giving his daughter to a Negro in marriage. . . . When she sinks with her mulatto children into the black abyss of Negroid life, then ask him!" That Dixon's "test" seems nearly a parody of the stock question hardly discredits its power; on the contrary, it reenforces the obvious continuity of Southern thought on its most elemental, visceral issue. The war transformed the Negro into a "Beast to be feared and guarded," wrote Dixon, and now, as then, "around this dusky figure every white man's soul was keeping its grim vigil."[55]

That this "dusky figure," this shadow, is indeed a figure rather than a person is what generates the ambiguous power of Faulkner's own "romances" of race. It is in *Absalom, Absalom!* and *Go Down, Moses*, which like Dixon's romances spread across the entire history of the South, that the contagion of the racist imagination must be measured; but it is in *Light in August* that Faulkner found the key to the mysterious country of Yoknapatawpha by finding in Joe Christmas and Joanna Burden the climactic realization of a hysteria that had necessarily been building since Reconstruction. He found in Christmas the utter, alienating paradox of that contagion, and he found in Joanna Burden its gestating, enclosing receptacle. To put it in such sexual terms—thus literalizing the anxiety implicit in Cash's figurative assertion that "negro entered into white," as white had into Negro—is not at all unwarranted; for the complementary converse of Joe's repeated aversion to both black and white women ("the lightless hot wet primogenetive Female" that seems to enclose him "on all sides, even within him") is Joanna's nymphomania, which reaches its rhetorical climax in her frenzied erotic exclamation: "Negro! Negro! Negro!"[56] By making Joanna a "nigger-lover" before making her a "nigger's lover," Faulkner deflected attention away from a more unsettling possibility he had already explored in the brilliant story "Dry September" (1931), in which the "rape" of a white Southern spinster by a black man is clearly suggested to be a product of her own diseased imagination.[57] It may be that Faulkner found this possibility too dangerous to elaborate in *Light in August* and thus countered Joanna's explicit desire for violation with her New England abolitionism. As we have noted, however, it hardly matters; once she is murdered, she becomes as white and respectable and Southern as the communal hysteria requires.

In Joanna Burden's frenzied embodiment of a state of seizure that, with all the characteristics of released repression, expresses a direct counterpoint of the South's greatest fear, we also find an ironic emblem of the more far-reaching observation of James Weldon Johnson: "The South today stands panting and almost breathless from its exertions."[58] Just as Joe has spent much of his life in a state of "physical outrage and spiritual denial," "trying to breathe into himself the dark odor, the dark and inscrutable thinking and being of negroes, with each suspiration trying to expel from himself the white blood and the white thinking and being,"[59] Joanna's correlative breathless exertions engulf and internalize him as the alien *other*—the invisible seed of black blood that should be, that *must* be mixed with her own. Their physical union enacts a "pantomime of violation," as Howe remarks,[60] but it represents as well the vivid climax of the historical fantasy that created it. Entering the "gutter filth," the "sewer," the "bottomless morass," the "swamp," the "pit [of] the hot wild darkness" of Joanna's desire, Christmas enters the actualization of a fantasy that creates his life and leads to his death: "It seemed to him that he could see himself being hunted by white men at last into the black abyss which had been waiting, trying, for thirty years to drown him and into which now and at last he had actually entered." The surge of "pent black blood" that accompanies his execution, rushing "from out the slashed garments about his hips and loins . . . like a released breath," expresses the origin and end of racial violence as it is transformed from twisted fantasy into grim reality, as it is raised from invisible menace into visible sacrifice. The medium of that transformation, the shocking sexuality of Joe and Joanna, bears all the fateful weight of inherited tragedy as their affair nears its conclusion, the two of them "peopled, as though from their loins, by a myriad ghosts of dead sins and delights, looking at one another's still and fading face, weary, spent, and indomitable." And her false pregnancy with his "bastard negro child," apparently the result of menopause, is the ironic culmination of the novel's romance of blood.[61]

Maxwell Geismar is thus absolutely right, for the wrong reasons, to complain that the tragic union of "the Negro and the Female, the twin furies of Faulkner's deep southern Waste Land," leads to no redemption or proper catharsis in *Light in August*, but rather can express only "the world of human perversions whose precise nature is that they are also infantile emotions . . . the reflections of our early animal instincts which have been blocked and forced out of their normal channels of maturing."[62] The failure of emotional catharsis in the mating of Joe and Joanna, because it holds in tension the adolescent rite of purification Joe performs and the greater communal effort at purification performed by Percy Grimm, makes further evident the infantilizing relationship between white and black, which in some respects the abolition of slavery could not eliminate but could only intensify. It is therefore essential that the brutal gothicism of *Light in August*—which grows out of a union among Calvinism, racism, and naturalism—be seen to derive from "infantile emotions," for it is these very emotions that require a (white) system of social and political convention to be justified on the basis of (black) primitive, animal, "natural" instincts. This has been the argument of every racist commentator from antebellum years through the twentieth century; it even lies behind the most disturbing aspects of Thomas Jefferson's thoughts on black slavery in *Notes on the State of Virginia* (1787). Troubled that emancipation might not be possible without the freed slave "staining the blood of his master," Jefferson was driven to an analogy whose apparent absurdity nevertheless had the sanction of centuries of thought on the origins of blacks. Situating his understanding of the natural difference between black and white in the neoclassical language of beauty, Jefferson noted that the superiority of elegant, symmetrical white physiognomy was proved even by the Negroes' own "judgment in favour of whites, declared by their preference of them, as uniformly as is the preference of the Oranootan for the black woman over those of his own species."[63]

Jefferson did not bother, or could not bring himself, to unpack the details of this explosive analogy. Perhaps for him, rumored to be the father of mulatto children—and so portrayed in one of the first novels by a black American, William Wells Brown's *Clotel, or, The President's Daughter* (1853)— the emotions were too complex and personal to admit of extended analysis. His assertion in any event, as Winthrop Jordan remarks, recapitulates with a "geyser of libidinal energy" some of the "major tenets of the American racial complex" and at the same time may transfer to others his own repressed "desires, unacceptable and inadmissible to his society and to his higher self," thereby draining them "of their intolerable immediacy."[64] Such a dramatic transfer of repressed desire to its complementary paranoid fantasy describes rather exactly the progression of racist thought from slavery through the equally tenuous justifications of Jim Crow. The myth of excessive virility and lust in the Negro as "beast" derived historically from his presumed direct descent from the ape, most commonly the orangutan; and Jefferson's minor displacement of that theory of descent into more liberal distinctions—the black man preferring the white woman, as orangutans prefer black women over their own species—did little to hide its bluntness. Confronted with "that immoveable veil of black which covers all the emotions of the other race,"[65] Jefferson retreated to the safety—behind the further veil—of primitive, infantile fantasy.

There may be no reason now to take Jefferson too much to task—and there would have been less reason, say, in 1940, the year Richard Wright's *Native Son* exploded into the American imagination, releasing the Jim Crow nightmare in splendid horror. Described by the press in the novel as an "ape," a "missing link in the human species," a "jungle beast . . . in the grip of a brain-numbing sex passion," Bigger Thomas is the paradoxical cry of oppression and its violent protest, of fantastic fear and its requited realization. His "rape" and murder of Mary Dalton is terrible precisely because of the double pressure of fate and coincidence that brings it about; but in the press it is ascribed to the "minor portion of white blood in his veins, a mixture which generally makes for a criminal and intractable nature." Exposing the brutal rebellion a misconceived liberalism can produce, *Native Son* nonetheless transcends the actual violence it depicts in the hallucination of protest that, like a mirroring image, like the mask of a mask, pervades and creates the character of Bigger: "He wished that he could be an ideal in their minds; that his black face and the image of his smothering Mary and cutting off her head and burning her could hover before their eyes as a terrible picture of reality which they could see and feel and yet not destroy." The prosecution's assertion that Bigger burns Mary's body in order "to destroy evidence of offenses *worse than rape*," to obliterate the "marks of his teeth . . . on the innocent white flesh of her breasts," reminiscent as it is of *The Clansman*, is unnervingly countered by the greater, more legitimate violence in Bigger's own mind: "He committed rape every time he looked into a white face. He was a long, taut piece of rubber which a thousand white hands had stretched to the snapping point, and when he snapped it was rape. But it was [also] rape when he cried out in hate deep in his heart as he felt the strain of living day by day."[66]

Had it been Jefferson, Mississippi, rather than Chicago, Bigger would perhaps not, as the prosecutor goes on to remark, "have been accorded the high honor of sitting here in this court of law!" and of being executed by the machinery of deliberate justice. The difference between Joe Christmas and Bigger Thomas as deliberate, even stylized symbols of requisite sacrifice should not be ignored; but the enslaving fate that surrounds each of them, expressing a thorough interpenetration of fantasy and reality, is as similar as the details of their crimes—similar to the point that Bigger, in what seems a deliberate echo of Faulkner's refrain concerning the fate of Christmas, says early on, "Sometimes I feel like something awful's going to happen to me."[67] Of course everything that happens to Bigger and to Joe Christmas is awful. But whereas Wright's risk lay in the lure of a Marxist ideology that threatens to flatten out Bigger's tragedy, the risk in the case of Faulkner's novel is that the awful, forced to extremity in the grandiose rhythms of the prose and in the relentless probing of depravity, will become comic. Indeed, *Light in August* often verges on the burlesque horror of *Sanctuary*, but only at two points—in its delineation of Joanna Burden's murder and in Percy Grimm's bicycle chase of Christmas—does it slip over the edge, at both points in recoil from the greatest acts of violence the novel contains. The second, because it leads to the slaughter of Christmas, has the greater significance as an ironic, anticipatory release of pressure; the first, however, increases in splendor for having come straight out of Faulkner's Southern precursor, Poe.

The passerby who discovers the fire and then the nearly decapitated body of Joanna Burden is afraid "to pick her up and carry her out because her head might come clean off."[68] Her throat slashed ear to ear, Joanna seems an intentional mirror image of Madame L'Espanaye, who in "The Murders in the Rue Morgue" (1841) is decapitated by an orangutan wielding his master's razor. When her corpse is picked up, the head falls off. Insofar as Poe's story should be read in part as an oblique, libidinous racial fantasy, the details of the murder, the fear of whipping that initiates it, and the focus on the beast's mimic shaving with his murder weapon all have their relevant analogues in *Light in August*.[69] Faulkner does not bring the razor into such powerful symbolic focus as Melville had in *Benito Cereno*, and nowhere in *Light in August* does he directly compare Joe Christmas to an orangutan: he did not have to, so much was the "Negro as beast" a part of Southern—and

American—racial iconography. And though we should note as well that he was probably drawing on a similar murder of a white woman by decapitation with a razor (followed by the lynching and castration of the black murderer) that occurred near Oxford in 1908,[70] it is the heritage of racial violence, surrounding this actual murder as well as its fictional counterpart and enveloping both in the convulsive fantasies of blood violation, that must be seen to contain *within* it the power of *Light in August*. As Christmas himself both contains, and is contained within, a myth, so the novel embodies within itself the many threads of a racial myth—unwinding and rewinding in both Faulkner's career and his nation's history—that in a larger way embodies it.

The murder of Joanna Burden, which appears as a kind of shadow play of weapons, revolver and razor,[71] and which follows from her final attempt to get Christmas to kneel with her in prayer, is the last, antagonistic expression of the violence their combative sexual affair has mimicked all along. As such it casts back to the ritual sacrifice Joe performs to cleanse himself of the horror of menstrual blood ("It's something that happens to them once a month," his companion had said) and forecasts the ambiguous absolution he finds kneeling behind a table when he is murdered in Hightower's house. Enveloping the two murders and the affair that produces them, and enveloping the novel and the heritage that produces it, is the potent symbol of "the black shadow in the shape of a cross" that Joanna invokes at the climax of her family's story. Although the shadowed cross is black, the crucified are white; the "shadow in which" all live, black and white, is the perfectly ambiguous expression of the burden of white *within* black *within* white—of what her father calls "a race doomed and cursed to be forever and ever a part of the white race's doom and curse for its sins."[72] There is no need to go through the contortions some readers have to see Christmas as a Christ figure; his career simply includes that potential significance (as, in a different fashion, Lincoln's career did) but surpasses any actual relevance it could have—except (here again like Lincoln) as the ironically tortured emblem that releases into the surging rhythms of racial fantasy the degeneration of Southern gynealotry (Joanna Burden), the tautological frenzy of zealous racism (Doc Hines), the last gasp of the Lost Cause (Hightower), and the dream come true of the Invisible Empire (Percy Grimm). What it does more conclusively is continue to depict the psychological confusion in (and quite nearly the inversion of) the relationship between master and slave, in which a literal and visible ascendancy is engulfed by one that is figurative and invisible. Joe Christmas lives between these two possibilities, passes between them, and it is there that he dies.

Faulkner began *Light in August* in August of 1931, the centennial anniversary of Nat Turner's bloody rebellion in Southampton, Virginia. The Turner insurrection, in which some fifty whites were murdered, erupted out of nowhere—or so it seemed to many Southerners. A religious fanatic who early in his life had apocalyptic visions of "white spirits and black spirits engaged in battle," of lighted figures in the sky stretched "from east to west, even as they were extended on the cross on Calvary for the redemption of sinners," Turner claimed in the purported confessions recorded by Thomas Gray that he was divinely inspired to take up Christ's yoke and "fight against the Serpent, for the time was fast approaching when the first should be last and the last should be first."[73] The threat of Turner's rebellion was thus mitigated in some minds by his madness; only insanity could lead otherwise contented slaves to such brutal atrocities. Aside from the crazed rebel slave in Harriet Beecher Stowe's *Dred* (1856), Turner received little significant literary attention until the appearance in 1967 of William Styron's *The Confessions of Nat Turner*, a novel designed to reassure no one, black or white.

The aspect of Styron's searing fictional account of Turner's life that has aroused most controversy is his explicit portrayal of Turner's imagined sexual attraction to several white women, most particularly to the white girl who appears to be the only person Turner himself actually killed. If this part of the novel is to be deprecated, however, it must also be measured, for example, against the portrayal of "rape" in *Native Son*. Turner's desire (as Styron depicts it) to fill his future victim with "warm milky spurts of desecration" or, in another instance, to repay the "pity" and "compassion" of a weak white woman with "outrageous spurts of defilement" and produce in her "the swift and violent immediacy of a pain of which I was complete overseer,"[74] is nothing less than the actualization of a fantasy that may have existed during slavery (although Turner's insurrection, among others, was remarkably free from such sexual retribution) but arose more clearly in the twentieth century *between* black and white, making deceptively confused the masks that faced and reflected each other, and enclosing both in the violence the threat of amalgamation could release. Without minimizing the important differences between the situations and the historical renderings of Bigger Thomas and Styron's Nat Turner, we should note as well that from the standpoint of their creators they are two sides of a coin, two masks of violence turning against itself in redoubled, nearly tautological frenzy. The power driving this frenzy, as James Baldwin has observed in the case of Bigger, is simply that of a "complementary faith among the damned," which may lead them at last to a forcing "into the arena of the actual those fantastic crimes of which they have been accused, achieving their vengeance and their own destruction through making the nightmare real."[75]

Faulkner was dead by the time Styron's novel appeared; he thought well of *Native Son*; and there is no evidence, aside from the coincidence of the date he began *Light in August*, that he knew or cared much about Nat

Turner. But the psychology of amalgamation, and the violence it responds to and extends, are rendered visible on nearly every page of Faulkner's novel. It is a psychology that thoroughly depends on the paradox of retributive violence—a paradox Faulkner often described in response to questions about violence in his fiction as something "man must combat" even when "he has been strangled by degradation and violence, when he has hated the violence he participated in, when he has resisted the violence, when he believed in something like honor and pride and compassion, even in degradation."[76] Sex, he added, has much the same function; indeed, it is difficult to conceive of their separation in his novels, so completely do they penetrate each other, like white and black. Because violence and sexuality determine the contours of the South's romance of blood, it is worth pointing out again that the relationship between *Sanctuary* and *Light in August*, Faulkner's two most violent and sexual novels, is an important one. As we noted earlier, the ambiguous delineation of Popeye as a "black man" casts back in the American tradition toward Hawthorne's probing of the secret thrills of Puritan repression, and at the same time prefigures Faulkner's confrontation in *Light in August*, *Absalom, Absalom!*, and *Go Down, Moses* of the more haunting, more historically immediate complexity of that repression. By making literal in Joe Christmas the figurative coloring of Popeye and extending by a single degree the nymphomania of Temple Drake into the comic depravity of Joanna Burden, Faulkner himself passed the color line that would define his major work and extend the boundaries of classic American fiction to include a tormenting problem that underlay each successive challenge to the failing vision of democratic freedom.

Faulkner's struggle with the problem of narrative form up to and including *Light in August* must therefore be seen to contain as well his evolving effort to include a tradition that is both larger than his own and yet in the twentieth century completely dependent on it. *Light in August*, heaving and bulging with the effort to integrate those traditions, barely survives the pressure it produces, but it turns Faulkner, as it would Styron, back toward the century in which the amalgamation of America and the South seemed least likely and became most crucial. The accounts of those readers of *Light in August* who have tried to emphasize that Christmas is characteristic of the "isolated, doomed heroes" of classic American fiction; that he takes his place in the "descending spiral of isolation, rebellion, and denial" that is "the heritage of American negation"; or that he personifies "the most extreme phase conceivable of American loneliness,"[77] are thus correct but require a different emphasis. The critics I quote from here hardly deny the importance of race, but they focus on a problem of literary characterization that in the case of *Light in August* both contains, and must be subordinated to, a more particular social one. "The problem of the twentieth century," W.E.B. Du

Bois remarked in *The Souls of Black Folk* (1903), "is the problem of the color-line."[78] By embodying that problem in a character whose very physical and emotional self embodies the sexual violence of racial conflict, Faulkner made the problem painfully visible and immediate.

He did so most evidently by enacting in the novel's form the crisis that motivates its action. We have already noted that Christmas both dominates the novel and threatens to tear it apart, and that the peculiar form of the novel derives in large part from the way in which the characters of Joanna Burden, Hines, Hightower, and Grimm come into being in the long plunges into the past that contact with Christmas brings about. The actualization of their lives, in bold, alienating movements away from a line of integrated narrative action, expresses in the novel's form a crisis responding to the violent crisis of blood that the contagion of Christmas represents. Donald Kartiganer is thus right to say that, because the novel's isolated characters and scenes all "revolve around, and blur into, [the] impenetrable center" of Christmas's story, even as that story itself "dissolves into expanding configurations of meaning," *Light in August* is a novel whose form "feeds on its own dissolution."[79] What is most striking about the novel is that despite the later novel's extraordinary increase in narrative and syntactical complexity *Light in August* is much harder to keep in focus than *Absalom, Absalom!* The radical involution of fiction within fiction in the story of Charles Bon has no equal moment in *Light in August*, in which the crisis of blood, the "containing" of black within white, white within black, derives its power from collision, penetration, and withdrawal rather than from the dramatic marriages of opposing forces that Faulkner would strive for in Quentin's and Shreve's imaginative reconstructions. Both the action and the form of *Light in August* answer violence with violence, tearing away from each other lives and stories as they threaten to become joined. At a psychological level they do indeed blur into each other; but at a narrative level that responds to the deepest need of that psychology, they remain vivid and powerless in their segregation.

It is for good reason, then, that in accounting for Christmas's flight to Hightower's house Faulkner first raises the possibility of "like to like" and then replaces it with Gavin Stevens's equally inadequate theory of a battle in Christmas between white blood and black blood. The long, most isolating plunge into the past of Hightower that follows Christmas's death offers little that is relevant to Christmas's life, or even to Hightower's act of providing him with a futile, last-minute alibi—little, that is, but one of the many tortured myths that lie behind the enslavement in which Joe Christmas, like Jim Crow, is still trapped. Christmas's act of striking down Hightower, like a "vengeful and furious god pronouncing doom," issues only in the overcharged, overcompensating rhetoric of Hightower's final visions of the haloed wheel and the tumultuous rush of cavalry. As though spending in wild abandon the accumulated fury he could not bring into the focus of dramatic involvement, Faulkner tears away from each other the two characters who might most conceivably have been linked. They remain connected only by the slender threads of Faulkner's recurring plot of skipped generations, tied and untied with merciless haste, and by the fanatical exclamations of abomination and bitchery that mercilessly isolate Christmas's grandfather. Both the sexual frenzy of Hines and the visions of Hightower that are its ironic, sublimated corollary are surpassed in significance by the act of sacrifice that the one leads toward and the other falls away from. The "single instant of darkness" in which each of them continues to live can neither approach nor further elaborate the visionary scene of Christmas's death that grows out of Percy Grimm's violent act and his swift, brutal proclamation:

> "Now you'll let white women alone, even in hell," he said. But the man on the floor had not moved. He just lay there, with his eyes open and empty of everything save consciousness, and with something, a shadow, about his mouth. For a long moment he looked up at them with peaceful and unfathomable and unbearable eyes. Then his face, body, all, seemed to collapse, to fall in upon itself, and from out the slashed garments about his hips and loins the pent black blood seemed to rush like a released breath. It seemed to rush out of his pale body like the rush of sparks from a rising rocket; upon that black blast the man seemed to rise soaring into their memories forever and ever.[80]

Christmas's passive, suicidal participation in this act is one of several features that have led readers to envision him as a Christ figure. When he was once asked about this, Faulkner simply replied that because there are, after all, very few plots in the world of literature and because "that Christ story is one of the best" that has been "invented," it is likely that "it will recur."[81] When Christmas rises "forever and ever" into the memories of his executioners, the Christ story recurs in a fragmented form that depends on it ironically at best. It certainly depends upon it less, for example, than does *Uncle Tom's Cabin* (1852), whose author quite rightly claimed to have depicted nothing "that equals the frightful reality of scenes daily and hourly acting on our shores, beneath the shadow of American law, and the shadow of the cross of Christ," but seemed also to believe that only the "sons of white fathers" among slaves, only those with the "haughty feelings" of Anglo-Saxon blood "burning in their veins," could rise in revolt "and raise with them their mother's race."[82] Stowe, of course, meant to increase her rhetorical power by these remarks rather than undermine it. But as Baldwin has trenchantly observed of the novel whose hero acquires his superhuman powers of humiliating endurance from a vision of the suffering Christ, *Uncle Tom's Cabin* wears the secret "mask of cruelty." Although it poses as a catalogue of actual crimes and heart-rending violence, its emphatic racist sentimentalism betrays a "theological terror, the terror of damnation," which in the end is "not different from that terror which activates a lynch mob." As Baldwin's challenging remarks suggest, the terror behind Stowe's mask may be the distinguishing characteristic of a drama of repression, which when it is inverted leads directly to Bigger Thomas, who is so much Uncle Tom's contemporary descendant, "flesh of his flesh," that if the books are placed together it seems Stowe and Wright (not at all unlike Joanna Burden and Joe Christmas, we might add) "are locked together in a deadly, timeless battle; the one uttering merciless exhortations, the other shouting curses."[83]

To see this inversion clearly and to measure the changing climate of racial fantasy that makes it possible, we need only to place *Light in August* between the two books and their authors. Welding together the suffering passivity of Uncle Tom and the violent rage of Bigger Thomas, Joe Christmas, his own blood violently released in retribution for the blood he has spilt and violated, is surrounded on the one hand by the theological terror of Joanna Burden and Doc Hines, and on the other by its twentieth-century machinery of execution, the hysterical, overbearing violence of Percy Grimm. Christmas's death is as much a "lynching" as he is a "Negro"; that is, technical details do not count here. What counts is the fantasy Christmas embodies and exposes in others by appearing to act "like a nigger," by releasing formally and actually what Walter White called "the Frankenstein monster" of lynching, which puts its creators in fear of their own creation and threatens to bring about more violence than it can ever control.[84] It is thus significant that Faulkner agreed with Cowley that the Percy Grimm section should be anthologized in *The Portable Faulkner*, for as Faulkner remarked at that later date, he had "created a Nazi" before Hitler did, a "Fascist galahad who saved the white race by murdering Christmas."[85]

The power of the analogy between slavery and fascism, both productive of complex psychological infusions of overt hatred with infantalizing dependency, has been noted by historians and literary critics alike.[86] We need not accept it in detail here in order to see that the sacrifice of Joe Christmas by Percy Grimm—a sacrifice made in the name of a thorough denial, not just of the threat Christmas poses, but of the one he already contains within him as its requisite opposite—is exceeded in actual violence by the hallucinating specter that momentarily coalesces into a physical act. The physical violence of the sacrifice, like the sexual contagion it responds to, is enveloped in a violence that knows no tactile, containing bounds. One might well speak, then, of a form of violence that corresponds in part to the novel's displayed struggle with the form of Christmas's life and story; as his very existence sets in motion, but cannot be controlled by, the fantasies it arouses, so his murder cannot in any clear or final way, can with no catharsis or resolution, control or make meaningful their pattern. In this respect, Christmas's death is utterly opposed, for example, to that of Billy Budd, which conforms in measured, stately fashion to the mechanisms of justice that create and define Captain Vere's fatherly authority and reenforce the Christology of his victim.

Christmas's death is a sacrifice not because he sees it that way, or because Percy Grimm necessarily does, or even because the novel suggests that it is; rather, it is sacrificial in that it depends on the "mechanism of reciprocal violence," which René Girard has shown to be the origin of, and to be fully expressed by, ritual sacrifice. The reciprocal violence Girard describes is a "vicious circle" from which the community, once it has entered, in unable to extricate itself without selecting a surrogate victim who can contain the spread of violence by taking it upon himself. As such, the surrogate victim may be seen as a "monstrous double," a figure who is both inside and outside the community, who embodies all its possible differences, and thus "constitutes both a link and a barrier between the community and the sacred."[87] In designating Christmas a surrogate victim, we should be quick to note that he is no more carefully selected to die as a way of warding off further violence than he is, in his death, able to do so. The violence continues to spread—in the lives of the novel and in Faulkner's own novels of the next twenty years; in the agony of Jim Crow that Faulkner's novels and public declarations could do little to stop; and in the fantasies of violated blood that racial equality paradoxically resists and promotes. Like the contagion of sexual violence represented in the menstrual blood that horrifies Christmas by its monstrous significance, the contagion of violence that grows out of the fear of miscegenation represents a menace that has visible actualizations but invisible meaning.

Although Faulkner apparently never witnessed a lynching, his life was surrounded by them.[88] From at least two of them he drew the materials of *Light in August* and *Intruder in the Dust*; in the second he would temporarily resolve the crisis of blood, but in the first he gave way to the full horror it could release. Christmas is not a surrogate victim in the precise sense Girard describes, but as the "white nigger" he is very much, almost too much a monstrous double, for he contains—mask to mask, in mirroring images—the community's own projected desires and fears as well as their reciprocal realization. Like Twain's monstrous double, Tom Driscoll, who wears charcoal blackface when he murders his white "father," Joe Christmas embodies the twin acts of vengeance and sacrifice, neither of them within his control nor clearly ascribable to a conscious act of will; but unlike Tom and unlike Bigger Thomas, Melville's Babo, or Nat Turner, Joe is not "decently hung by a force, a principle" but, as his grandmother fears, is "hacked . . . dead by a Thing." That "thing" is not simply Percy Grimm (who is only its symbol, as Christmas himself is the symbolic embodiment of miscegenation) but an awesome power Faulkner can only account for by the mystic invocation of Fate—the "Player." Likewise, Christmas's castration, the mirroring affirmation and denial of sexuality, is a grotesque distortion of violent reciprocity. Occurring outside the sacrificial process of justice whose machinery may take the place of surrogate victimization in the control of contagious violence, the form of Christmas's death ensures, as White and Twain observed of lynching, that such violence will go on. The legitimized, legal violence with which *Native Son*, *Pudd'nhead Wilson*, *Benito Cereno*, and Nat Turner's rebellion all end serves to remind us that the shocking violence of *Light in August* depends in large part on its vitiating and overwhelming a system that cannot control it. As Faulkner put it quite appropriately in an episode that is otherwise humorous (the useless bloodhounds employed to track Christmas): "It was as if the very initial outrage of the murder carried in its wake and made of all subsequent actions something monstrous and paradoxical and wrong, in themselves against both reason and nature."[89]

This loss of control; this monstrous swelling of paradoxical actions is expressed, again, not just in the blasphemous character of Christmas himself, but also in the novel's form from beginning to end—most particularly, of course, from the moment the murder of Joanna Burden begins a third of the way into the novel. It is precisely at that point that the nearly uncontrollable fury of Faulkner's narrative is released. The threat of physical amalgamation, of the disintegration of racial distinctions, erupts into a violent assertion of distinctions—one that radically denies the physical amalgamation that already exists and the psychological amalgamation that follows from it; and one that leads Faulkner, in the face of such a blurring of emotions, to an equally violent and alienating narrative form. The attempt to unite the crisis of blood and the crisis of narrative form continues beyond *Light in August* in the more precisely probed and controlled violence of *Absalom, Absalom!* and *Go Down, Moses*, and it may be said to continue in the consciously measured and carefully worded rhythms of Faulkner's later public statements on the question of race. Like Twain's "imitation nigger," no less the "monstrous freak" than the Siamese twins his character grew from, and like Twain himself, Faulkner was haunted by an unanswerable question: "Why were niggers *and* whites made? What crime did the uncreated first nigger commit that the curse of birth was decreed for him? And why this awful difference made between white and black?"[90] *Light in August* begins Faulkner's stunning explorations of that question, explorations that would lead him deeper into his own past and into the past of his own first fiction; deeper into a history that came more visibly and paradoxically into focus as his career became more public and his native country more stridently recalcitrant on the question of race; and deeper into a moral and psychological problem that engulfs the promise of freedom. It would lead him next to an epic rendering of his country's epic trauma: the trauma of the house divided.

NOTES

24. James Weldon Johnson, *The Autobiography of an Ex-Coloured Man* (New York: Alfred A. Knopf, 1927), p. 21.

25. Kenneth Burke, *A Rhetoric of Motives*, quoted in Joseph Skerrett, "Irony and Symbolic Action in James Weldon Johnson's *The Autobiography of an Ex-Coloured Man*," *American Quarterly* 32, no. 5 (Winter 1980): 558. On Johnson's incest novel, see Skerrett, p. 550. On Dixon's novel, also published in 1912, see pp. 143–44 below.

26. Irving Howe, *William Faulkner: A Critical Study*, 2nd ed. rev. (New York: Vintage-Random, 1960), p. 65.

27. *Light in August*, pp. 321, 326, 331.

28. The best considerations of the novel's form along these lines are Donald M. Kartiganer, *The Fragile Thread: The Meaning of Form in Faulkner's Novels* (Amherst: University of Massachusetts Press, 1979), pp. 37–68; and Alfred Kazin, "The Stillness of *Light in August*," in Frederick J. Hoffman and Olga W. Vickery, eds., *William Faulkner: Three Decades of Criticism* (New York: Harcourt, Brace & World, 1963), pp. 247–65.

29. *Selected Letters*, p. 66.

30. Malcolm Cowley, *The Faulkner-Cowley File: Letters and Memories, 1944–1962* (1966; reprint ed., Baltimore: Viking-Penguin, 1978), pp. 28–29.

31. Cleanth Brooks, *William Faulkner: The Yoknapatawpha Country* (New Haven: Yale University Press, 1963), p. 54.

32. *Light in August*, pp. 376, 388—ellipsis Faulkner's.

33. Walter White, *Rope and Faggot: A Biography of Judge Lynch* (New York: Alfred A. Knopf, 1929), pp. 69–75. This would seem far-fetched if the official United States census for 1930 had not itself carried the following instructions: "A person of mixed white and Negro blood should be returned as a Negro, no matter how small the percentage of Negro blood." See Woodward, *American Counterpoint*, p. 86.

34. Howe, *William Faulkner: A Critical Study*, p. 129.

35. Brooks, *William Faulkner: The Yoknapatawpha Country*, pp. 51–52, 60–62.

36. White, *Rope and Faggot*, pp. 54–55.

37. *Light in August*, p. 439.

38. For the best discussion of this problem, see Carolyn Porter, "The Problem of Time in *Light in August*," *Rice University Studies* 61, no. 1 (Winter 1975): 107–25.

39. In this regard Wright Morris is correct to point out that, although she is "the great mother, the abiding earth, the patient and enduring force of life," it is the reciprocally "surrounding tension and incipient violence that give Lena Grove such serenity, and *Light in August* a ballast, an emotional stability, almost unique in the works of Faulkner." See *The Territory Ahead*, p. 181.

40. *Light in August*, pp. 330, 6.

41. Gwynn and Blotner, eds.., *Faulkner in the University*, p. 77.

42. W. J. Cash, *The Mind of the South* (1941; reprint ed., New York: Vintage-Random, 1960), p. 51.

43. Charles Carroll further maintained, for example, that at the time of the Flood, Noah and his wife were the only pure whites left on the earth; unfortunately, there was a pair of Negroes among the beasts on the Ark, and amalgamation began again soon after

the Flood. Christ was then sent to "redeem man from atheism, amalgamation, and idolatry" and "to rebuild the barriers which God erected in the Creation between man and the ape." Miscegenation, Carroll argued (and here he was more in line with some more rational antebellum abolitionists), was the reason for God's destruction of slavery; but he concluded from this that the "cursed" and "degenerate" mulattoes descended from these and more recent couplings had no right to live. See I. A. Newby, *Jim Crow's Defense: Anti-Negro Thought in America, 1900–1930* (Baton Rouge: Louisiana State University Press, 1965), pp. 92–98; and George M. Fredrickson, *The Black Image in the White Mind: The Debate on Afro American Character and Destiny, 1817–1914* (New York: Harper & Row, 1971), p. 277.

44. *Light in August*, pp. 120, 159, 189, 173–74, 146–47.

45. René Girard, *Violence and the Sawed*, trans. Patrick Gregory (Baltimore: Johns Hopkins University Press, 1977), pp. 34–36.

46. *Light in August*, pp. 32, 271–72.

47. On this problem in particular and the attitudes and theories that produced it, see Cash, *Mind of the South*, pp. 85–89, 117–20; White, *Rope and Faggot*, pp. 54–81; Newby, *Jim Crow's Defense*, pp. 122–40; Claude H. Nolen, *The Negro's Image in the South: The Anatomy of White Supremacy* (Lexington: University of Kentucky Press, 1967), pp. 29–39; Forrest G. Wood, *Black Scare: The Racist Response to Emancipation and Reconstruction* (Berkeley and Los Angeles: University of California Press, 1967), pp. 143–53; Lawrence J. Friedman, *The White Savage: Racial Fantasies in the Postbellum South* (Englewood Cliffs, NJ.: Prentice-Hall, 1970), pp. 140–68; and Fredrickson, *The Black Image in the White Mind*, pp. 256–88.

48. Thomas Dixon, *The Clansman: An Historical Romance of the Ku Klux Klan* (Ridgewood, NJ.: Gregg Press, 1967), pp. 304–8. Throughout his life Faulkner owned a copy of the novel that had been presented to him by his first-grade teacher in 1905. See Blotner, *Faulkner: A Biography*, 1:94.

49. William Hannibal Thomas, *The American Negro: What He Was, What He Is, What He May Become* (New York: Macmillan, 1901), pp. v, 180, 182.

50. Thomas Nelson Page, *The Negro: The Southerner's Problem* (New York: Charles Scribner's Sons, 1904), pp. 80–85, 99–100, 112–13.

51. Thomas, *American Negro*, pp. 407, 411.

52. James D. Sayers, *Can the White Race Survive?* (Washington, D.C.: Independent Publishing Co., 1929), pp. 11, 171.

53. See Arthur F. Raper, *The Tragedy of Lynching* (Chapel Hill: University of North Carolina Press, 1933), p. 20.

54. Frederick Douglass, "The Color Line" (1881), in *The Life and Writings of Frederick Douglass*, ed. Philip S. Foner, 4 vols. (New York: International Publishers, 1955), 4:343. In "Why Is the Negro Lynched?" (1894), Douglass noted that from Reconstruction through the early 1890s, the South employed on behalf of lynching an "orderly arrangement" of excuses that "show design, plan, purpose and invention." As the old lies of insurrection and Negro supremacy lost their ability to deceive, Douglass wrote, the "heart-rending cry of the white women and little white children" took their place. See pp. 491–523.

55. Thomas Dixon, *The Leopard's Spots: A Romance of the White Mane Burden, 1865–1900* (Ridgewood, N.J.: Gregg Press, 1967), pp. x, 336, 463–64, 5.

56. *Light in August*, pp. 107, 245.

57. See *Collected Stories of William Faulkner* (New York: Random House, 1950), pp. 169–83. Unlike *Light in August*, the crisp power of "Dry September" derives from Faulkner's not depicting the "attack" or the lynching but dwelling instead on the surrounding actions. The last image we get of Minnie Cooper, who had attended a motion picture while her accused attacker is being beaten or killed, is particularly revealing: "They removed the pink

voile and the sheer underthings and the stockings, and put her to bed, and cracked ice for her temples, and sent for the doctor. He was hard to locate, so they ministered to her with hushed ejaculations, renewing the ice and fanning her. While the ice was fresh and cold she stopped laughing and lay still for a time, moaning only a little. But soon the laughing welled again and her voice rose screaming. . . . 'Do you suppose anything really happened?' [they said,] their eyes darkly aglitter, secret and passionate. 'Shhhhhhh! Poor girl! Poor Minnie!'" As Walter White remarked, "the Southern white woman's proneness to hysteria where Negroes are concerned . . . needs investigation by a competent psychologist" (*Rope and Faggot*, p. 57).

58. Johnson, *Autobiography of an Ex-Coloured Man*, p. 75.

59. *Light in August*, p. 212.

60. Howe, *William Faulkner: A Critical Study*, p. 69.

61. *Light in August*, pp. 99, 242, 246, 248, 255, 313, 440, 264, 251.

62. Maxwell Geismar, *Writers in Crisis: The American Novel, 1925–40* (1947; reprint ed., New York: E. P. Dutton, 1971), pp. 164–68. The same half twist of logic that makes Geismar's argument useful also betrays him in his further insistence that Christmas is "the 'emancipated' new negro, who must be punished with all the devices of Faulkner's hatred." Because the pair "symbolize for Faulkner all the evils which have befallen his land," Geismar remarks, "what better expression of his scorn can the southern writer produce than to have the sterile female accept the emancipated negro as her sexual partner, to have her humiliated by the negro, and to have her murdered by the negro" (p. 174).

63. *The Portable Thomas Jefferson*, ed. Merrill D. Peterson (New York: Viking Press, 1975), pp. 193, 186–87.

64. Winthrop Jordan, *White over Black: American Attitudes Toward the Negro, 1550–1812* (1968; reprint ed., New York: W. W. Norton, 1977), pp. 458–59. On this aspect of Jefferson's thought and life in general, see pp. 457–99; and John C. Miller, *The Wolf by the Ears: Thomas Jefferson and Slavery* (New York: The Free Press, 1977). The evidence for Jefferson's fathering of mulatto children has been widely disputed and is not conclusive.

65. *Portable Thomas Jefferson*, p. 187.

66. Richard Wright, *Native Son* (New York: Harper & Row, 1966), pp. 260, 261, 123, 376, 214.

67. Ibid., pp. 376, 23. Cf. *Light in August*, pp. 97, 110, 256, 261.

68. *Light in August*, p. 85.

69. Overshadowed by *The Narrative of A. Gordon Pym*, the peculiarly Southern dimensions of several of Poe's stories is often overlooked. The most relevant passage in "The Murders in the Rue Morgue" runs as follows:

As the sailor looked in, the gigantic animal had seized Madame L'Espanaye by the hair (which was loose, as she had been combing it), and was flourishing the razor about her face, in imitation of the motions of a barber. The daughter lay prostrate and motionless; she had swooned. The screams and struggles of the old lady (during which the hair was torn from her head) had the effect of changing the probably pack purposes of the Ourang-Outang into those of wrath. With one determined sweep of its muscular arm it nearly severed her head from her body. The sight of blood inflamed its anger into phrensy. Gnashing its teeth, and flashing fire from its eyes, it flew upon the body of the girl, and imbedded its fearful talons in her throat, retaining its grasp until she expired. Its wandering and wild glances fell at this moment upon the head of the bed, over which the face of its master, rigid with horror, was just discernible. The fury of the beast, who no doubt still bore in mind the dreaded whip, was instantly converted into fear. Conscious of having deserved punishment, it seemed desirous of concealing its bloody deeds, and skipped about the chamber in an agony of nervous agitation; throwing down and breaking the furniture as it moved, and dragging the bed from the bedstead. In conclusion, it seized first the corpse of the daughter, and thrust it up the chimney, as it was found; then that of the old lady, which it immediately hurled through the window headlong.

See *The Complete Tales and Poems of Edgar Allan Poe* (New York: Modern Library, 1938), p. 167. Poe's representation of the murderous ape, as well as Dupin's procedure of capturing him by placing an ad in the newspaper, is reenforced by the perhaps typical example of an ad for a runaway slave placed in the *South-Carolina Gazette* of 1734: "Whereas a stately *Baboon* hath lately slipp'd his Colar and run away; He is big-bon'd full of flesh, and has learn'd to walk very erect on his two Hind-Legs, he grins and chatters much, but will not bite, he plays Tricks impudently well, and is mightily given to clambering, whereby he often shews his A—. If any one finds him. . . ." Quoted in Jordan, *White over Black*, p. 238.

     70. Blotner, *Faulkner. A Biography*, 1:113–14.

     71. Olga Vickery remarks that the razor and revolver are "phantom weapons directed at phantom opponents. For each sees embodied in the other that racial myth which has dominated their lives and which they must destroy if they are to be free." There remains, of course, some question about the degree of freedom achieved. See *The Novels of William Faulkner: A Critical Interpretation* (Baton Rouge: Louisiana State University Press), p. 72.

     72. *Light in August*, pp. 173, 239. Joanna reports moreover that her father had told her that "the curse of the black race is God's curse. But the curse of the white race is the black man who will be forever God's chosen own because He once cursed Him" (p. 240), a passage that only makes sense if we think ahead to *Go Down, Moses* and read "Ham" (the supposed biblical progenitor of the African races) for "Him." See *Selected Letters*, p. 374.

     73. "The Confessions of Nat Turner," reprinted in Herbert Aptheker, *Nat Turner's Slave Rebellion* (New York: Humanities Press, 1966), pp. 136–38.

     74. William Styron, *The Confessions of Nat Turner* (New York: Signet-Random, 1968), pp. 349, 255–56.

     75. James Baldwin, "Many Thousands Gone," in *Notes of a Native Son* (1955; reprint ed., New York: Bantam, 1964), p. 29.

     76. Meriwether and Millgate, eds., *Lion in the Garden*, pp. 206–7.

     77. Richard Chase, *The American Novel and Its Tradition* (1957; reprint ed., Baltimore: Johns Hopkins University Press), p. 214; Geismar, *Writers in Crisis*, p. 144; Alfred Kazin, "The Stillness of *Light in August*," in *William Faulkner: Three Decades of Criticism*, p. 253.

     78. W.E.B. Du Bois, *The Souls of Black Folk* (New York: Fawcett World, 1967), p. 23.

     79. Kartiganer, *Fragile Thread*, pp. 37, 68.

     80. *Light in August*, pp. 419, 438, 425, 439–40.

     81. Gwynn and Blotner, eds., *Faulkner in the University*, p. 117.

     82. Harriet Beecher Stowe, *Uncle Tom's Cabin* (New York: Collier Books, 1962), pp. 506, 325.

     83. James Baldwin, "Everybody's Protest Novel," in *Notes of a Native Son*, pp. 10, 13, 17. Faulkner's opinion of Stowe's novel was more generously mixed: "I would say that *Uncle Tom's Cabin* was written out of violent and misdirected compassion and ignorance of the author toward a situation which she knew only by hearsay. But it was not an intellectual process, it was hotter than that; it was out of her heart." See Joseph L. Fant III and Robert

Ashley, eds., *Faulkner at West Point* (New York: Random House, 1964), p. 104. On the intellectual climate of which Stowe was a part see Fredrickson, "Uncle Tom and the Anglo-Saxons: Romantic Racialism in the North," *The Black Image in the White Mind*, pp. 97–129.

84. White, *Rope and Faggot*, p. 57. Twain had reached a similar conclusion when he wrote in "The United States of Lyncherdom" (1901) that, because "communities as well as individuals are imitators," lynchers are themselves the worst enemies of their women. As each Negro crime begets others, Twain believed, so each lynching begets other crimes and other lynchings, eventually breeding "a mania ... a fashion which will spread wider and wider, year by year, covering state after state, as with an advancing disease." See *The Portable Mark Twain*, ed. Bernard DeVoto (New York: Viking Press, 1968), p. 586.

85. Cowley, *Faulkner-Cowley File*, p. 32.

86. The most important and debated is that of Stanley M. Elkins, *Slavery: A Problem in American Institutional and Intellectual Life*, 3rd ed. rev. (Chicago: University of Chicago Press, 1976), pp. 103–39, 242–53. Geismar (*Writers in Crisis*, pp. 181–82) invokes the analogy and extends his attack on Faulkner's Negro–Female obsession by asserting, strangely enough, that Faulkner's "infantile preoccupation with scapegoats" diverts attention away from the "genuine ills" of society. But compare Fanon's claim that "the scapegoat for white society—which is based on myths of progress, civilization, liberalism, education, enlightenment, refinement—will be precisely the force that opposes the expansion and the triumph of those myths. This brutal opposing force is supplied by the Negro" (*Black Skin, White Masks*, p. 194).

87. Girard, *Violence and the Sacred*, pp. 81, 271. Cf. Girard's observation that masks, because they do not efface differences but rather "incorporate and rearrange them," are "another aspect of the monstrous double" and thus stand "at that equivocal frontier between the human and the 'divine,' between a differentiated order in the process of disintegration and its final undifferentiated state—the point where all differences, all monstrosities are concentrated, and from which a new order will emerge" (pp. 167–68).

88. Blotner, *Faulkner: A Biography*, 1:113–14, 189–90, 301, 601, 880; 2:1246.

89. *Light in August*, pp. 421, 437, 280.

90. Twain, *Pudd'nhead Wilson*, pp. 103, 303, 117.

THADIOUS DAVIS

The Signifying Abstraction:
Reading "the Negro" in
Absalom, Absalom!

A black presence dominates *Absalom, Absalom!* as it does perhaps no other Faulkner novel. Nowhere else is it so apparent that the Negro is an abstract force confounding southern life both past and present even while, paradoxically, stimulating much of that life and art. The material or experiential realities of black people do not figure into the conception of "the Negro," an essentialized, always already "typed" configuration. A symbolic statement of this idea is suggested by the action of Miss Rosa Coldfield, one of the participants and narrators, who attempts to lift the weight of a coffin bearing the body of Charles Bon (whom she has never seen either alive or dead) in order to ascertain whether Bon's body is, in fact, inside. In essence, she desires to validate Bon's existence from sensory evidence; she is determined to know whether he is flesh or an imaginative construct. However, Miss Rosa is forced to apply not the most expedient sensory mechanism (that is, sight) but the only one available to her, and that one is insufficient for such a determination. She recalls:

> I tried to take the full weight of the coffin to prove to myself that
> he was really in it. And I could not tell.... Because I never saw
> him.... There are some things which happen to us which the
> intelligence and the senses refuse ... occurrences which stop us

From *Faulkner's "Negro": Art and the Southern Context*, reprinted in *William Faulkner's Absalom, Absalom!: A Casebook*, pp. 69–106. © 2003 by Oxford University Press.

dead as though by some impalpable intervention, like a sheet of
glass through which we watch all subsequent events transpire as
though in a soundless vacuum, and fade, vanish; are gone, leaving
us immobile, impotent, helpless; fixed, until we can die.[1]

Her metaphorical language suggests the white South confronted
with the Negro—its morally paralyzing abstraction. No one sensory test is
capable of validating the existence of the Negro; even sight has traditionally
been insufficient, not only because blacks who are visibly white in color
exist, but also because the white southerner has persistently refused to
see blacks, despite living and dying with the effects of their presence. In
Rosa Coldfield's mind, Charles Bon becomes "the abstraction which we
nailed into a box" (153), but like the Negro in the South, the abstraction in
this novel refuses to remain in a box. Bon is always flesh and imaginative
construct, both of which excite the rational and creative faculties of the
narrators. His presence, whether seen or felt, is an inescapable reality. He
becomes, like the Negro in general, the metaphorical embodiment of all
that is invisible in southern life.

The Negro supplies the central focus—albeit the most illusive—and the
major tensions in the pre- and postwar South of Thomas Sutpen, a man born
into the poor white mountain culture of western Virginia. Sutpen formulates
a grand design for living, labors to execute his design, and comes extremely
close to completing it. A synopsis of the Sutpen legend without the inclusion
of the Negro is a story without motivation or significant meaning. In June
1833, Sutpen mysteriously arrives in Jefferson and resolutely establishes a
plantation, wealth, and respectability. He marries Ellen Coldfield, whose
sister Rosa is one of the principal narrators, and he begets two children,
Henry and Judith. Prior to the outbreak of the Civil War, Sutpen's son
renounces his birthright and departs from Sutpen's Hundred, his father's
plantation, with a University of Mississippi classmate, Charles Bon, a New
Orleans Creole and Judith Sutpen's intended husband. The two youths do
not reappear until the end of the war when Henry shoots Bon at Sutpen's
Hundred and then disappears. Sutpen himself returns from the war a
decorated colonel but poverty ridden (having lost both his only son and most
of his plantation). He salvages a mile of land, consorts with a poor white,
Wash Jones, and opens a small store with Jones as partner; he is eventually
killed by Jones.[2]

The addition of the Negro lifts the Sutpen legend from a flat canvas
and transforms it into a powerful vehicle of individual will, of complex
human motives and emotions, of personal, social, historical interactions.
From the beginning, the Negro shapes, motivates, and determines Sutpen's
design. As a boy of thirteen or fourteen, Sutpen approaches the big house on

a Tidewater Virginia plantation with a message from his father to the owner, Pettibone. He is thwarted in his attempt to deliver the message (and see the inside of the house) by a black house slave who turns Sutpen away from the front entrance and directs him to the back door. The black man becomes the "monkey nigger" in Sutpen's accounts, and the young Sutpen becomes "the boy-symbol."

According to Sutpen's own version, which he gave to General Compson, Quentin's grandfather and Sutpen's sole confidant if not friend:

> He had never thought about his own hair or clothes or anybody else's hair or clothes until he saw that monkey nigger, who through no doing of his own happened to have had the felicity of being housebred in Richmond maybe, looking at them and he never even remembered what the nigger said, how it was the nigger told him, even before he had had time to say what he came for, never to come to that front door again but to go around to the back. (232)

Sutpen regards the incident as a denial of his individual value by the "monkey-dressed nigger butler" and the plantation owner and the system he represents. This recognition forces Sutpen to evaluate his personal and societal estimations of human worth. He has an epiphany regarding himself and his society:

> Not the monkey nigger. It was not the nigger anymore than it had been the nigger that his father had helped to whip that night. The nigger was just another balloon face slick and distended with that mellow loud and terrible laughing so that he did not dare to burst it, looking down at him from within the half-closed door during that instant in which, before he knew it, something in him had escaped and—he unable to close the eyes of it—was looking out from within the balloon face just as the man who did not even have to wear the shoes he owned, whom the laughter which the balloon held barricaded and protected from such as he, looked out from whatever invisible place he (the man) happened to be at the moment, at the boy outside the barred door in his patched garments and splayed bare feet, looking through and beyond the boy, he himself seeing his own father and sisters and brothers as the owner, the rich man (not the nigger) must have been seeing them all the time—as cattle, creatures heavy and without grace, brutely evacuated into a world without hope or purpose for them, who would in turn spawn with brutish and vicious prolixity,

populate, double treble and compound, fill space and earth with
a race whose future would be a succession of cut-down and
patched and made-over garments bought on exorbitant credit
because they were white people, from stores where niggers were
given the garments free, with for sole heritage that expression on
a balloon face bursting with laughter which had looked out at
some unremembered and nameless progenitor who had knocked
at a door when he was a little boy and had been told by a nigger
to go around to the back. (234–35)

Compressed into Sutpen's epiphany are all the tensions of caste and
class struggles in the South, the brutalization of human beings, black and
white, inherent in the slave system, and the moral ambiguities engendered
by social problems. In closing the door, the "monkey nigger" opened the
young Sutpen to a painful awareness of the inner dynamics of southern life.
Because of his action, the "monkey nigger" balloons up larger than life; he
becomes at once a visible metaphor for social reality and an allusive, invisible
presence in the boy's life. The incident precipitates Sutpen's rejection of his
family's simple way of life in favor of all that the "monkey nigger" held the
door against. As a result, Sutpen desires not simply wealth, but slaves and a
plantation, all the trappings designating the value of a human being in the
antebellum world. He realizes, "'You got to have land and niggers and a fine
house to combat them with'" (238). He works for the indisputable, visible
and material, right to assert his superiority over the "monkey nigger" and his
kind, whom he further abstracts by means of the "balloon" metaphor. The
intent, then, of Sutpen's design is to elevate himself into the landed gentry
against whom no "nigger" can close doors. Sutpen feels compelled to prove
that he is better than the "monkey nigger" and of course better than his
owner. His self-image, personality, and life goals are shaped by the "monkey
nigger," who is ultimately the personification of an entire society, its values
and ideology.

Sutpen's eventual downfall may be read as inevitable because he
substitutes his personal design in place of an existing moral and social order;
however, his encounter with the "monkey nigger," as well as the resulting
self-debate, leads to a recognition of his design as one complying with the
existing social order and the prevalent moral order. In fact, because Sutpen's
way of life is so in tune with the dominant southern way, his personal history
can become one, in Quentin and Shreve's construction, with the progress
of southern history. The South's retreat and surrender, in particular, are
imagined as occurring simultaneously with the failure of Sutpen's design
(347–50). What Sutpen violates in accepting the principles of the "monkey
nigger" and plantation-society Virginia is precisely a personal code of honor

and moral behavior derived from the social and ethical order of his own mountain society.

Sutpen's design is preeminently a drive toward completion of self. The irony is that he strives to complete an image of self constructed from models alien to his "natural" state. His failure is ordained from the moment he loses touch with that inner self which demands of the aware individual a completing of self. That initial loss of harmony is irreparable. Sutpen strives vaingloriously to complete Pettibone and his kind. Like those slave owners who upon seeing the African's black skin deemed him animal rather than human, Sutpen settles for appearance rather than substance as an estimate of human worth. Thus, he is essentially always about the business of duplication instead of true self-completion. Because an imitation is, by its very nature in the usual order of things, less than the original, his process of duplication, despite its unfinished state, can never attain the status, albeit morally questionable, of the model.

Moreover, because Sutpen's understanding of completion is literally a body fitted to the prescribed mold of Pettibone's kind, his design has as its ultimate goal the heir, the male figure, a replica of the model, which is again Pettibone's kind, not Sutpen himself but the Sutpen who is an imitation of Pettibone. Therefore, Charles Bon appears as a threat to Sutpen's design, not simply because Bon himself by virtue of his blood from the slave class cannot duplicate Pettibone's model, but primarily because Bon exercises such a powerful hold over Henry Sutpen, the heir apparent to Sutpen's design, that Bon possesses the potential of becoming himself a Pettibone, a model for Henry instead of the one laid out for Henry by his father.

Because he bases his design mimetically upon a negative, unwholesome model, Sutpen lacks the stature of a man who has failed in the attempt to achieve something magnificent or laudable. He, finally, can be reduced to a pathetic old man literally killing himself by trying to place his seed in an available and remotely acceptable (that is, "white") female in order to produce a male child. His ultimate failure is not a tragedy; he has denied his "central I-Am" (139). Yet because Faulkner presents that poignant boy symbol and with it the possibility of harmonious self-completion, he shows in that moment of faulty, but private, individual choice, Sutpen's lost potential. Though haunted by the boy symbol and the "monkey nigger," Sutpen understands neither the proportions nor the implications of his choice. Consequently, he never knows that his choice of Pettibone as a model for self-completion corrupts the boy symbol and signals waste and loss, which ultimately justify the laughter of the balloon-face "monkey nigger."

The Negro provides the modern survivors of Sutpen's South (specifically, three of the four narrators: Jason Compson, his son Quentin, and Rosa

Coldfield) with one means of approaching, understanding, and living with their past, the collective southern past, if they prove capable of reading the meaning of Sutpen's story. The opportunity that the story represents for them is reminiscent of an observation on race relations made by Joel Chandler Harris: "The problems of one generation are the paradoxes of a succeeding one, particularly if war, or some such incident intervenes to clarify the atmosphere and strengthen the understanding."[3]

The four narrators help to clarify the novel's intricate design and to determine the Negro's relationship to the verbal design, because narrating or "telling" in this novel is a way of establishing the concrete reality of narrator characters, both those participating in the legend and those attending its recreation. At the same time, the lack of telling by the blacks who inhabit the world of *Absalom, Absalom!* reduces them to an involved dependency upon the actual narrators, and their lack of telling functions, inversely, to establish the abstract quality of their existences.

Mr. Compson suggests the narrative method in his attempt to grasp the reality of the legend from "a few old mouth-to-mouth tales" and "letters without salutation or signature" exhumed "from old trunks and boxes and drawers" (100–101). He recognizes that fragments from the past are "almost indecipherable, yet meaningful" (101) and that the "living blood and seed" of people "in this shadowy attenuation of time" (101) create him and generate his absorption in their lives. He tells and sees both as himself, a sardonic and disillusioned southerner (an image which results from narrative voice rather than his actions), and as his father, General Compson, who had been Sutpen's lone intimate among the Jefferson townspeople, and whom the reader gets to know from his reported voice as much as from his interactions with the Sutpens. Although Mr. Compson understands the magnetic nature of the past and its inhabitants, he cannot explain the legend, not even in his own version, because "something is missing" (101). He has "the words, the symbols, the shapes themselves," but they remain "shadowy inscrutable and serene" (101). When, for example, he spins the tale of Charles Bon and his octoroon, Mr. Compson withdraws his final approval of it because his rational vision that "something is missing" is at odds with his creative impulse. He emphasizes Faulkner's main point: there is no true design for the telling, only the most expedient, practical, or communicative in a given situation.

Mr. Compson's acknowledgment that "something is missing" reminds the reader that *Absalom, Absalom!* is not about Sutpen, Charles, Henry, or Judith; but about Rosa, Mr. Compson, Quentin, and Shreve—about those inhabitants of a modern world (which is growing increasingly more complex) as they reveal and react, by force of habit, inclination, curiosity, or need, to aspects of themselves which appeared long ago, were illuminated, and faded only to be dusted off and held up to the light at the time of an impending personal crisis. At the same time, "something is missing" also suggests the absence of the Negro from the narrators' initial formulations of the past. The Negro's place in the whole pattern is revealed gradually.

The narrators themselves construct the Negro. Independently, they invent their own "Negro" in defining themselves and in expressing the limits of their imaginations, personalities, and humanity. Miss Rosa creates Clytie, Sutpen's slave daughter, and the "wild niggers" who build Sutpen's Hundred. Mr. Compson draws the New Orleans octoroon and her son, Charles Etienne St. Valery Bon. Quentin and Shreve imagine Charles Bon and his mother, Eulalia. They have the most complete authorial control over the Negro because his actual physical presence is the least documented by "facts" from the past. All of their projections operate to enrich the significance of "Negro" as both abstraction and metaphorical reality in *Absalom, Absalom!*

The most readily apparent example of this process is Rosa's construction of the "wild niggers," Sutpen's original band of slaves. She sees them as "his band of wild niggers like beasts half tamed to walk upright like men, in attitudes wild and reposed" (8). This recurring image of the slaves grounds her telling in a recognizable, if distorted, reality which attempts to wrench a personal moral order out of confusion. Because Sutpen is her private demon, she makes the "wild niggers" an extension of Sutpen himself and synonymous with Sutpen's Hundred. The "wild niggers" are her stage props and stage crew, just as they are the actual work horses who clear the virgin land and build Sutpen's plantation.

Beginning with the early segments of Rosa's narrative, the "wild niggers" become an obsessive presence in her mind. She calls them "a herd of wild beasts that he [Sutpen] has hunted down single-handed because he was stronger in fear than even they were in whatever heathen place he had fled from" (16). She imagines their origins "in the mud" of a "dark swamp" (24) in order to complete her construction of their bestiality. The slaves, according to Rosa, are from a nameless "heathen place," which is a "much older country than Virginia or Carolina but it wasn't a quiet one" (17); her statements link Sutpen to the same place reference. She perceives Sutpen's "wild niggers" as his mirror reflection (somewhat similar to Quentin Compson's view in *The Sound and the Fury* of blacks as an "obverse reflection of the white people" among whom they live). The appearance of the blacks becomes the irrevocable proof of Sutpen's nature ("anyone could look at those negroes of his and tell," 17). They are imaginative projections of Rosa's feelings about Sutpen, about blacks, and about Sutpen's Hundred.

The "wild" slaves as an imagined reality in the novel serve to create psychological atmosphere and mood similar to the function of natural landscape or setting in some nineteenth-century novels (such as the moors in *Wuthering Heights*). For instance, every appearance of Sutpen in Jefferson is colored by Rosa's association of him with his "wild" slaves and land. Her version of the arrival of the Sutpen family for Sunday church services is typical of her perception of Sutpen's union with his slaves:

> This is my vision of my first sight of them which I shall carry to my grave: a glimpse like the forefront of a tornado, of the carriage ... and on the front seat the face and teeth of the wild negro who was driving, and he [Sutpen], his face exactly like the negro's save for the teeth (this because of the beard doubtless)—all in a thunder and a fury of wildeyed horses and of galloping and of dust. (23)

The words are aptly chosen, because Rosa is shading a real incident with her own peculiar way of seeing Sutpen.

Mr. Compson's narrative, gathered primarily from his father, General Compson, but also from other members of the community, serves as a corrective to Rosa's presentation of Sutpen and his "niggers." The townspeople and Mr. Compson are by no means egalitarian when it comes to the slaves, yet they do not display Miss Rosa's fanatical view of the blacks. Mr. Compson admits that there is a legend of the wild blacks and that there is some element of "truth" contained in the legend:

> So the legend of the wild men came gradually back to town, brought by the men who would ride out to watch what was going on, who began to tell how Sutpen would take stand beside a game trail with the pistols and send the negroes in to drive the swamp like a pack of hounds; it was they who told how during that first summer and fall the negroes did not even have (or did not use) blankets to sleep in, even before the coon-hunter Akers claimed to have walked one of them out of the absolute mud like a sleeping alligator and screamed just in time. (36)

The view of blacks in this less emotional account is still that of primitive men close to instinctual communication with animals and nature. Mr. Compson suggests, however, that the "wild men" were the mental projections of Sutpen created by the town, as well as Miss Rosa, in its ignorance. Sutpen's slaves, for instance, are not using a heathen tongue, but are West Indians (either from Haiti, as is Sutpen's first wife, or from Martinique, like the architect) speaking a French dialect. Akers and the other townspeople, Rosa included, fill in the shadowy outlines of the real Sutpen slaves with information that appeals to their imaginations.

Other versions balance Miss Rosa's misplaced emphasis, although they, too, represent Sutpen's relationship with his slaves as different from that traditionally depicted between master and slave. For example, General Compson told his son that "while the negroes were working Sutpen never raised his voice at them, that instead he led them, caught them at the psychological instant by example, by some ascendancy of forbearance rather than brute fear" (37). Sutpen, in other versions besides Miss Rosa's, worked intimately with his twenty slaves, all of them "plastered over with mud against the mosquitoes and . . . distinguishable one from another by his beard and eyes alone" (37). The others, too, stress the primitive nature of Sutpen's slaves and actively mythologize them into an integral part of the community legend. But they do not resort to calling them wild beasts; for example, one quite civil reference is to Sutpen's "crew of imported slaves"—though the added comment is that Sutpen's "adopted fellow citizens still looked upon [his slaves] as being a good deal more deadly than any beast" (38). Another reference terms the slaves "human," even while exalting their animal instincts: "human beings who belonged to him body and soul and of whom it was believed (or said) that they could creep up to a bedded buck and cut its throat before it could move" (40).

These views reflect a matter-of-fact depiction of blacks as slaves and whites as masters; they are glimpses of the minds of individuals thoroughly in tune with the dominant social practices. But these other observations of Sutpen's slaves are secondary; Rosa's vision of the "wild niggers" dominates the narrative. Her image of the "wild" slaves emanates from a mind out of joint with reality; it becomes a metaphor that the reader comes to identify, not with the demon Sutpen, but with the dark mysterious force at the center of southern life that, as portrayed in *Absalom, Absalom!* the southerner creates out of an unfailing reserve of self-flagellation and mental anguish.

When Rosa takes fragments of the actual and constructs an extensive, self-satisfying whole, she duplicates in microcosm the process of the novel as a whole. She projects precisely what she has made herself see and what she has come to feel after forty-five years of static rage. Her imaginative process is a more exaggerated version of Quentin's, Shreve's, and Mr. Compson's (as well as of the collective mind of Jefferson, because Rosa's view of Sutpen's slaves is but an exaggeration of the one held less rigidly by the town). In transforming Sutpen's human chattels into an extension of his demon self and into a synonym for his plantation, Rosa reveals the narrow limits of her personality and her humanity. Her picture of the slaves is the most revealing in what it reflects about Rosa herself, her mental condition and conflicting emotions.

Rosa's creation of the "wild niggers" is related to the larger implications of the novel. It brings into the open the hysterical image of blacks which undermines the rational appeal of Charles Bon, Sutpen's elegant mulatto son, who seeks paternal acceptance without regard to race. Because of its intensity and obstinacy, Rosa's distorted vision of the slaves pervades the entire novel and operates as a psychological backdrop for Sutpen's rejection of Bon and his black blood. The struggle between father and son can take on colossal proportions with far-reaching historical and cultural consequences in part because Rosa has so effectively created a forceful, larger-than-life, demonic landscape for the action.

All of the anonymous blacks in the world of *Absalom, Absalom!* represent the paradox of "a soil manured with black blood from two hundred years of oppression and exploitation until it sprang with an incredible paradox of peaceful greenery and crimson flowers" (251). The blacks appear to specify the paradoxical nature of the southern world constituting the novel, and at the same time their presence insinuates that the Negro's "place" is not simply subordinate to whites, but that its dimensions are different, smaller by comparison. Their presence suggests that the Negro is intended, in the proper order of things, to serve the white man. Generally, it is this provincial view of "Negro" growing out of his social functions in the South to which Sutpen adheres in formulating his design and to which the narrators conform in creating the legend.

The major black figures emerge out of conceptions of blacks accommodating themselves to the white world. They evolve out of two rather conventional literary images of blacks; significantly both involve mixed-blood people. One is the free mulatto during the pre- and postwar years who, envisioned as searcher, occupies the tragic "noplace" in southern life; the second is the slave daughter of the master who remains on the family plantation in an ambiguous maternal role as a member and nonmember of the family. In fact, all of the blacks in Absalom who are given names and delineated in detail are of mixed blood, or presumed to be by the narrators. Clytie and the Bon men are representative characters. Whereas the Bons are obviously crucial to the resolution of the novel, Clytie reveals the most about Faulkner's art and the Negro in this novel.

Throughout the work, Clytie is the felt black presence that pervades the South. She embodies this presence much more than Charles Bon, the abstraction who is made "nigger" in order to complete the pattern of the legend. She, more than any other character, reveals the ultimately inexplicable nature of human motivation. Both the tension of her existence and the obscurity of her involvement in the lives of others manifest Judith Sutpen's metaphor:

> You get born and you try this and you dont know why only you
> keep on trying it and you are born at the same time with a lot of

other people, all mixed up with them, like trying to, having to, move your arms and legs with strings only the same strings are hitched to all the other arms and legs and the others all trying and they dont know why either except that the strings are all in one another's way. (127)

The process of life, as Judith describes it, means that Clytie is irrevocably connected to other individuals, so that her very existence, not merely her actions, affects and is affected by others.

Clytie is symbolically and literally a fusion of the two worlds of southern life; yet like the other mixed-blood people in the novel, Clytie does not experience the black world as a black person. Nonetheless, like Charles Bon and his son, Charles Etienne St. Valery, Clytie knows what it is to be treated as a "nigger" in the white world. She is, for instance, greeted differently by Sutpen upon his return from the war. Instead of the kiss and touch he gave Judith, Sutpen merely "looked at Clytie and said, 'Ah, Clytie'" (159). And Rosa Coldfield, who recoils from Clytie's "nigger" touch on the day of Charles Bon's death, has from childhood "instinctively" feared her and shunned objects she has touched (140).

Bereft of all that gave meaning to black life, Clytie is denied access to the only two institutions available to blacks—the family and the church. She is deprived of the sustenance of communal identity. Clytie is far from Elnora, the hymn-singing cook-housekeeper of Faulkner's *Flags in the Dust*, who is also the daughter of the white master. In addition, she is unlike Dilsey of *The Sound and the Fury*, who so staunchly endures with the help of the religion of the black community. Clytie is neither hymn-singing nor churchgoing; for her there is no refuge in a private life as a black person. Her lack of affiliation with the black world illuminates Faulkner's development of the black housekeeper-servant in his fiction, for in portraying Clytie he moves away from the character type as it appears in the earlier novels.

Clytie is an attempt at a more innovative, and psychologically modern, character, though she is a less successful characterization than Dilsey. Dilsey is conventionally a more imposing and prominent character; however, Faulkner creates her primarily as a character who obviously and symbolically elucidates and embodies his theme. Despite the innate nobility with which Faulkner endows her, Dilsey is and remains the Compsons' servant who on Easter Sunday emerges phoenix-like, encompassing the extant possibility for human survival with dignity and love. But Clytie is not simply a member of the Sutpen household. She is a member of the family, marked, according to all accounts, with the Sutpen face. She has no connections with individuals who are not Sutpens; her mother, one of Sutpen's original band of slaves, is not even given to her as a memory. Legally chattel before the war and an institution afterward, Clytie is a coffee-colored Sutpen. She is defined mainly in terms of her Sutpen heritage and blood. In terms of traditional place and order, then, she is where she belongs. There are no possibilities suggested for her living apart from Sutpen's Hundred; she has no alternative form of existence.

Clytie's singular position may initially suggest a realistic mode of characterizing blacks; however, the fictional method by which she achieves life, primarily through Rosa Coldfield's imaginative construction of her, is a break with conventional portraits. Clytie's presence, unlike Dilsey's, is not intended to provide ethical certainty or emotional comfort. Instead it evokes the duality of human nature. Whereas Dilsey lacks close personal identification with any member of the Compson family, Clytie is closely identified with both her half sister, Judith, and her father, Sutpen. Described as "at once both more and less Sutpen" (140), she is an extension of the physical selves of Judith and Sutpen, as well as an imaginative projection by the narrators of some dark essence of the Sutpen being. Whatever reality Clytie attains as a character, she attains in the minds of her narrators, but that reality primarily reinforces their central visions. All that readers know of her is filtered through the consciousness of others.

Clytie is preeminently a silent, shadowy presence which, imaginatively delineated, assumes force in the lives of those around her. Her position in the narrative challenges conventional mechanisms contrived for identifying family members and for defining the "central I-Am" of the individual. At the same time, her personal responses to her status as a slave daughter and to her world go unarticulated by words or gestures. What Clytie herself feels remains a mystery, despite the fact that she is one of the participants in the Sutpen legend who survives into the novel's present.

Although Judith and her brother, Henry, are described as "that single personality with two bodies" (9–10), the description is even more fitting when applied to Clytie and Judith. Except for physical coloring, the two could be twins. They appear together initially, and from that first appearance, they are twin, silent, and calm figures of strength. Both frequently are called "inscrutable," "impenetrable," and "serene." As they age, they become more alike and gradually assume the status of living legends in the Jefferson community. Clytie is the shadowy complement of her white sister. In a sense, she is Judith's double, functioning to complete Judith's fragmented self. For example, after Bon's death Judith tells the Compsons that she will not commit suicide because "somebody will have to take care of Clytie" (128). Yet because a Clytie who needs Judith's care is never visible, the reader may speculate that she is instead another part of Judith's own self, which cannot be denied as long as there is some external manifestation of it. Symbolically,

Clytie represents both Judith's inner self and the social environment in which Judith functions and exists.

Because Clytie is Judith's complementary part, she follows to conclusion the pattern of action established by Judith and supported by the two of them while Judith lived. She pays for Judith's and Charles Etienne's tombstones, raises Jim Bond, and harbors Henry. Her final action, the burning of the Sutpen mansion, is a desperate attempt to preserve the house and the family from violation by outsiders because the Sutpens have earned that right. As she observes, "Whatever he done, me and Judith and him have paid it out" (370).

Clytie, as black twin to Judith, becomes a subtle statement of the oneness of humankind. The common bonds of temperament, interests, duty, and affection unite the two women in a sisterhood that transcends race. Their relationship is a more sustained and meaningful version of that between Henry and Charles. Because Clytie and Judith relate to each other as "womenfolk" first, then as "daughter" and "sister," they partly escape the racial burden placed on their brothers. Their personal relationship provides a model of sibling cooperation and harmony in the novel, and by extension it suggests the possibility of a different order of social interaction between races in the South.

The limits of Clytie's existence are set not by her slave status but by her identity as a Sutpen, and in that regard she is also Judith's counterpart. The two are locked into a narrow existence; uncomplaining and stoical, they make the best of their lives. They share the "*indomitable woman-blood*" (153) and are as close to survivors as Faulkner comes in *Absalom, Absalom!* They accept a life without joy or frivolity; they assume the burden of existence and accept each other as human beings. Consequently, Clytie and Judith emerge together as the most admirable characters in the novel. Certainly, Faulkner endows them with dignity and endurance, with pity and love—the virtues he esteemed most and identified with his beloved mammy, Caroline Barr, whom Clytie alone of his black women characters resembles.

The relationship between Clytie and Judith is critical to the novel because it achieves a level of communication and kinship across social barriers, but also because it precipitates the destructive cycle of Charles Etienne St. Valery Bon, the son of Charles Bon and a New Orleans octoroon. Charles Etienne's story moves the Sutpen legend into the postwar period and enlarges its social significance. Clytie prevents the boy on his first visit to Sutpen's Hundred from playing with a black youth. Even after Charles Etienne arrives to live on the plantation, he is not allowed to have contact with blacks or whites. By watching him with a "brooding fierce unflagging jealous care" (200), Clytie virtually isolates him from members of either race. It seems that as long as she can keep him on Sutpen's Hundred,

Clytie believes that she can protect Charles Etienne from the knowledge that barriers exist between races and that those barriers are socially real. She knows that the plantation is a self-contained world sustained only by Judith and herself, for whom racial distinctions no longer have social meanings. Clytie—not Judith—is the boy's guardian and protector. She becomes "the fierce, brooding woman" (197) who in a "curious blend of savageness and pity, of yearning and hatred" (198) cares for Charles Etienne. Clytie's efforts, nevertheless, lead the boy to a much more painful and premature knowledge: the awareness that the barriers between races and individuals are psychically real. Sutpen's legacy to his rejected black son, Charles Bon, is thus perpetuated in the next generation.

When taken abruptly from the "padded and silken vacuum cell" (199) of his life in New Orleans, Charles Etienne encounters the "gaunt and barren" (197) world in which Clytie and Judith live. Once he crosses the threshold of Sutpen's Hundred, his "very silken remaining clothes, his delicate shirt and stockings and shoes which still remained to remind him of what he had once been, vanished, fled from arms and body and legs as if they had been woven of chimaeras or of smoke" (197). His silk clothing is symbolic of more than the white world; it represents the hedonistic, cosmopolitan world of New Orleans, "where pigmentation had no more moral value than the silk walls . . . and the rose-colored . . . shades, where the very abstractions which he might have observed—monogamy and fidelity and decorum and gentleness and affection—were as purely rooted in the flesh's offices as the digestive processes" (199). The city with less rigid racial codes and more indulgent mores forms a contrast to the closed world of the plantation and Jefferson. Compared to the delicate, mythical existence Charles Etienne experiences in New Orleans, Sutpen's Hundred (as introduced by Clytie and the denim jumper) is the abrasive "actual world"; Mr. Compson envisions Charles Etienne as

> produced complete . . . in that cloyed and scented maze of shuttered silk as if he were the delicate and perverse spirit symbol, immortal page of the ancient immortal Lilith, entering the actual world not at the age of one second but twelve years, the delicate garments of his pagehood already half concealed beneath that harsh and shapeless denim cut to an iron pattern and sold by the millions—that burlesque of the Sons of Ham. (196)

When Clytie covers Charles Etienne with a coarse denim jumper, she burdens him with a second existence without explanation. She begins the process of alienating the boy and destroying the world he knows to be real. Neither Clytie nor Judith recognizes his loneliness. He is irretrievably an outsider—alien to Sutpen's Hundred and lost to the two women who, in their simplicity, fail to realize that he does not understand (indeed, has no basis for understanding) his new life, the two women themselves, or their awkward protective gestures. Clytie and Judith, for all their strength and endurance, are extremely naïve women; they are, like their father and brother, independent country people. Thus, they are unable to see the beginning of Charles Etienne's dividedness. Their naïveté and ignorance compound the boy's problem with identity and place. Both women fail Charles Etienne; he, in turn, fails them and himself. These joint failures emphasize the reciprocal nature of the tragedy resulting from defining human beings in terms of race and caste. The tragedy is social as much as private; it affects whites as well as blacks.

Charles Etienne rejects the white world, which he mistakenly perceives as being peopled by the two stern, shadow women, Judith and Clytie, who seem to need only each other. By their inability to express their feelings for him in terms he can clearly comprehend, his two Sutpen "aunts" propel Charles Etienne into a constant battle with racial barriers, which are mainly presented as social restrictions against open, public displays of interracial activities. (He is reminiscent of Joe Christmas of *Light in August*, who is similarly propelled by a restrictive Puritan disciplinarian into a rootless, embattled life.) Charles Etienne marries a "coal black and ape-like woman" who "existed in that aghast and automaton-like state" (205). He makes his wife, a "black gargoyle" (209), an external projection of his black self. He abuses his wife's humanity, even though Faulkner presents her as physically grotesque and inhuman ("resembling something in a zoo," 209). By his treatment of the helpless woman, he dehumanizes himself and alienates himself from the rest of humanity. After a period of moving through a series of cities and towns as if driven by fury, Charles Etienne returns to Sutpen's Hundred, rents a parcel of land on shares, and lives in an old slave cabin on the place. Nonetheless, he does not penetrate the black world. He remains as alienated from it as he is from his black wife and the Sutpen women.

Clytie's fierce guardianship of Charles Etienne corresponds to mythical allusions evoked by her name, Clytemnestra. According to Mr. Compson, Sutpen "named her himself" (61), though perhaps "he intended to name Clytie, Cassandra, prompted by some pure dramatic economy not only to beget but to designate the presiding augur of his own disaster, and . . . he just got the name wrong through a mistake natural in a man who must have almost taught himself to read" (62). Mr. Compson seems inaccurate here because Clytie is not so much Cassandra, mad prophetess of doom, as she is Clytemnestra, fiercely maternal wife mother figure of vengeance.

The allusions to the name Clytemnestra seem appropriate, if not precisely so. Clytemnestra is wife/mother, who out of complex motives brings disaster to her children and herself by willfully exacting revenge for her daughter Iphigenia's death. Despite the reference to Clytie's "fierceness," she does not seem to be a personality motivated by a personal fury (such as revenge). However, the mythical Clytemnestra is responsible for Cassandra's death; their two visions of reality and duty fatally conflict. Clytie is related to the mythical Clytemnestra in this sense, because she finally thwarts Rosa's efforts to control the Sutpens by taking charge of Henry. She burns the mansion rather than have Rosa remove Henry and assume responsibility for him. Shortly thereafter, Rosa dies, somehow mortally wounded by her last encounter with Clytie. Clytie's action represents a kind of dual expiation on the part of both races in the South and particularly on the part of the planter class. In burning Sutpen's Hundred with herself and Henry inside, Clytie destroys the two surviving Sutpens, who along with Judith are similar to the mythical Orestes in their attempts to expiate the old crimes, their own sins and those they inherit from their father.

While Mr. Compson speculates that Sutpen intended to name Clytie "Cassandra," he and Quentin actually describe Rosa Coldfield as "Cassandralike." Quentin sees her as having "an air Cassandralike and humorless and profoundly and sternly prophetic out of all proportion to the actual years even of a child who had never been young" (22). And before his explanation of Clytie's name, Mr. Compson speaks of the "Puritan righteousness and outraged female vindictiveness [in which] Miss Rosa's childhood was passed, that aged and ancient and timeless absence of youth which consisted of Cassandralike listening beyond closed doors" (60). Shreve, too, refers to Rosa as "Cassandra" in his description of her peculiar relationship with Sutpen: "instead of a widowed Agamemnon to her Cassandra an ancient stiff-jointed Pyramus to her eager though untried Thisbe" (177).

In linking both Clytie and Rosa to Cassandra, Faulkner reiterates that his characters flow into one another and merge with historical or mythological figures as well. The figurative association of Clytie with Rosa joins the Negro to the white southerner who is the most reactionary about race. Their union is tense because, in Rosa's words, they are *"open, ay honorable, enemies"* (157). Clytie and Rosa, the daughter and the sister-in-law, the slave and the "not-wife," share a relationship with Sutpen that is as tortured as that of either Clytemnestra's or Cassandra's to Agamemnon.

When Rosa and Clytie confront each other on the stairs of Sutpen's Hundred after Charles Bon's murder, they participate in one of the most dramatic, and revealing, scenes in the work.[4] At the moment of their meeting, Rosa sees Clytie as an extension of Sutpen and as her own twin sister because of their joint connection to him: "the two of us joined by that hand and arm which held us like a fierce rigid umbilical cord, twin sistered

to a fell darkness which had produced her" (140). Though Rosa, like Charles
Etienne, rails against the order of things in her world, she recognizes the
complex nature of human interconnectedness (thereby accentuating one of
Faulkner's major themes). She describes herself as well as Clytie as "sentient
victim" and admits the private, mysterious connection to Sutpen, who is
Clytie's biological father and who gives Rosa life (that is, provides her with
a raison d'être which in its negative capacity links her even more closely to
the negative aspect of Sutpen's indefatigable and undefeated will to duplicate
himself). At the same time, Rosa acknowledges the connection between
two individuals who share a deeply felt experience: "*we seemed to glare at one
another not as two faces but as the two abstract contradictions which we actually
were, neither of our voices raised, as though we spoke to one another free of the
limitations and restrictions of speech and hearing*" (138). Rosa and Clytie are
yoked so that their differences are grossly exaggerated, even though the very
intensity of their union destroys ordinary impediments to communication.
This yoking of "abstract contradictions" is central to the structural and
thematic progress of the novel. For instance, it is one way of approaching
Quentin and Shreve as creators, or Henry and Charles as friends.

Rosa's meeting with Clytie is a central scene because it reverberates
with all the tensions between blacks and whites, between classes and races
that have been used to define the South and to establish the major concerns
of the novel. One of the most starkly honest scenes in the Faulkner canon,
this meeting probes the psychological and cultural realities of race and
kinship. It suggests all of the dramatic meetings which take place in *Absalom*
(Sutpen and the "monkey nigger," Charles Bon and Henry, even Shreve
and Quentin). Superseded in intensity only by Quentin's encounter with
Henry, it is the single extended narration of a confrontation between black
and white in a work clearly dependent upon a series of such confrontations
for meaning.

Rosa, in her moments of knowing, her "epiphany," encounters Clytie
as "Negro" and "woman" but also, paradoxically, as "sister": "*we stood there
joined by that volitionless . . . hand, . . . I cried 'And you too? And you too, sister,
sister?'*" (140). Prior to this moment, Rosa has neither recognized nor accepted
Clytie as Sutpen's daughter, sister to Judith and metaphorically sister to Rosa
herself. Still, Clytie is not a person to Rosa. She is "nigger" and a sphinxlike
presence invented by Sutpen solely to confound Rosa; she is "*the Sutpen face
. . . already there, rocklike and firm . . . waiting there . . . in his own image the cold
Cerberus of his private hell*" (136).

Clytie's presence reminds Rosa that she is cut off from significant areas
of life, particularly from family participation, just as the Negro, symbolically
represented by the "balloon face" and the "monkey nigger," serves to remind
Sutpen of his poor white origins. It is not only that Rosa is not a wife, but

that finally she is not sister, daughter, aunt, or niece. She is and remains an outsider. Begrudgingly, Rosa recognizes her own inadequacies, Clytie's essential harmony with her world, and their psychological union. But she does so by making Clytie not merely like Sutpen, a demon, but the personification of all that has prevented her full participation in life. Clytie becomes an "*immobile antagonism*," "*that presence, that familiar coffee-colored face*" (137), which Rosa "sees" as both an object blocking her passage up the stairs and as a force confounding her entire life.

Clytie stands for Sutpen's continuing reality and his insult to the spinster who hurls herself into

> *that inscrutable coffee-colored face, that cold implacable mindless (no, not mindless: anything but mindless, his own clairvoyant will tempered to amoral evil's undeviating absolute by the black willing blood with which he had crossed it) replica of his own which he had created and decreed to preside upon his absence, as you might watch a wild distracted nightbound bird flutter into the brazen and fatal lamp.* (138)

Clytie is the proof (and for the sight-oriented Rosa, the visible therefore incontrovertible proof) of Sutpen's sexual activity, in particular his mating with someone other than a "wife," with someone more animal than human, with the "black willing blood" of one of the original "wild niggers." It is an insult to the spinster that Sutpen, who represented her one opportunity for marriage (here, specifically sex and children), would "grace" even a "nigger" but would deny her. Thus, Sutpen himself, not Clytie, has condemned Miss Rosa to ignorance and blind, futile thrusting. Sutpen is, paradoxically, "clairvoyant," and Clytie is a "brazen and fatal lamp," while Rosa is "a wild distracted nightbound bird." For all their negative capacity drawn by Miss Rosa, Sutpen and Clytie symbolize vision and light for her. On the other hand, Rosa with ironic aptness sees herself as a sightless bird enmeshed in darkness and fluttering blindly into destruction.

Clytie's command, "*Dont you go up there, Rosa*" (138), causes Rosa to assert the authority of her race and the superiority of her position as a white woman in the South: "*Rosa? . . . To me? To my face?*" (139). Yet even while speaking the words, Rosa knows "*it was not the name, the word the fact that she had called me Rosa*" (139); Rosa believes that "*while we stood face to face . . . she did me more grace and respect than anyone else I knew; . . . to her of all who knew me I was no child*" (139). She infers that Clytie recognizes her as "woman," intuits her female urges and sexual drives. Perhaps Clytie alone, with her "brooding awareness and acceptance of the inexplicable unseen, inherited from an older and a purer race" (138), understands Rosa's frustrated sexual energy, understands that Rosa is denied access to marriage and familial intimacy (and in this instance, specifically, denied access as well to the knowledge and experience of life and death she seeks in the upper regions of the Sutpen house).

Nonetheless, Rosa perverts the meeting into a racial confrontation; she is otherwise unable to cope with its implications (that is, Clytie as a Sutpen "belongs" at Sutpen's Hundred and has a natural place in the affairs of the family, whereas Rosa, though white, is relegated to a lower, nonprivileged status). Rosa's tactic reiterates the ultimate tragedy of the Sutpen legend: the son's meeting with the father is reduced to a racial confrontation; kinship, whether physical or spiritual, may be denied when one party is "Negro."

Clytie's hand on Rosa raises the specter of a "nigger" violating racial barriers. Symbolically, the gesture duplicates the larger violation attempted, according to Quentin and Shreve, by Charles Bon, the "nigger" who desires to sleep not with the abstract "white woman," but with the individual "sister" and "daughter" (which Judith personifies). Rosa experiences "*a shocking impact . . . at that black arresting and untimorous hand on* [her] *white woman's flesh*" (139). Her response is automatic: "*Take your hand off me, nigger!*" (140). She retreats into the sanctity of race, and to the safety of racial epithets.

In this moment Rosa exposes the process by which the individual makes "nigger" a scapegoat; it is a microcosm of the larger societal process which the community acts out in *Light in August*, and it is a tableau extending Sutpen's treatment of his son Charles Bon to the conduct of an entire society. Rosa, in attempting to convert Clytie into "nigger" and the physical embodiment of all blackness, reveals her own duality and asserts herself as the flawed component of a flawed society. Clytie is, after all, more Sutpen than black and more Sutpen than woman, primarily as a result of Rosa's own imaginative constructions, which she has made "true" in the progress of the narrative. The two visible realities that Clytie embodies ("Negro" and "woman") are denied and rendered meaningless by her "Sutpenness," which is the true abstraction confronting and confounding Rosa on the stairs. "*Yes,*" Rosa declares, "*I stopped dead—no woman's hand, no negro's hand, but bitter-curb to check and guide the furious and unbending will—I crying not to her, to it; speaking to it through the negro, the woman*" (139–40).

Since Rosa believes that Clytie is most vulnerable because of her race and the social stigma it carries, she can deny her own egalitarian emotions and subvert her own compelling logic:

> *There is something in the touch of flesh with flesh which abrogates, cuts sharp and straight across the devious intricate channels of decorous ordering, which enemies as well as lovers know because it makes them both—touch and touch of that which is citadel of the central I-Am's*

private own: not spirit, soul; the liquorish and ungirdled mind is
anyone's to take in any darkened hallway of this earthly tenement. But
let flesh touch flesh, and watch the fall of all the eggshell shibboleth of
caste and color too. (139)

Rosa's perception is fleeting; her spoken word, "nigger," does not coincide
with her internal analysis of the meaning of touch.

Although "touch" seems emblematic of larger possibilities for interracial
contact, Clytie's touch is not an ambivalent gesture. Nor is Rosa's response
ambiguous; Rosa means to issue her command in terms that carry the weight
of social sanction. Rosa's response to Clytie is an overt expression of Sutpen's
implicit response to Charles Bon. Sutpen's drama is an internal process not
witnessed by the reader, yet the essence of his complex reaction to Bon is
mirrored symbolically in the extended development of Rosa's physical and
emotional response to Clytie. For all of the characters, touch crystallizes the
"eggshell shibboleth of caste and color" and the taboos against interracial
union; touch creates, too, the necessity for southern customs, and laws against
miscegenation (specifically here because the "secret" of the legend is solved
in terms of miscegenation—actual miscegenation for the father, Sutpen,
and intended by the son Charles Bon). Nonetheless, southern interracial
restrictions, according to one theme of this novel, are not about preventing
touch but rather about affirming all of the negative implications of touch
when they serve the ends of white society.

Clytie's reactions to this meeting are not provided; she remains as
nonverbal as she has been throughout the novel; however, her presence, as
a mixed-blood person within the Sutpen family, suggests that either race
or kinship must be denied if caste and color are to continue to sustain fixed
meanings in a changing world. Clytie's involvement in the lives of other
characters forwards the conclusion that in order to avoid self-destruction,
and perhaps ultimately social disintegration, bonds of kinship on every level
must be honored, even if they exist across racial lines (or most especially
when they do, as Faulkner suggests both with the resolution of *Absalom,
Absalom!* and with a later novel, *Go Down, Moses).* This idea of kinship, most
apparent in the portraits of Clytie and Charles Bon, is, in one sense, an
insightful development of the idea of family (both white and black) Faulkner
first employs in *Flags in the Dust* and uses more intensively in *The Sound and
the Fury;* it partakes, too, of the conception of "blood" and racial definitions
from *Light in August.* Blood and family become in *Absalom, Absalom!* human
kinship and interconnection—larger abstractions—which Faulkner presents
as confused and conflicting, but by means of them he aims toward a more
comprehensive way of portraying the divided world of his South. He attempts
to probe imaginatively into the causes behind the Sutpen legend, but because

neither incest nor fratricide provides him with a means of transcending the inner tensions of his narrative situation, he returns to the Negro. He relies upon conventional beliefs about "Negro" to solve his narrative dilemma.

In *Absalom, Absalom!* Faulkner seems to have pulled a neat trick. Both Quentin and Shreve are convinced that they have found the "truth" of the Sutpen puzzle in the Negro, technically in their uncovering the secret of Bon's black blood. Almost inevitably their view has been accepted. In a sense their resolution amounts to a discovery of the proverbial "nigger in the woodpile," a not-so-unexpected way for southerners to resolve the complexity of human interactions and motivations. (Shreve is, of course, Canadian; however, his notions of the South are stereotyped, literary exaggerations.) Both Shreve and Quentin, in conjecturing "Negro" as the key, reflect something basic about their conformity to the ideology of the South. They retrace what Mr. Compson relates as the opinion of the townsmen regarding Sutpen once he became successful:

> There were some among his fellow citizens who believed even yet that there was a nigger in the woodpile somewhere, ranging from the ones who believed that the plantation was just a blind to his actual dark avocation, through the ones who believed that he had found some way to juggle the cotton market itself and so get more per bale for his cotton than honest men could to those who believed apparently that the wild niggers which he had brought there had the power to actually conjure more cotton per acre from the soil than any tame ones had ever done. (72)

The "nigger in the woodpile" to which Mr. Compson refers takes on a literal meaning in the resolution as it is constructed by Shreve and Quentin. The old saw becomes an indispensable part of Faulkner's complex structure and narrative scheme.

In their reconstruction of the final confrontation between Henry Sutpen and Charles Bon, Quentin and Shreve assign Bon the fateful words: "*I'm the nigger that's going to sleep with your sister. Unless you stop me, Henry*" (358). The imagination of the two narrators is frozen into the clichés of southern thinking. Quentin and Shreve do not intuit the terms in which to couch Charles's decisive statement; they know. Shreve's knowledge is a result of his melodramatic vision of the South, Quentin's of his long personal and historical experience of the South.

Shreve deflates the finely tempered rhetorical reality the two have created by calling Bon in his very next reference "the black son of a bitch" (358). Somehow it all becomes very ordinary, so ordinary in fact that Shreve at last is

ready to end the night: "Come on. . . . Let's get out of this refrigerator and go
to bed" (359). The Negro is, after all, an expected part of the tissue of southern
life. Instead of penetrating something unfathomable about human conduct
or life, the two narrators (and Faulkner himself, for all the brilliant shape
of the novel) resort to the pedestrian—though it is the pedestrian that has
tyrannized conscious and subconscious levels of thought. Perhaps the problem
that the Negro represents to the southern white man clouds his perceptions
and constricts his imaginative faculties; however, that problem is so enduring
and realistic that its power to affect mental processes does not dissipate. Even
Shreve's mental capacity to make enlightened conjectures is stimulated as well
as circumscribed by the Negro's actual presence in the South. Shreve comes
to the legend with an image of the South's depravity, and he concludes with a
confirmation of it. The South and the Negro are once again inextricably bound
together, though this time it is the result of a piecemeal and tortuous logic.

On one level, that of narrative structure, it is a long way around to a
"solution." But on another level, a certain ease is apparent in the way the
narrators head with an inevitable, dead reckoning to the Negro, though they
themselves try to delay it and prolong the resolution in order to savor or
reconstruct all of the elements possible from a logical base. Their fabrications
create an illusion of reality; their construct is quite believable. All rational
investigations lead to a basic reality: Charles Bon as "nigger."

Nonetheless, the process by which the two young narrators come to
Bon as "nigger" suggests an analogy to Rosa Coldfield's poetic analysis of
remembering: "That is the substance of remembering—sense, sight, smell,
the muscles with which we see and hear and feel—not mind, not thought:
there is no such thing as memory: the brain recalls just what the muscles
grope for: no more, no less: and its resultant sum is usually incorrect and
false and worthy only of the name of dream" (143). The image of the brain's
recalling "just what the muscles grope for" is analogous to Shreve and
Quentin's simultaneously moving toward Bon's blackness out of separate
and distinct conditionings of their muscles. In recreating the past, they are
remembering what their experience of life has taught them.

Authority for Bon's black blood, then, is not the point. The point is
rather that both for Faulkner in the construction of his novel and for his
various narrators in the telling of the tale, meaning hinges upon somehow
coming to the "fact" of Bon's being "Negro," when ironically he is the one
character the furthest removed (by all narrative accounts) from "Negro" and
"nigger" as the novel and society have presented them; even Clytie, whose
Sutpenness primarily defines her, remains a "coffee-colored," "dark essence."
Mr. Compson's images of Bon as "a young man of a worldly elegance and
assurance beyond his years, handsome" (74) and as "watching, contemplating
them from behind that barrier of sophistication in comparison with which

Henry and Sutpen were troglodytes" (93) function effectively to separate Bon from all social images of Negro as subordinates and servants which Faulkner incorporates into the novel.

What the narrators finally make of Bon as "nigger" is prefigured by Mr. Compson: "Bon with that sardonic and surprised distaste which seems to have been the ordinary manifestation of the impenetrable and shadowy character. Yes, shadowy: a myth, a phantom: something which they engendered and created whole themselves; some effluvium of Sutpen blood and character, as though as a man he did not exist at all" (104). It is only a short step from the conception of Bon that Mr. Compson reports to the two youths' conjecture that Bon is a "nigger." Bon becomes "the abstraction" and "the Negro" created to satisfy the needs of the characters and narrators. His situation, like Clytie's, stresses the force and inevitability of the Negro as a presence, "impenetrable and shadowy," at the center of the South and of Faulkner's creative imagination.

Absalom, Absalom! returns the reader and each of the four narrators to those myths about the southern past (the myth of racial purity is just one) out of an acknowledged helplessness and inability ever really to know or understand the South, and by extension both themselves and the past. The view of miscegenation, or a pathological fear of it, as the primary cause of destruction in *Absalom, Absalom!* ignores the fact that miscegenation is only one piece of the larger race question and only one part of the total pattern of life represented in the novel.

For Quentin and Shreve, it is not slavery alone which accounts for the South's moral deficiency. It is, as well, the white southerner's failure to respond to the black human being; the response instead is to an abstraction—"the Negro" myth. Unfortunately, Quentin's conjecture that Henry kills Bon because of the threat of the Negro points to the individual seeking something outside of himself to hold responsible for his situation. Quentin needs the myth of the Negro in order to escape a personal confrontation of complex moral problems, incest and fratricide. Sutpen, too, is guilty of a similar evasion of self when he fails to ask where he himself went wrong. Whereas Sutpen distorts his understanding of morality to fit the contours of the morally reprehensible, slaveholding South, Quentin rationalizes a morally complex situation by resorting to the scapegoat sanctioned by his society. Ultimately, Quentin in the modern age repeats the mistake of Sutpen in the past. He seeks an external cause which, because of the social composition of the South, is readily available in the Negro.

Regarding the interpretation of Sutpen's story, Faulkner has observed:

I think no one individual can look at a truth. It blinds you. You look at it and you see one phase of it. Someone else looks at it and

sees a slightly awry phase of it. But taken all together, the truth is
in what they saw though nobody saw the truth intact. . . . It was,
as you say, thirteen ways of looking at a blackbird. But the truth,
I would like to think, comes out, that when the reader has read all
these thirteen different ways of looking at a blackbird, the reader
has his own fourteenth image of that blackbird, which I would
like to think is the truth.[5]

What makes *Absalom, Absalom!* ultimately such a fine literary experience is
that it succeeds remarkably well in creating the illusion of open-endedness,
of expanding possibilities and realms of interpretations.

   Although *Absalom* engages the reader in a continuing creative process
as detective and interpreter, it retains a hard and fast central core. There is no
escaping the conjecture of "the nigger that's going to sleep with your sister,"
as Shreve has Bon identify himself (358). Faulkner may skillfully execute
the illusion of myriad possible interpretations; however, he signals through
his omniscient narrator's comment, "probably true enough," a corroboration
of precisely what he wishes. And one of these corroborations involves the
Negro (the "nigger in the woodpile") at the center, one to whom many
narrative clues lead. "Negro" is a central metaphor, albeit a most difficult
one to explicate. Representative major black figures in the novel are all as
much white as black, and in practically every case, they are more white than
black. The visibly "white" product of miscegenation has confounded sight as
a test of racial identity. Yet the cognitive image of "Negro," the traditionally
conceived and conventionally executed abstraction, provides the prism
through which all the black figures are refracted.

   The problem suggests Mr. Compson's consideration of Charles Bon
among the Sutpens:

> He is the curious one to me. He came into that isolated
> puritan country household almost like Sutpen himself came
> into Jefferson: apparently complete, without background or past
> or childhood—a man a little older than his actual years and
> enclosed and surrounded by a sort of Scythian glitter . . . yet from
> the moment when he realized that Sutpen was going to prevent
> the marriage if he could, he (Bon) seems to have withdrawn
> into a mere spectator, passive, a little sardonic and completely
> enigmatic. He seems to hover, shadowy, almost substanceless,
> a little behind and above all the other straightforward and
> logical, even though (to him) incomprehensible, ultimatums and
> affirmations and defiances and challenges and repudiations with
> an air of sardonic and indolent detachment. (93)

Bon is detached, older than his years, a completely enigmatic spectator. It is a long way from Bon to Sutpen's "monkey nigger." However, Bon's presence, as Mr. Compson describes it, hovering "a little behind and above all the others" (93), duplicates the stance of the balloon-face "monkey nigger":

> You knew that you could hit them [blacks] . . . and they would not hit back or even resist. But you did not want to, because they (the niggers) were not it, not what you wanted to hit; that you knew when you hit them you would just be hitting a child's toy balloon with a face painted on it, a face slick and smooth and distended and about to burst into laughing, so you did not dare strike it because it would merely burst and you would rather let it walk on out of your sight than to have stood there in the loud laughing. (230)

The Negro as a "toy balloon with a face painted on it" represents the helplessness and powerlessness of the existence of poor whites in general and Sutpen in particular. Sutpen's awareness of the futility in taking action against a balloon, which, paradoxically, is concrete yet insubstantial and symbolic in terms of the real world, suggests his attitude toward Charles Bon. Bon, like the balloon face, is an artificial configuration. He is the abstraction that Sutpen refuses to see or acknowledge because Bon's very presence mocks Sutpen, and any action against Bon exposes Sutpen to the possibility of that mockery being extended into the general public or community. Sutpen ignores Bon because he cannot accept Bon's reality. Like the black housekeepers in Sherwood Anderson's *Dark Laughter*, Bon is and remains the anonymous "nigger" ready to burst into laughter at the slightest provocation. Acceptance of Bon would make Sutpen's design an "ironic delusion," while rejection of him foists upon Sutpen and his design an "ironic reality."

This metaphorical presence of the enigmatic "Negro" pervades the entire novel, especially the conclusion. Shreve, for example, presents the metaphor of the "two niggers" to get rid of one Sutpen: "So it took Charles Bon and his mother to get rid of old Tom, and Charles Bon and the octoroon to get rid of Judith, and Charles Bon and Clytie to get rid of Henry; and Charles Bon's mother and Charles Bon's grandmother got rid of Charles Bon" (377–78). The metaphor suggests the omnipresence and the obstinacy of "the nigger" in the lives of white southerners. Shreve concludes his summary with the theory that "You've got one nigger left. One nigger Sutpen left. Of course you can't catch him and you don't even always see him and you never will be able to use him. But you got him there still. You still hear him at night sometimes. Don't you?" (378).[6] Despite the destructive eliminations basic to Shreve's summary and the legend, the oppressive presence of "the Negro" remains.

The illusive, disturbing "nigger," Jim Bond specifically, is a metaphor perhaps for the unknowable, or the contradictions, inherent in southern life and in life generally.

The stubborn "nigger" refuses extinction, and paradoxically, in the sense of Jim Bond being an authentic Sutpen descendant, "the nigger" belongs; he has his place in the physical and mental space of the South. Significantly, because no one—none of the narrators, none of the participants, not even Faulkner's omniscient narrative voice which sometimes interpolates and sometimes intrudes—comes away with an understanding of the Negro as metaphor at work or with an interpretation of the Negro, the herculean efforts (in vision, experience, and telling) remain somewhat mysterious. As long as there is one "nigger" left, southerners (reconstructed or not) and outlanders (sympathetic or not) alike can create myths out of the interaction of "the South" and "the Negro." Faulkner has left the flood gates of Yoknapatawpha open once again.

Literally, Shreve, the outlander who has vicariously experienced it all, revives the process, begins the myth anew, with his fanciful theorizing that the howling idiot and surviving Sutpen haunt the physical place (Sutpen's Hundred) and the psychological space (Quentin's dreams) that make up the South. Shreve concludes with the notion that

> in time the Jim Bonds are going to conquer the western hemisphere. Of course, it won't quite be in our time and of course as they spread toward the poles they will bleach out again like the rabbits and the birds do, so they won't show up so sharp against the snow. But it will still be Jim Bond; and so in a few thousand years, I who regard you will also have sprung from the loins of African kings. (378)

Shreve continues the process right up to and through the ending. His image of the Jim Bonds is a fine mythologizing that is not in the least unfamiliar. The myth of the Negro endures, as rigid and inflexible as the old one even though it may reflect a diminishing of the traditional racial hatred and fear.

Shreve pushes the mythology through to another inevitable conclusion from his analytical perspective. The result is Quentin's emotional breakdown at the end of *Absalom, Absalom!* which comes about as a result of the breakdown of his defense mechanism. Shreve and Quentin conclude their probing of the Sutpen legend, but Shreve turns the tables and wants to probe Quentin as a personal representative of the South. "Now I want you to tell me just one thing more," Shreve states. "Why do you hate the South?" (378). The reply is instantaneous: "'I dont hate it,' Quentin said, quickly, at once, immediately; 'I dont hate it; he said. *I dont hate it* he thought, panting in the cold air, the iron New England dark; *I dont. I dont! I dont hate it! I dont hate it!*'" (Faulkner's italics; 378). Shreve's analytic question shatters Quentin's forced composure. Shreve destroys the spell which their introspective process of constructing a total (that is, harmonious with all known and conjectured details) fiction has produced. The asking of the question is as much to blame as any inherent validity the question might have. The question itself is a violation of a code, and that violation is even more destructive to Quentin's uneasy equilibrium than the psychological process of putting together a compelling whole story from individually biased, fragmented perceptions.

Shreve, concerned all along with the southerner's negative identity, forges a negative affirmation of Quentin's southernness by the question and the response to it. Given the moral and psychological dualism intrinsic to southern society, Quentin, paradoxically, is telling the truth, as he knows it. It is no illusion: he does not hate the South. The tendency, of course, is to accept that Shreve has put his finger squarely on Quentin's problem, that Quentin does indeed hate the South. However, Quentin's emotional response can also be attributed, at least partially, to Shreve's violation of a code to which southerners tacitly agree. Shreve, the outlander, forces Quentin to respond to a question that lies outside the boundaries of accepted social interchange. Shreve seeks a union of internal and external realities; for the southerner in this novel, that is an impossibility, and both the Sutpen legend and its reconstruction are confirmations of this "fact."

Both as a participant in a resolution of the Sutpen drama and as a narrator of it, Quentin is an enigmatic figure. Faulkner has put it another way: "It's incidentally the story of Quentin Compson's hatred of the bad qualities in the country he loves."[7] However, Quentin is as mysterious about revealing what it is he hates about his South as he is about what he loves. He does not make emphatic or judgmental statements regarding Sutpen's or the South's morality. Neither does he make specific valuations of slavery and the South's racial dilemma. But what Quentin succeeds in doing as a character is to involve the reader in the large, complex, and shady areas of being, almost because of his inability to provide answers or to identify problems.

Quentin, from the outset, is a ghost because of the past; Henry Sutpen, at the end, is a ghostlike apparition from the past. Together the two remind us of Faulkner's statement that the South is "dead." Henry, once the promise of the South's future, is a death-in-life figure who retains a deathlike grip on Quentin's imaginative and rational faculties. Henry Sutpen, Miss Rosa, Mr. Compson, and the Sutpen legend all mark Quentin for an irreparable, nightmare stasis. He is impotent and unable to resolve the moral dilemma posed by the legend and the southern past, yet he has the ability to involve Shreve actively in it. Similarly, Quentin is alienated from the southern past while at the same time completely absorbed in the South by means of the telling of the tale. In the process of the novel, Quentin condemns, justifies, expiates, and absolves the South from "sin"; nonetheless, the experience of the "sin" remains.

What Quentin goes up the stairs at Sutpen's Hundred to discover is not the same thing that compels Miss Rosa; that is, he does not ascend the stairs, as Rosa does, in order to see for certain that Henry is in the house. The purpose for Quentin is to meet his guilt-ridden, death-in-life double, to ascertain the waste of Henry's life, to acknowledge the lost potential of the South's young manhood, and to witness the reckoning of time and futility. Quentin recognizes that Henry embodies all of the "ghosts" of the southern world which haunt Quentin himself. Even though Henry is of an earlier generation, his subjective experiences as a son of the South mirror Quentin's. Henry's suffering makes Quentin self-conscious, and Quentin suffers the more because, while meaningful synthesis is possible for him, it is not necessarily accurate or sufficient for solving his personal dilemma. When the two meet at Sutpen's Hundred, they represent a form of self-confrontation for which the imaginative constructions of the legend throughout the novel have prepared the reader. The horror of self-confrontation in this meeting is Quentin's most illuminating vision. He can no longer experience his world vicariously; the imagination is not enough, because, in this case, it implies a retreat from reality.

Attempting to use this encounter in order to prove empirically that Quentin did or did not learn of Bon's black blood from Henry appears inconsequential ultimately because the heart of the enigma is not the black blood, but the unknown, the mysterious, and the inexplicable written into Henry's wasted life and read on Quentin's "waking and sleeping" face. Henry shows that the pariah is not necessarily the Negro and that there are fugitive southern sons, just as there were fugitive black slaves. The black blood is a device, a red herring in the sense that it suggests a false significance to the meeting between the two sons of the South, the old and the new, who are linked in a death grip from which neither will emerge to tell, in specific terms, the "truth" of his existence and his experience because neither can— given both human frailty and the inexplicable in individual motives.

Henry's guilt and Quentin's fear (of life's possibilities for him) join in presenting a powerful image of the dark at the core of southern life and the southern imagination as Faulkner demonstrates. The image has power because it is a unique turn of the tradition; the Negro in the South (either slave or free) usually stands for the dark that has overshadowed and blighted the South, and Faulkner himself sometimes uses this notion. However, in *Absalom, Absalom!* it is, as the ending suggests, the southerner himself, his own mind—conscience (Henry) and imagination (Quentin)—that encompasses and creates the dark. The Negro, whether Clytie, Charles Bon, or Jim Bond in type, becomes in comparison a rather benign force. There is, then, in the ending a marginal pulling away from the myths of southern existence, although the retreat is not strongly verbalized. Faulkner relies upon an emotional experience (as he does in resolving *The Sound and the Fury*) to imply an abandoning of a traditional position: Look at what the black man has done to me; look at what the black man has made me do. Even though the new position is more of a felt experience than a statement, it seems to be: See what I have done to myself. This recognition, which Faulkner can present only obliquely, is one that Quentin cannot thoroughly absorb.

Whether external elements are real or imagined, the individual has to come to terms with them because they are aspects of himself. If the individual does not, he is doomed. Whether dream or waking reality, the "Nevermore of peace. Nevermore of peace. Nevermore Nevermore Nevermore" (373) which punctuates Quentin's thoughts after he reveals his meeting with Henry echoes neither "Negro" nor "nigger" but the powerful namelessness, the metaphysical "dark" that has wasted Henry's life and promises to waste Quentin's as well. It is Faulkner's ability to portray, not the meaning of that dark in the human heart, but so surely its multifaceted existence there that contributes to the power and intensity of *Absalom, Absalom!*

NOTES

1. William Faulkner, *Absalom, Absalom!* (1936; New York: Random House, 1964), 151–52. All parenthetical references are to this edition.

2. A possible source for Wash Jones is a character by the same name, Washington Jones, which is shortened to Wash Jones, in "Ananias," a short story by Joel Chandler Harris. I do not wish to emphasize the coincidence of the name; however, the situation is suggestive. Wash Jones, a lower-class white, is the one-time overseer of Colonel Benjamin Flewellen's plantation who becomes rich after the war and is the colonel's chief creditor. Jones is a commission merchant who forecloses the mortgage on the Flewellen plantation and thereby becomes the owner. See Joel Chandler Harris, "Ananias," in Harris, *Balaam and His Master* (Cambridge: Riverside, 1891), 113–48.

3. Joel Chandler Harris, "Free Joe and the Rest of the World," in Harris, *Free Joe and Other Georgian Sketches* (New York: Scribner's, 1887), 1. Harris's fiction resonates throughout *Absalom, Absalom!*

4. One measure of the importance of the encounter between Rosa and Clytie is the care that Faulkner took in revising the scene. According to Gerald Langford, there were four stages of revision apparent in Faulkner's presentation of the meeting between the two women. The manuscript shows that much of Faulkner's rewriting of the scene involves emphasizing the dramatic impact of the confrontation. Specifically, Faulkner added to the section in such a way as to extend the significance of the touch of Clytie's coffee-colored hand on Rosa's white flesh. See Langford, *Faulkner's Revision of "Absalom, Absalom!": A Collation of the Manuscript and the Published Book* (Austin: University of Texas Press, 1971), 29–31.

5. Frederick L. Gwynn and Joseph L. Blotner, eds., *Faulkner in the University* (New York: Vintage, 1959), 273–74.

6. According to Langford, "The most significant revision in Chapter IX is the added emphasis given to Jim Bond in the closing pages of the book" (*Faulkner's Revision of "Absalom, Absalom!"* 40). Faulkner added the image of Bond's howling to the manuscript, but the impact of the addition does not seem to be "the heritage of man's long inhumanity to man," as Langford suggests (41), but rather an enduring concern with the presence of the Negro as a symbol of the tensions in the southerner's existence. See, for instance, Langford's reproduction of the manuscript and book revisions (360–61).

7. Gwynn and Blotner, eds., *Faulkner in the University*, 71.

DIANNE LUCE COX

A Measure of Innocence:
Sanctuary's *Temple Drake*

The charges that have been leveled against Temple Drake of Faulkner's
Sanctuary since its publication in 1931 are often astonishing both in their
substance and in the subjective involvement betrayed in these accusations. She
is said to be a man-devouring nymphomaniac, a murderess, a pathological liar,
a whore, a siren, a snare for innocent men, a psychopath, a masochist; depraved,
sluttish, frigid, promiscuous; evidence of Faulkner's hatred of women and his
premarital performance anxiety. It has been written of Temple that "She wants
Popeye to assault her; she tells the sordid tale to Horace Benbow. . . 'with actual
pride.' She could escape from the Memphis house, but she doesn't because she
loves life there. She could save Goodwin's life. She does not because she has
no compassion whatsoever."[1] And elsewhere; "Subconsciously, she desires to
be raped at the Goodwin place. She stays in the Memphis bordello to rebel
against her father and the accepted moral code. She testifies against Lee
Goodwin, among other reasons, merely to perform another sinful act. . . .
The only character who senses Temple's unhealthy state of mind is Horace
Benbow. . . ."[2] And similarly: "In the events to follow: the rape, the sojourn in
the Memphis brothel, in the trial of the innocent Godwin [*sic*], she is a driven
helpless creature, progressively degenerate. At last she causes the death of an
innocent man by refusing to bear witness. She has nothing against him; it is
just that she has no capacity for responding to moral stimuli."[3]

From *Mississippi Quarterly* 39, no. 3, 1986, reprinted in *William Faulkner: Six Decades of
Criticism*, pp. 105–126. © 2002 by Michigan State University Press.

These are judgments about a character who herself suffers the most outrageous betrayals and violations in the course of the novel.

Though the character of Temple drawn in *Sanctuary*—young, irresponsible, playing at life—is not in many ways admirable or likeable, Faulkner asks us to read her story with pity for what she suffers, much as one reads the story of Darl Bundren or Joe Christmas. The initiation into evil, the realities of death, destruction, and injustice, that Temple undergoes, and her reactions to the progressive phases of that initiation are treated realistically but not unsympathetically.

Though there have been judicious readings of the book, too, many of them ultimately dismiss Temple as one who succumbs without a struggle to sexual and moral corruption. The prevailing view seems to be that if she is a victim, she was a victim waiting for Popeye to happen to her. Much of the hostility critics have directed toward Temple seems to result from their accepting Horace Benbow's view of her. It is important to keep in mind, as Warren Beck's perceptive analysis of Faulkner's techniques and achievement in *Sanctuary* has noted, that this novel is Horace's story, and its depiction of events and characters is colored by his sexual obsessions even in omnisciently narrated scenes where he is present.[4] His desire for justice is genuine, but his view of Temple is deeply biased because he is himself a deeply ambivalent character: "He stands . . . as an anxiously striving champion of human rights and security for Goodwin and the woman and child, but also as self-hypnotized victim of a veiled but tolerated lust."[5] But in counterpoint to Horace's perspective, we are also provided several other points of view of differing degrees of reliability, including those of the omniscient narrator in scenes when Horace is not present, of Temple herself, and of Ruby, who witnesses portions of Temple's ordeal at the Old Frenchman's Place. It is helpful, I think, to read *Sanctuary* (and all of Faulkner's novels) as one reads *The Sound and the Fury* and *As I Lay Dying*—with a careful use of each narrative perspective as a touchstone for the reliability of the others and as a supplement to the evidence supplied in the others.

Further, if we are to understand Temple Drake, we must not approach her as we do the "opaque" Popeye.[6] While the enigma of evil is at the center of *Sanctuary* in the figure of Popeye, the other characters are usually given plausible motivations for their actions, even their evil ones. Thus, before we conclude with the self-castigating Temple of *Requiem for a Nun* that she merely "liked evil," or with many critics that the novel provides inadequate evidence of her motives for perjury,[7] we should proceed on the assumption that Faulkner is sufficiently in control of his creation to know why Temple lies—just as he knows why Horace fails to take her from the Memphis brothel and why he fails to cross-examine her—and that therefore he has probably provided sufficient evidence of these motivations, though in his typically indirect manner. In fact, if we proceed from this assumption, we find quite a bit of evidence about the actions of Popeye, Temple, Narcissa Sartoris, Eustace Graham, Clarence Snopes, Judge Drake and the Memphis lawyer in the few days before the opening of Lee Goodwin's trial that has direct bearing on Temple's motivation for perjuring herself.

At the opening of the novel Temple, like her counterpart Horace Benbow, is an innocent. She is the only daughter of her respectable father, Judge Drake, and the sister of four protective older brothers, one of whom has threatened to beat her if he finds that she has been in the company of a drunken man.[8] She has been raised in a household of men in which her experience has been strictly limited, but where she has apparently been given instruction about the danger that exists in the world and about the need to avoid the appearance of contamination by it at all costs (much as Horace Benbow instructs his stepdaughter Little Belle not to soil her slippers by forming acquaintances with college boys she meets on trains) (15). Apparently Temple is restive in this sheltered environment, because when she goes away to college at Oxford, she sets about doing whatever she can get away with to broaden her experience. She is not very imaginative about these opportunities, but she does sneak out of the dorm at night to go riding with the town boys who have cars, dating them on weeknights and reserving the weekends for the college boys.

However, she is not very practiced at breaking rules, and she gets herself into trouble of two kinds. Most immediate is her being put on probation by the school. But in addition, she angers several of her acquaintances with her lack of restraint and judgment—especially the town boy, Doc, who is jealous of her attentions to them, and that "Virginia gentleman," Gowan Stevens, who sees her name written on a lavatory wall.

Temple is pretty and popular, and she relies on her attractiveness to secure the dates she wants, and also to help her placate the various competitors for her attentions. But she is not entirely successful at this last, partly because she is, in her relations with the boys, an opportunist. "Cool, predatory and discreet" (32), she apparently cares little for any of them, and as a virgin, too, she is little troubled by the sexual arousal they must deal with. Nevertheless, they are a necessary adjunct to her social life: the fins and wings of her existence. Temple knows how to act only through men—and, in addition, only through men who accept the conventions of her social world. But she is no different from her peers in this. Except for some whom Temple does not understand, they measure their self-worth by the standards of popularity and the amount of "damage" they can do to boys without losing their respectability. When Temple thinks of the girls' shared preparation for the school dances, she thinks with pity of the ugly girl who swears she has lost her virginity, sacrificing her reputation to affirm her attractiveness (181–82).

Thus, when Temple willfully jumps off the train[9] to join Gowan and finds that he has broken the cardinal rule that one does not drink heavily in the presence of a lady (his discovery of her name on the lavatory wall having raised doubts in his mind that she is a lady), she is at a loss for a course of action. The logical thing for her to do is to take the next train back to Oxford, but after a look at the dingy train station and the overalled men watching her (31), she instinctively chooses the drunken Gowan as one who will, she believes, honor his obligation as a gentleman to protect her. She has no confidence in her ability to deal with the country folk at the train station, she opts for one of her own class, passively putting herself in his hands (though as the day proceeds she becomes less hopeful that she will extricate her from this very compromising situation).

Temple's fear of the overalled men at the train station prepares for her reaction when Gowan drives the car headlong into the felled tree obstructing the entrance to the Old Frenchman's Place. She accepts the impact without a sound, seeing, as she is thrown violently from the car, the gangster Popeye and the half-wit Tommy, armed with a shotgun, emerge from the roadside foliage:

> She scrambled to her feet, her head reverted, and saw them step into the road. . . . Still running her bones turned to water and she fell flat on her face, still running. (44)

This running with head reverted characterizes much of Temple's behavior while at the Old Frenchman's Place. Like Isabella of *Measure for Measure*, though there are important differences, Temple recognizes evil; she fears it, tries to escape it, but is not unwilling to face it.[10] Paradoxically, though, this is because in her childish innocence she doesn't quite believe in it. Like Horace and Gowan, she believes that the things she fears don't really happen. And given her background, there is some justification for Temple's inability to believe in a violent, unjust world. Sheltered as she has been, she has no experiential basis for such belief. She has always been admonished to preserve respectability, but not especially to avoid evil. It is as if her social class alone will protect her from that. Indeed, she seems to think that evil resides only in other social classes and perhaps even that it is only a matter of social class—like having a different set of manners. She tells Ruby, "'Things like that don't happen. Do they? They're just like other people. You're just like other people. With a little baby. And besides, my father's a ju-judge. The gu-governor comes to our house to e-eat'" (64). She repeatedly uses the incantation "My father's a judge" in the face of danger at the Old Frenchman's Place—and her gradual discovery that it is an impotent talisman parallels her acceptance of the reality of evil. So while Temple's primary emotion at the

Old Frenchman's Place is fear, it is mixed with a strange denial that evil can touch her; and both are manifested in a childish sort of assertiveness that might best be called whistling in the wind.

Contrary to seeking violation, from the moment that Temple arrives at the bootlegger's camp where she is so out of her element she begins looking for sanctuary, and this search lasts until the end of the novel. In this world Temple is an infant, and her desire for protection is nowhere more painfully obvious than when she takes an army canteen, a vessel suggesting her absent mother but endowed with the protective aspects of the father, to bed with her, or when she projects her fear on Ruby's baby, mothering it to console herself: "'Now, now; Temple's got it. . . . I'm not afraid'" (64). She looks in turn to each of the others first to help her get back to her dormitory and then just to remove her from the growing danger; but except for Tommy each not only refuses her protection but adds to her fear. Though Ruby has stressed that she must leave before dark, Gowan knows Popeye carries a pistol and refuses to ask him for transportation. When Temple takes the initiative in her jaunty, collegiate style, attempting a winning smile that is transmuted into a "cringing grimace" (57) by her fear, Popeye sees through her naïve coquetry and responds, "'Make your whore lay off of me, Jack'" (58). By reflex Gowan objects, and encouraged by her assumption that she has a gentlemanly ally after all, Temple retorts saucily, "'What river did you fall in with that suit on? Do you have to shave it off at night?'" Appalled, Gowan hurries her away and then goes in search of more alcohol, and Temple realizes that her protector is himself terrified of Popeye. At this point she panics, sinking down tearfully into a corner next to a rifle, an ambiguous image of masculine strength and potential protection, but as it anticipates Popeye's pistol, also of threat.

Temple's inexperience and self-centeredness make a failure of her attempt to enlist Ruby's aid, too. Temple's story of her father and brothers' political power and her thoughtless social condescension anger Ruby and prompt her to lecture Temple on her lack of self-reliance and to upbraid her for her failure to carry her own weight in life—truths of which the events of the day have made Temple increasingly aware. What's more, Ruby realizes that Temple's obvious fear of sexual violation is arousing to the men there, and her compassion for the girl is stifled by her own fear that their reactions to Temple will disrupt the life with Lee that she has purchased at great cost, prostituting herself to get him released from jail for murdering another man in a fight over a Filipino woman (68).

Most of Temple's actions are ill-judged and counterproductive. She is, as Ruby calls her, a "little gutless fool" (70).[11] She envies and wonders at Ruby's ability to cope with these frightening men without really understanding what gives Ruby her assurance. The immediate lesson of Ruby's story of her own courage in trying to save the life of her lover Frank

and of Frank's courage in standing up to her father and his rifle is mostly
lost on Temple. However, she listens attentively enough to Ruby's tale to
learn the dubious lesson that to earn the protection of a "real man" one
must be a "real woman," or sexually active. Ruby's account of her father's
killing Frank and calling her a whore (67) may lead Temple to recognize
more clearly that before that the repressive man—the father—is a captor
who would enforce innocence by denying sexual experience and love, and
to conclude that the cost of gaining love and protection may be losing
respectability. Later on, in the scene at the roadhouse, Temple will imitate
Ruby and draw on some of these lessons in her attempt to escape Popeye.
Here the story only serves to convince her of her powerlessness because
she recognizes the truth of Ruby's criticisms of her. Ruby's perceptiveness
about Horace and Temple and her loyalty to Lee should not blind us to
the fact that she fails Temple just as surely as do the men in this novel. The
frightened girl looks to her for comfort and advice, but the older woman's
selfish concerns lead her to deny any human sympathy with Temple and to
humiliate her for the fear she exhibits. Her response to Temple is exactly as
she tells Horace it was: "I've lived my life without any help from people of
your sort; what right have you got to look to me for help?" (195–96). Ruby
would use people according to their deserts, but as Hamlet reminds us (II.
ii.), under the application of that philosophy how shall she herself escape
whipping when she needs help from Temple?

Temple hasn't the courage to walk away partly because she continues
to hope that she will get away with this venture—that she will get back to
Oxford in time for one of her friends to sneak her into the dorm. She fears
violation, but she also fears the consequences of breaking her social code, of
being caught being indiscreet, of suffering a lapse in respectability; and all
her life this, not violence, has been the most immediate danger. So, terrified
though she is of the men who are gradually becoming more threatening, she
removes her dress and carefully folds it before going to bed, lest it appear
rumpled when she returns to the safety of the campus (83). There can be
no doubt of the sincerity of her fear of rape, given the fantasies she reports
having that night of turning into a boy or wearing a chastity belt, and given
her loss of consciousness when Popeye puts his hand into her underwear. Her
version of the story is corroborated in large part by the omniscient narration
of the same scene. Why, then, does she fluff out her hair and powder her
nose before lying down in the bed (83–84), an action that has been cited as
evidence that she is subconsciously preparing for a desired sexual encounter?[12]
It is plausible that she does this precisely because she fears an intrusion from
the men. Her preparations for bed are, on the one hand, a kind of denial; the
primping is a habit, and going through these motions reassures her that it is
still an orderly world. On the other hand, Temple sees her beauty as her only

tool with which to control men; even in her frightened fantasies she does not think of rebuffing them by turning ugly. The rigidity of Temple's thinking is equally clear during her abduction from Frenchman's Bend to Memphis. She has been brutally raped, has witnessed a murder, and has been subtly threatened with a pistol herself. She rides passively with Popeye as she had with Gowan, but this should not be construed as an affirmation of her rape or a desire to go with Popeye. The girl has suffered a series of traumas. The countryside passes her seemingly blind eyes until Temple subconsciously notices the lush spring flora and sees in it a reflection of her recent experience:

> It had been a lavender spring. The fruit trees, the white ones, had been in small leaf when the blooms matured; they had never attained that brilliant whiteness of last spring, and the dogwood had come into full bloom after the leaf also.... But lilac and wisteria and redbud, even the shabby heaven-trees, had never been finer, fulgent, with a burning scent.... The bougainvillea against the veranda would be large as basketballs and lightly poised as balloons, and looking vacantly and stupidly at the rushing roadside Temple began to scream. (164)

With a new knowledge of the evil her father and brothers have been sheltering her from while warning her only against the appearance of evil, teaching her to be discreet but not how to live in a world that contains evil, Temple now perceives that evil invading even her garden at home. She has shown every indication of wanting life and experience—of chafing under the watchful protection of her male kin. Now that she has experienced a violent sexual initiation into evil and can no longer deny its existence, she is horrified at it.

However, Temple's initiation is not accomplished in a single lesson. She is still naïve enough to assume that now that she has lost her virginity—presumably the worst fate her family has warned her of—the ordeal is over. Thus she does not attempt to escape from Popeye because she believes he is driving her to a town where he will release her, and when they arrive in Dumfries she begins "to look about, like one waking from sleep. 'Not here!' she said. 'I cant—'" (166). Her fear of compromising appearances again controls her behavior. It is terrible to be raped but equally terrible to have it known. When Popeye leaves the car to get food and Temple sees an acquaintance, she disobeys Popeye's instructions to stay in the car and hides around the corner of a building lest the boy recognize her and see the blood still running down her legs. She ought to understand her situation when Popeye approaches her threateningly, his right hand freed to reach the pistol in his pocket,[13] but she doesn't. It is only when Popeye hands her a sandwich, a gesture of nurturance, and takes the road toward Memphis, that she comprehends he means to keep her:

> Again, the bitten sandwich in her hand, she ceased chewing and opened her mouth in that round, hopeless expression of a child; again his hand left the wheel and gripped the back of her neck and she sat motionless, gazing straight at him. . . . (168–69)

In the brothel, Temple's violation continues, and still she finds no help either from older women or from men. Probably willfully, and because she doesn't suspect his impotence, Reba does not recognize that Popeye has kidnapped Temple. She keeps referring to Temple as his "girl" and tells her that she is lucky Popeye is such a free spender. Still, in her shock, Temple is slow to understand the terms of her imprisonment. Popeye has told her he'll buy her a new coat (168), but when Reba tells her they'll shop for new clothes tomorrow, Temple thinks despairingly that she has only two dollars (187). But she understands well enough that she is a prisoner and that her keepers repeatedly violate her privacy. Temple's fear is now numbed because she believes the worst has already happened to her, but she writhes in anguish as Minnie and Reba ruthlessly expose her shame—taking her knickers to wash them, discussing the blood, checking the arrangement of the towels around her loins.

Given the first opportunity, Temple locks Reba and Minnie out of her room, and she is reluctant to admit the doctor. That she finally does so suggests that she hopes a professional man—someone like her father—will help her to escape. But Reba will not leave them alone, so she has no opportunity to ask him to rescue her. Further, Dr. Quinn is a coarse, insensitive man who reaches toward her with "a thick, white hand bearing a masonic ring, haired over with fine reddish fuzz to the second knuckle-joints" (179). The violations both of the night before the rape, when Popeye touches her, and of the rape itself are about to be re-enacted, and so, "Lying on her back, her legs close together, she began to cry, hopelessly and passively, like a child in a dentist's waiting-room" (179). After suffering these repeated attacks upon her helplessness and innocence, Temple is disoriented, wrenched by time and experience out of the orderly garden created for her by her father and brothers; and her view of life temporarily takes on a dark sensibility (ironically heightened by gin) of which she has not previously been capable:

> She watched the final light condense into the clock face, and the dial change from a round orifice in the darkness to a disc suspended in nothingness, the original chaos, and change in turn to a crystal ball holding in its still and cryptic depths the ordered

chaos of the intricate and shadowy world upon whose scarred flanks the old wounds whirl onward at dizzy speed into darkness lurking with new disasters. (180–81)

By the time that Horace Benbow learns of Temple's whereabouts, she has been there nearly three weeks. He has heard part of her story from Ruby already, and so he fears what he will hear from Temple because he is not certain he can bear it. Even before he meets Temple, Horace has begun to associate her with his step-daughter, Little Belle. What he thinks he fears for both girls is their exposure to irresponsible young men like Gowan Stevens and through them to evil, but what he really fears is that they may be impervious to evil, that they may be able to survive it. Indeed, in his nausea at his relationship with his pampered, twice-married wife, Belle, and his manipulating sister, Narcissa, Horace is prepared to believe that all women of his social class are thoroughly corrupt though they hide behind a façade of respectability. But his disgust at respectable women is largely a projection of his lustful feelings for his step-daughter, Little Belle, whose experience with college boys he would like to curtail but whom he compulsively watches in the grape arbor (i.e., garden) in a manner that Faulkner tellingly pairs with Popeye's watching Temple and Red, who "looked like a college boy" (283). His jealousy over Little Bell's emerging sexuality leads him to project the guilt for his own lust onto her and onto Temple. Temple's story of her night of terror at the Old Frenchman's Place will excite in Horace, who fortifies himself with a drink, "'A big one'" (254), just before listening to it, a hallucination in which the two girls merge in the photograph of Little Belle, and through some action of his own "the small face seemed to swoon in a voluptuous languor, blurring still more, fading, leaving upon his eye a soft and fading aftermath of invitation and voluptuous promise and secret affirmation like a scent itself" (267–68). He vomits as he imagines Temple/Bell's violation, his body position suggesting that he himself is the violator: "he . . . leaned upon his braced arms while the shucks set up a terrific uproar beneath her thighs." However, the truth revealed in this hallucination is something Horace must deny, so he spends a good deal of energy inwardly railing at the hypocrisy of women. This is why he is so interested in Ruby: because he thinks that she, with her frank sexuality and capacity for loyalty, is categorically different from the "chaste" women he knows.

Horace arrives in Memphis well prepared to believe that Temple is there because she wants to be, and expecting—even hoping—to be shocked at her. Nothing Reba tells him beforehand would lead him to think differently. She even refers to Temple as one of "my girls" (253). Again, as with the doctor, Temple is ashamed to face Benbow. He is a lawyer as are two of her brothers, and he is of her social class. But she agrees to see him, and again it is likely that she hopes he will take her away from Popeye. But again, Miss Reba quietly insists on staying in the room and hearing their conversation. Having agreed to see Horace, then, Temple hides under the covers until he and Reba explain that they want her to testify on Lee's behalf. Then she suddenly emerges from them utterly shamelessly and with a "black antagonism" directed at Horace. This is because he has unwittingly made it perfectly clear what he thinks of her, while professing to know how she feels:

> "I just want to know what really happened. You wont commit yourself. I know that you didn't do it. I'll promise before you tell me a thing that you wont have to testify in Court unless they are going to hang him without it. I know how you feel. I wouldn't bother you if the man's life were not at stake." (255)

What Horace doesn't offer speaks volumes. For Temple there is to be no sanctuary in the law. Reba has made it even clearer, assuring her that Popeye will not be arrested and that they'll still be together. When she adds, "'The lawyer'll take care of you'" (256), Temple thrusts back the covers demanding a drink. (She has been given a lot of alcohol at Miss Reba's both to make her feel better and to control her.) If nice-girl-turned-whore is what Horace wants, that's what she'll give him, and with a vengeance. The two innocents face each other, he punishing her for his disillusionment with women, she punishing him for her betrayal by men. She gives Horace only one hint that all is not as he thinks, but predictably he fails to perceive it. When Horace repeats that she needn't tell Popeye's location, she protests, "'don't think I'm afraid to tell. . . . I'll tell it anywhere. Don't think I'm afraid'" (257). But of course she is afraid of Popeye, and she skillfully avoids telling Horace anything that would incriminate her kidnapper because she sees that Horace will not protect her from him. Horace misinterprets even her anxious attention to her auditors' reactions. He sees that she is trying to affect them, "looking from him to Miss Reba with quick, darting glances like a dog driving two cattle along a lane" (259), but he cannot see that her behavior is prompted by fear of reprisal from Popeye were she to reveal anything. Instead he ascribes it to feminine vanity: "She went on like that, in one of those bright, chatty monologues which women can carry on when they realise that they have the center of the stage; suddenly Horace realised that she was recounting the experience with actual pride, a sort of naïve and impersonal vanity, as though she were making it up" (258–59).

Reba apparently is moved by the recounting of Temple's night of terror, for she tells Horace as he leaves, "'I wish you'd get her down there and not let her come back. . . . She'll be dead, or in the asylum in a year, way him and her go on up there in that room. . . . She wasn't born for this kind of life!'" (264–65). But Horace refuses to feel compassion for Temple, thinking, "Better for her if she were dead tonight. . . . For me, too" (265). That is, he thinks he would be better off if Temple were dead. He thinks he can't bear to see this symbol of innocence exposed. But subconsciously he desires her violation and yet cannot admit that he takes a secret relish in it, so in that way, too, he would be better off—safer from his own intolerable desires—if she were dead. He leaves her in the brothel to serve his own purposes, both his conscious and unconscious ones. He certainly knows that were he to remove her Popeye would kill Goodwin—and possibly Temple, too—and that even if Popeye didn't kill her, Temple's respectable father would very likely prevent her from testifying. It is a fact that Temple is more accessible to him as a witness right where she is, under Popeye's "protection" rather than Judge Drake's.

Abandoned by Horace as by Gowan, Temple casts the next man she has access to in the role of her savior. We learn that Popeye has brought her a lover for four consecutive days. The most apparent reason for this is that Popeye wants to achieve sexual gratification through voyeurism, since he cannot do it in any other way. But both impotence and rape are often motivated by hostility. Like Horace and many other men in this novel, Popeye is attracted by Temple's immaturity, by her provocative innocence, and he wants to see it (literally) violated. Red, like the corncob, is Popeye's instrument in this repeated rape. But Popeye may also want to do the violation. At the Old Frenchman's Place, he is aroused to imitate Van's abusive behavior the night before Temple's rape. Having entered the room just in time to see Van rip open the raincoat she is wearing and be torn away from her by Goodwin, Popeye approaches her himself: "His right hand lay in his coat pocket. Beneath the raincoat on Temple's breast Tommy could see the movement of the other hand, communicating a shadow of movement to the coat" (87–88). It may be that Popeye's decision to bring Red to Temple is motivated by his hope that he can visually "learn" the potency to act out his hostility. Certainly he chooses in Red someone who is known to be sexually potent. If Red awakens Temple's sexuality without sufficiently awakening Popeye's potency, Popeye must be doubly frustrated by his experiment. He apparently decides it is a poor idea, and Red comes to Temple no longer.

But this brief relationship has been enough to demonstrate to the naïve Temple the difference between Popeye and a "real man." In her innocence she not only reverts to the law of the college dance floor and expects that her preference for Red will make Popeye retire in dudgeon, but also she assumes that Popeye's sexual impotence means he is less potent in other matters than she had thought—that this discovery makes him less a power to be reckoned with. She finds the courage, with the help of more gin, to steal out to arrange to meet Red, but ironically she cannot find it within herself to use that same opportunity to leave Memphis. She still fears Popeye enough to think that she needs a man to take her away from him, and she hopes that Red can do so. When she returns, in gloating repudiation but highly agitated, she tears all of the clothes Popeye has bought her out of the closet, flinging them on the floor, followed by bottles of perfume (270). Then she extracts the only one of these dresses she thinks she will ever wear again and hangs it up (274). But later that evening when Temple dresses for her "date" and sneaks out, she finds Popeye waiting for her.

The confidence born of her discovery of Popeye's impotence and her knowledge that he has left his pistol in her room stays with her only until she realizes that Popeye is carrying another pistol (280–81) and that he means to kill Red, whom he now sees as a threat to his possession of Temple and thus to his impunity for the murder of Tommy. Then all her attentions are turned to averting the disaster. As at the Old Frenchman's Place, she is again filled with terror, and she tries to placate the men she must control. But now she has learned what sex is and what, for Popeye, Red, and women of their class, sexual behavior is. She is still the scared college girl grinning in abasement, but now the gestures are different ones. Caressing him and whispering, she tries to vamp Popeye into turning over his pistol—even stroking him seductively: "'Give it to me,' she whispered. 'Daddy. Daddy.'" But then she abruptly stops in confusion and revulsion, saying "'I forgot . . . ; I didn't mean . . .'" (284), undoing in a moment her attempt at allurement by implicitly referring to his impotence.

Temple's language here and her taunting Popeye that Red is a "better man" (278) indicate that she associates the pistol-carrying Popeye with Ruby's shotgun-wielding father and probably with her own possessive father, the judge. In certain ways the events at the Grotto re-enact details of Ruby's story about her lover Frank, and at some level of consciousness Temple must recognize the analogies because she acts on them. When she realizes that Popeye intends to kill Red, she tries, like Ruby, to give Red a chance to escape. She offers to return to Miss Reba's, but Popeye rejects her efforts to placate him. When she sees Red enter the roadhouse, she urges Popeye to dance, frantically manipulating him to keep his back to Red. But Red, like Frank, does not run, and he asks her to dance. Again like Ruby, she tries to send him away, refusing the dance.

Her fear leads her to drink heavily; she becomes disoriented, and a sense of intense bereavement overcomes her, accompanied by desire. As with Laverne in Faulkner's novel *Pylon*, Temple's fear of loss triggers a desire for intimacy,[14] and when she can speak to Red alone for a moment, she flings herself on him, demanding that they escape together immediately and declaring that she's "on fire" (289). It is important to distinguish between

Temple's ugly and exaggerated behavior here and her feelings. The narrator tells us that she feels both grief and desire, and that is reasonable and understandable. But an unselfconscious passion that could make Temple writhe and gape like a "dying fish" (287) is simply not consistent with her vanity and immaturity. Furthermore, it is patently incredible that, after being brutally raped once and made love to under the randy eye of an abductor a total of four separate times, now inebriated and wrung with terror and exhaustion, Temple or anyone could generate quite this kind of urgent passion. Rather, it seems logical that Temple is pathetically trying to arouse passion in Red, to reach him through "sexual" behavior to get him to take her away in spite of Popeye and his goons. This is perfectly consistent with her earlier behavior with men; it's just that now she has overt sexual tactics in her repertoire. Once she leaves Red in the room, she is no longer described as manifesting or feeling any desire.

Further, Temple's use of sexual manipulation is also related to her memory of Ruby's story of Frank. Red's continued presence is grounds for Temple's hope that he, like Frank, might have enough will and courage to take her away from "Daddy." But to arouse him to be a "real man" she feels she must be a "real woman." Her behavior mimics what she imagines Ruby's sexual behavior to be. She is playing out Ruby's romantic illusion of the courageous lovers, but her naïveté makes her behavior a parody of adult sexuality. Moreover, she forgets that Frank's courage, like Tommy's, counted for nothing in the face of a loaded gun and remembers only the courage to defy Ruby's father that her sexual love had inspired in Frank. Temple needs a man with the courage to defy Popeye. She certainly doesn't want Red to die; she wants him to live to defeat Popeye and rescue her. But once again Temple's tactics fail. Red has not run because he does not know of Popeye's intent to kill him until Temple herself tells him at the same moment that she tries to arouse him (288). Despite her telling him repeatedly that he is a man, Red is afraid of Popeye and is not aroused by Temple's grotesque attempt at seduction. Possessing neither Tommy's mental limitations nor Frank's love, Red is unmanned by Popeye, and he chooses the reverse of Frank's course; he sends Temple away, hoping that Popeye will ignore the incident. Popeye does not. So Temple is left with yet another failure to find a protector, she has seen yet another instance of Popeye's murderous intent, and she has acted in such a way that she might expect him to retaliate violently against her. Through a turn of events, though, she is given a chance to ransom herself from his custody, and she takes it.

Popeye kills Red on June 17.[15] On the day following Horace's interview with Temple,[16] Narcissa has told the ambitious and unscrupulous district attorney that Clarence Snopes gave Horace some information that caused him to go to Memphis. He'll have to find out why for himself, she says

(317–18). Presumably, then, Graham has contacted a lawyer in Memphis to take care of the investigation because on the 18th, two days before court opens,[17] Clarence is in Oxford bitterly complaining that while he was in Jackson selling information to a certain judge, he had the same information beaten out of him by a "Memphis jew lawyer" (320). The information, of course, is that Horace knows Temple is a witness to Tommy's murder and that both Horace and Judge Drake now know where Temple is. The evidence of the courtroom scene suggests the following. The Memphis lawyer has underworld connections (he is probably the same Memphis lawyer who attempts to defend Popeye when he is arrested for murder in Alabama in the last chapter), and he warns Popeye—probably as early as the 17th, before Red is killed, thus giving Popeye additional motivation for that murder. Then the lawyer negotiates a three-way arrangement to satisfy Popeye, Graham and Judge Drake. Temple disappears from the night of Red's death (322) until she appears in court.[18] It seems likely that some time between the 18th and the 20th, Popeye or his henchmen turn her over to the Memphis lawyer and Eustace Graham, who coach her on her testimony just as Horace coaches Ruby on the night of the 20th (325). If Temple does as they instruct her and testifies that Lee Goodwin raped her and killed Tommy, then she will be free to leave with her father and brothers. If she does not perjure herself convincingly, clearing Popeye of the murder and preempting any later charges against him for the rape, he will be waiting for her outside the courtroom. Temple must choose to save herself or to save Lee, who has been too afraid of Popeye to testify in his own behalf.

On June 21, Temple arrives in court in a new, stylish black dress, probably purchased by Graham (342), and is called as a witness by the district attorney, not by Horace Benbow, who has allowed her to be sworn in as his witness (339) but does not call her to testify because he has promised not to question her unless he thinks they will execute Lee without her testimony (255). With the Memphis lawyer there to observe her behavior (338), and her father and brothers there expecting her to be returned to them after her testimony, she testifies as though drugged and with the parrot-like answers apparently taught her by Graham, who skillfully phrases his questions so that she can answer in a single word and insists that she not run ahead of him to tell anything in her own way. During her entire testimony, Temple compulsively watches the back of the room, both before and after her father arrives, and she never looks at Judge Drake until he takes her from the witness stand. Her intent, distracted gaze, mirroring Lee Goodwin's gazing at the narrow window in his cell through which he expects Popeye to shoot him, is evidence of her continued fear of Popeye and his gun. Even when the Court releases her to go back to the protection of her father and brothers, she cringes in fear at the doorway until all five men close in a tight bodyguard around her and force her to move outside with them (347–48). Temple's dropping of the platinum bag Popeye had given her[19] and her father's kicking it out of their way are the only signs of defiance they make toward Popeye. Judge Drake's gesture implies not only his awareness of the bag's significance but also that he is cooperating with Popeye's plan though he is disgusted at having to. Temple's perjury and public humiliation are the ransom she and her father are required to pay. Now that it is over and Popeye is out of danger, the judge can afford to show his feelings even in the presence of the Memphis lawyer, who does not watch them but gazes "dreamily" out the window through which he might have given a sign if all had not gone as planned (348).

The testimony about the rape and the well-timed interruption of the court proceedings by Judge Drake are both calculated to prevent Horace's cross-examination of Temple. Graham has evoked such a strong feeling of sympathy for her and her father in the courtroom that Horace stands to lose more than he can gain by insisting that she stand cross-examination. The day before, he himself had assured Lee that their case was won because Graham was "'reduced to trying to impugn the character of your witness [Ruby]'" (324). Had he called Temple as his own witness and questioned her first, he would have avoided testimony about the rape because he thinks that she liked whatever Popeye did to her, and he himself can't bear to expose the evil he projects on her. The only objection he raises during Graham's questioning of Temple (though the Court expresses surprise that there are no objections to the district attorney's incendiary questions) is to Graham's statement to Temple about her whereabouts after Tommy's death: "'You were in hiding, then, because something had happened to you and you dared not'" (343). Horace objects, then, when Graham leads the witness to reveal her rape and when he realizes that Goodwin is to be accused of that, too. As the testimony continues along these lines, he has nothing further to say. Graham moves Temple quickly to naming Goodwin as the murderer/rapist, and Horace knows he has been defeated.

Furthermore, it is likely that Temple's testimony shakes Horace's faith in Ruby and Lee and thus in himself. Temple's version of the events surrounding Tommy's death is as plausible as Ruby's. Horace has believed from the start that Temple wanted to be in Memphis while never fully believing that she had been raped. Now he must consider the possibility that Goodwin raped her and that she has been hiding from him and from her shame. Of Horace's four informants, Lee will tell him nothing, Ruby and Reba do not know the facts of the rape, and Temple herself makes only one ambiguous reference to it.[20] If this daughter of respectable society will testify publicly to having been raped by Goodwin, a man who has been convicted previously of murdering a man over a woman other than Ruby (Horace has learned this only the night before; 331–34), how can Horace

prove even to himself that Temple is not telling the truth? Surely Horace
is confronted with the truth about himself here: that he has been willing to
believe Ruby and to condemn Temple just because the one is so different
and the other so like his respectable womenfolk against whom he harbors
intense anger. Horace is not prepared to cross-examine Temple because he
has never been objective enough to consider alternative explanations of the
evidence—to anticipate, as any good trial lawyer should do, the case that
could be made for the opposing side. Indeed, he has been too personally
involved to follow Narcissa's quite practical advice that he hire a better
criminal defense lawyer for Goodwin, rejecting that advice partly because it
comes from his sister, who wants him, he thinks, to put appearances before
justice, and partly because this case has become his personal crusade not
so much to get justice for Lee as to champion the lowly, loyal, pure-of-
heart womanhood that Ruby symbolizes for him, the idealized woman that
he wishes to possess, a woman who will repeatedly sacrifice herself for her
man no matter how self-indulgent his desires or how wayward his behavior.
(One wonders if this is not why Horace chose to marry "somebody else's
wife" [17]: to possess a woman who would make that sacrifice to his desires.
Once possessed, however, Belle reveals herself to be a "real" woman in quite
another sense than Ruby means, and Horace is inordinately disgusted at her
flawed nature.) Horace is not the best criminal lawyer, but he is an intelligent
man. He cannot escape the recognition, however quickly denied, that his
idealization of Ruby and his condemnation of Temple have contributed to
the conviction of Lee Goodwin. He has been too self-blinded, he does not
know enough, to cross-examine Temple effectively.

Temple does, then, actively participate in the killing of Lee Goodwin,
an act which involves the direct or indirect complicity of almost every major
character in the novel and of the community as a whole. His lynching is
part of the well-laid plan. He must die immediately both to lay to rest
the question of who killed Tommy and as punishment for Ruby's earlier
testimony implicating Popeye. This is partly why Temple is made to testify
to her rape as well as to the murder. Graham uses that testimony to incite
the mob, suggesting the precise means by which Goodwin is to be killed:
"'this is no longer a matter for the hangman, but for a bonfire of gasoline'"
(340). Again, though hardly an admirable or imaginative response to evil,
Temple's behavior is perfectly understandable. She implicates Lee under
great duress, fearing for her own life. More than anything else, she wants to
escape Popeye, and everything she has tried for six weeks has failed: everyone
she has turned to has failed her. Now Popeye and the law and her father
and brothers are giving her an opportunity to free herself and helping her
to take advantage of it. It is not evidence of a liking for evil that she does
so. But, as is often demonstrated in this book immaturity, the confusion of

social respectability with moral responsibility, lack of self-knowledge, lack of human empathy—all of the failings of flawed humanity—will suffice as evil's tools.[21] Or with only a slight shifting of perspective does Faulkner not also ask us to see the enigmatic and impotent Popeye as the tool, the nightmare shape embodying the concerted impulses toward evil exhibited by all of the novel's characters, the self-righteous Horace and Ruby included?

Temple survives her exposure to evil, as Horace fears she will. At the end of the novel, both have returned to their ironic sanctuaries of home and family, but Horace is a defeated man. With his failure to vanquish evil in the courtroom, he simply gives up and returns to Belle and Little Belle, over whom he hovers even more protectively, having learned nothing that allows him to establish a healthier acceptance of reality. In another closing chapter, Popeye demonstrates a comparable desire for retreat from the emptiness of his life, and he finds it in death; but Temple survives.[22] She is not happy in the sanctuary chosen for her by her father, sitting "sullen and discontented and sad" (379) in the Luxembourg Gardens. But she should not be. She has exchanged a brief life of evil with Popeye for the death-in-life with her father. Her gazing with discontent on the gardens in the embrace of the season of rain and death seems a slightly optimistic note. One cannot withdraw from life to remain in an artificial garden of innocence forever. It may be that Temple is anxious to get on with life; she is ready for another season.

NOTES

1. Lewis P. Simpson, "Isaac McCaslin and Temple Drake: The Fall of the New World Man," in *Nine Essays in Modern Literature*, ed. Donald E. Stanford (Baton Rouge: Louisiana State University Press, 1965), 100.

2. James R. Cypher, "The Tangled Sexuality of Temple Drake," *American Imago* 19 (fall 192): 249.

3. R. F. Haugh, "Faulkner's Corrupt Temple," *English Studies in Africa* 4 (1961): 9.

4. "Realist and Regionalist," in *Faulkner* (Madison: University of Wisconsin Press, 1976), 222–25.

5. Beck, 230. However, Beck's study, which has relatively little to say of Temple, sees her as "grossly lecherous" (226) and morally irresponsible.

6. This is Beck's apt description of Popeye and Flem Snopes, characters who are "unamenable to evocation through instancings of their consciousness in progress and [who] must be realized at some remove, by what they do and say and by others' overt and subjective response to them" (208).

7. The most thorough of several attempts to deal with the evidence is by Cleanth Brooks, *William Faulkner: The Yoknapatawpha Country* (New Haven: Yale University Press, 1963), 121–27, but even he misses some relevant details and concludes that some questions can't be answered.

8. *Sanctuary* (New York: Jonathan Cape & Harrison Smith, 1931), 63. All further references to this novel are noted in the text.

9. Like that of Conrad's *Lord Jim*, Temple's is an untested innocence; her "fall" from that innocence is emblematized in a leap.

10. Michael Millgate has pointed out that the title, themes, and some details of setting in *Sanctuary* may derive from Shakespeare's *Measure for Measure* (*The Achievement of William Faulkner* [New York: Random House, 1966], 120–21). I think the parallels are even more extensive than those he details. For instance, Isabella's predicament points to the paradox that to maintain one's innocence, one must be sufficiently knowledgeable to recognize and avoid evil. Horace paraphrases but fails to follow this principle when he tells Ruby, "'Damn it, don't you know that putting yourself in the position for disaster is the surest way in the world to bring it about? Hasn't your own experience shown you that?" (327).

Further, Horace's willingness to cast blame on the women who tempt him, his hypocrisy, his self-righteousness, his very lack of the self-knowledge required for acting with moral responsibility make him the central Angelo-figure in *Sanctuary*. Like Shakespeare's Angelo, like Milton's Satan, like Melville's Claggart, Horace (and perhaps Popeye) wants to see innocence defiled because he believes that it is corruptible and therefore already corrupt. Actions in defense of innocence provoke these characters' desire to violate it. Consider the conversation of Temple and her classmates about the effect of modesty on the sexual desires of men. One girl, in a childish revision of Biblical myth, asserts that "the Snake had been seeing Eve for several days and never noticed her until Adam made her put on a fig leaf" (181). In her naïveté, Temple rejects the truth of this because the girl who asserts it is physically unattractive. Had she accepted it, she might have anticipated the effect her own fear would have on the men at the bootlegger's camp. Again like Angelo, Horace cannot acknowledge his rapacious desires. Repressed, they nevertheless do their work as Angelo's do theirs. At the end of both works, both men return to women whom they had set aside, Horace to his wife, Angelo to his betrothed. For both, this return is punishment for their inability to recognize their own corruption in time to act with moral responsibility.

11. Ruby also calls Horace a "poor, scared fool" (18), emphasizing Faulkner's pairing of these "innocent" intruders into the world of evil epitomized, as Beck says, by Popeye.

12. See, for instance, Robert L. Mason, "A Defense of Faulkner's *Sanctuary*," *Georgia Review* 21 (winter 1967): 430–38. This question is also addressed by Elisabeth Muhlenfeld, "Bewildered Witness: Temple Drake in *Sanctuary*," *Faulkner Journal* 1 (spring 1986): 43–45. On this point, and other questions about Temple's behavior at the Old Frenchman's Place, Muhlenfeld's conclusions are compatible with mine. Though I disagree with her argument that Temple perjures herself primarily because Lee's persecution of her and indifference to her suffering make him a convenient choice on which to place blame, Muhlenfeld makes a strong case that Lee is the foremost object of her fear. Certainly this, together with her knowledge that Lee has a criminal record, may allow Temple to rationalize her decision to save herself at his expense.

13. "When he [Popeye] saw the car it was empty. He stopped ten feet away and changed the sandwich to his left hand.... The mechanic ... saw him and jerked his thumb toward the corner of the building" (167). Popeye's purpose in freeing his right hand is clarified by repeated references to his concealed pistol and his placing his hand in his right pocket when he wants to assert his control in the scenes at the Old Frenchman's Place. See, for example, pp. 87–88.

14. (New York: Harrison Smith and Robert Haas, 1935), 193–96. See also Joseph McElrath's helpful interpretation of this scene in "*Pylon*: The Portrait of a Lady," *Mississippi Quarterly* 27 (summer 1974): 285–88.

15. "It was on the night of June 17 ... when Red had been killed" (361).

16. At the beginning of the chapter relating Narcissa's betrayal of Horace, he sees Clarence Snopes, who had followed him to Miss Reba's, warned him of her high prices, and tried to get him to spend the night at a Negro whorehouse (248–250; 252); Snopes tells

Horace, "'Too bad I missed you last night . . . I could have took you to a place most folks don't know about" (313–14). "Later in the morning" Horace sees Narcissa disappear near the entrance to Graham's law offices, but he does not think to look for her there (314).

17. "The trial was set for the twentieth of June" (321). Faulkner also specifies this date on page 318. Clarence's complaint occurs "Two days before it opened" (319).

18. Temple is taken from the roadhouse by Popeye's henchmen (290; 361). "On the night of the nineteenth [Horace] telephoned [Reba]. . . ." "'They're gone,' she said. 'Both of them. Don't you read no papers? . . . I don't know nut-tin about them . . .'" (332).

19. The platinum bag is described and mentioned several times as Temple prepares to meet Red on June 17. See pages 271, 273, 276.

20. Temple tells Horace that when she feared violation at the Old Frenchman's Place, she imagined wearing a chastity belt, which she has heard about but never seen. She says, "'I was thinking maybe it would have long sharp spikes on it and he wouldn't know it until too late and I'd jab it . . . all the way through him and I'd think about the blood running on me. . . . I didn't know it was going to be just the other way . . .'" (261). Though Temple's language hints that she was raped, she never asserts it unequivocally, and as if frightened that she has nearly done so, she abruptly asks for a drink and changes the subject.

21. Conversely, in *Measure for Measure*, the nearly inhuman Isabella refuses to commit an evil act even to save her brother's life; and the Law, in the person of the disguised Duke, works behind the scenes as a force for justice and morality. But the issues are not simple in Shakespeare's dark comedy either: in choosing to preserve her chastity rather than her brother's life, Isabella, like Temple, shows herself willing to sacrifice the life of another in order to spare herself.

22. Warren Beck emphasizes the passivity of all three characters in the closing chapters, which he finds a triumphal tonal conclusion to the book, except for the interpolation of the naturalistic account of Popeye's past. I agree with Beck, but find in Temple's restiveness under the protection of her father a less acquiescent and defeated withdrawal from life than those of Horace and Popeye.

DEBORAH CLARKE

Erasing and Inventing Motherhood:
The Sound and the Fury *and* As I Lay Dying

In 1946 Random House reprinted *The Sound and the Fury* and *As I Lay Dying* in one Modern Library volume, a decision which caused Faulkner some distress: "It's as though we were saying 'This is a versatile guy; he can write in the same stream of consciousness style about princes and then about peasants'" (*Letters* 228). Despite his concern at being typed as a writer with a single prose style, this pairing makes sense, for the two books have much in common beyond their narrative structures. Faulkner may have labored long, hard, and lovingly over *Sound and the Fury* and written *As I Lay Dying* as a tour de force in only six weeks, but both books reverberate with the paradoxical power of women's bodily absence and presence, of women's silence and language. Both examine men's desperate attempts to deal with maternal absence, to use language as a replacement for the mother. Caddy and Addie, caught in a world which vanquishes women's bodies, nonetheless exert a powerful control over the literal and figurative, bodies and language, forcing brothers and sons to confront the fragility of their egos in the face of maternal power.

Faulkner's inspiration for *The Sound and the Fury* is well known. Most of his remarks about the genesis of his favorite novel center on Caddy, his "heart's darling," the "beautiful and tragic little girl" who was created to compensate for the sister he never had and the infant daughter he was to lose (*Univ.* 6; "Intro." 710). Other comments also locate Caddy at the center of

From *Robbing the Mother: Women in Faulkner*, pp. 19–50, 155–156. © 1994 by the University Press of Mississippi.

the novel, as he claimed that the central image of the book was the picture of three brothers looking up the tree at their sister's muddy drawers (*Lion* 245). Yet Caddy, who forms the core of the novel, is never actualized in the text, which "grows out of and refers back to an empty center," as André Bleikasten puts it (*Failure* 51). That center—Caddy herself—in its simultaneous absence and presence marks Faulkner's first major attempt to confront the relation between gender and art, between female sexuality and narrative authority, between mothers and language. If Caddy is the empty center, then Faulkner has robbed the novel of its mother by robbing the mother of her voice.

This is not a novel about Caddy, despite Faulkner's claims, but about her brothers' responses to her, about how men deal with women and sexuality. In fact, Faulkner's almost obsessive insistence on Caddy's importance begins to sound defensive, an apology, perhaps, for essentially writing her out of the text. Caddy's linguistic absence from the novel undercuts her centrality in a text formed and sustained by voice. If she is his heart's darling, why does she not rate a section of the novel, the chance to tell her own story? But Faulkner goes further than just silencing Caddy; he ties her silence to her beauty, her femininity, and claims that "Caddy was still to me too beautiful and too moving to reduce her to telling what was going on, that it would be more passionate to see her through somebody else's eyes" (*Univ.* 1). David Minter has suggested that Faulkner found "indirection" a useful strategy "for approaching forbidden scenes, uttering forbidden words, committing dangerous acts" (103). Yet the "forbidden words" and "dangerous acts" appear not to be Caddy's but those of her brothers: Quentin's incestuous desires, Jason's criminality, and Benjy's groping for the language "to say" which culminates in attempted rape. Indirection may approach male forbidden desires, but it does not approach Caddy except as the object of those desires.

Particularly in Faulkner's work, however, silence does not necessarily confer marginality. Paul Lilly has called Caddy's silence "a hallmark of the perfect language that Faulkner the artist knows can never be realized but which he knows he must keep on 'working, trying again' to reach" (174). But why must it be women who speak the perfect silence instead of language, even imperfect language? Linda Wagner argues that, despite their full or partial silences, Caddy and her mother control the narrative:

> Linguistic theory would define the narrator of any fiction as the person whose speech act dominates the telling of the fiction, yet Caddy and Caroline Compson are in many ways essential narrators of the Compson story. So much of their language, so much of their verbal presence, emanates through the novel that they are clearly and vividly drawn. Rather than being given one section, they take the novel entire. (61)

They are indeed "clearly and vividly drawn." Yet the fact remains that they are drawn rather than draw-ers, constructed rather than constructor, while the Compson brothers draw not only themselves but also "their" women.

Caddy's voice may never be restored, but the evidence of her physical substance remains. If her "speech act" does not dominate the text, her creative act does. Caddy's presence makes itself known less through her voice than through her body and its literal replication. Her physical procreation essentially engenders the linguistic acts which form the novel, thereby making this text, in a sense, her child. Yet it is difficult to claim that she "mothers" the novel when the process of mothering—and, particularly, Caddy's participation in that process— is hardly presented within the book as a triumphant creative experience. Her abandonment of her daughter to Jason and his malicious exploitation seriously undermines both her idealized status and her maternal position. While she serves as an admirable if temporary mother to Benjy, her treatment of Miss Quentin merits her no consideration as Mother of the Year. Faulkner has robbed the mother not just of her voice but her maternity. Because the brothers control the terms of the narrative, Caddy exists as sister rather than mother.

The problem, however, is that she serves as a mother as well, not just to Benjy but to all of her brothers, who find themselves confronted with problematic maternal ties to both their biological and symbolic mothers. Thus while their narratives, except for Jason's, lack the overt condemnation of Caddy which they all display towards Caroline (and even Jason saves his strongest complaints for Miss Quentin, displacing much of his resentment toward Caddy onto her daughter), they also reveal their unbreakable ties to Caddy, ties which deny them full control over their own identities. By his indirection, Faulkner has allowed Caddy to approach the position of all-powerful and all-encroaching mother rather than simply mother of Miss Quentin. Doubly abandoned, first by Caroline and then by Caddy, the Compson men achieve a kind of revenge in fixing both, in allowing each woman to be defined only through the perspective of her son/brother.

They fail to score a significant victory, however, because just as each brother inscribes his vision of Caddy, he also finds himself defined through his own relation to her. Quentin is trapped by being the weaker older brother to a powerful sister, by his own attraction to her, and by his sexual innocence as opposed to her experience:

> youve never done that have you
> what done what
> that what I have what I did (174)

Jason struggles against his sense of being unimportant and unloved, the brother whom Caddy never valued. Benjy cannot perceive himself as anything other than connected to Caddy, as his entire life constitutes an elegy of her loss. As both a presence and absence, Caddy's maternity determines the fate of the Compson family.

The novel, in fact, is full of mothers; besides Caroline and Caddy, we also have Dilsey, Frony, and Damuddy. But Damuddy dies before we ever meet her, and Frony, Luster's mother, functions as a daughter rather than a mother. Dilsey, more a mammy than a mother, primarily mothers ungracious and unappreciative children she did not give birth to: the Compson children and Luster. Thus, there are at once too many and too few mothers in this novel. These replacements, substitutions, and reversals in the function of mothering all undermine Faulkner's professed admiration for Caddy by linking her most disturbingly to her own mother—and to the failure of mothering, which holds such a crucial position in this text.

The lack of adequate mothering, as so many scholars have noted, causes many of the problems within the Compson family. Quentin's often quoted remark, "*if I'd just had a mother so I could say Mother Mother*" (197), lays the blame for his numerous problems squarely at Caroline Compson's feet, a reading many critics tend to uphold. Interestingly, Mr. Compson's alcoholic disregard for his family finds much more sympathetic treatment. Lack of adequate fathering is apparently not seen in as nefarious a light.[1] Even Thomas Sutpen, surely one of the worst fathers in literary history, is granted a Faustian grandeur which Caroline Compson certainly lacks. While Faulkner may overtly distance his "heart's darling" from such a problematic function, enough symbolic connections remain to call her idealized position into question. If even Caddy fails as an adequate mother, can there be any hope left in motherhood, or is the dungeon mother herself, as Quentin says? (198). The fact that we see remarkably little of Caddy once she becomes a mother—only a few glimpses from Jason, the most hostile of the narrators— suggests that Faulkner was chiefly concerned with Caddy prior to maternity, before she becomes wholly identified as female; as a child, not only does she lack sexual maturity but she genders herself as male: "she never was a queen or a fairy she was always a king or a giant or a general" (198). In growing up she loses her childhood appeal and her sexual innocence as she moves toward femininity and motherhood.

Indeed, what chiefly disturbs her family about Caddy's motherhood appears to be the sexual activity that generates it, for Western culture idealizes mothers but condemns female sexuality. As Julia Kristeva has pointed out in "Stabat Mater" (*Reader*), the cornerstone of Christianity is the virgin mother, an icon perpetuated by a patriarchal system in an effort to deny women's sexuality as a necessary ingredient of motherhood. Faulkner, with his interest in unravished brides, seems well aware of the difficulties inherent in attempting to privilege both virginity and motherhood. Quentin quotes his father as remarking that "it was men invented virginity not women" (89). This closely resembles Addie Bundren's comment in *As I Lay Dying*, that men invented motherhood (157). These inventions serve to define women by their sexual status and yet avoid female sexuality itself as women's identifying characteristic, for virginity and motherhood exist in relation to male possession, male sexuality. Before a woman can become a mother, a position of considerable power, she must bear the cultural mark of male domination: a wedding ring. These labels control a woman's body until she herself comes under the control of a man. One can see why men, and not women, invented them.

Quentin finds, however, that the invention doesn't work. Imposing such terms as virginity and motherhood may construct a cultural discourse regarding the role of female sexuality, but it does not restrict women's bodies to their linguistic functions, as Mr. Compson realizes. "Women are never virgins. Purity is a negative state and therefore contrary to nature. It's nature is hurting you not Caddy and I said That's just words and he said So is virginity" (132–33). Virginity, a lack, a "negative state," is "just words," thereby implying that language itself represents a lack and explaining why all the language of the Compsons can never replace Caddy's loss. In identifying women, nature, and sexuality as distinct from "just words," Mr. Compson inscribes a cultural split between women and language and yet retains the words which have proved ineffectual, the words, which Addie Bundren says, "dont ever fit even what they are trying to say at" (*AILD* 157). This, then, explains why female sexuality and, by extension, motherhood, are so threatening. They represent something that cannot be controlled, or even defined, by symbolic discourse. Madelon Sprengnether asserts, "At the heart of phallogocentrism lies the terror as well as the certainty of its own undoing. And this undoing is associated with the body of a woman, who must be controlled, who must be prevented from achieving a condition of power from which she can exercise this threat" (244).

The Compson men fail, of course, to control the woman's body. Consequently, in the face of Caddy's sexuality, they are left to confront their own impotence and undoing. Warwick Wadlington has observed that Caddy represents the deathly alienation of experience for each brother, the passions that should be theirs rather than inflicted on them" (98). She has robbed them of their masculinity and hence of their cultural identities. The Compson brothers take refuge in discourse, using language in an attempt to recover what is irreparably lost—the narcissistic union with the mother, in this case figured as the sister. As Shoshana Felman notes, an incestuous desire for the sister can represent a "fantasy of a return to the womb, to femininity as mother" (40). Cut off from both mother and sister, forced to experience himself as separate, each brother in his narrative finds that language only leads to further alienation and ultimately, to a nonbeing similar to an embryonic state.

Benjy, who appears never to have left that embryonic state, comes as close as anything can to expressing what is essentially unrepresentable—what Kristeva terms semiotic discourse, the prediscursive communication with the mother. As far as we know, Benjy verbalizes only whimpers and bellows. Indeed, though constrained by the need to use symbolic discourse to present Benjy's interior thoughts, Faulkner strips as much reasoning power as possible from his language. When Benjy describes golf, he presents exactly what he sees. "Through the fence, between the curling flower spaces, I could see them hitting" (3). Likewise, when Luster closes the stove door Benjy notes, "The long wire came across my shoulder, and the fire went away" (67). Benjy's focus on the literal vision, his inability to deduce meaning, links him to the semiotic *chora*, Kristeva's term borrowed from Plato, to describe the mode which "precedes and underlies figuration" (*Reader* 94). His mental deficiencies render him unable to conceive of language as a symbolic structure; for him, it is a literal expression of what he sees and hears.

Because he cannot use symbolic discourse to replace his lost sister/mother, he formulates Caddy not through language but, as John Matthews suggests, through objects like the slipper, the cushion, and the fire (72). While his association of Caddy with these things does suggest the presence of some sort of imaginative process, it does not succeed in its attempt to replace the thing—Caddy—with a symbol, because the symbol lacks reality for him. It only evokes Caddy; it does not restore her. Faulkner claimed in the Appendix that Benjy remembers not his sister but only her loss. Rather, to remember Caddy is both to possess and to lose her. Thus he is trapped between union and separation. Because he cannot substitute language for his prediscursive tie to Caddy, he cannot enter into the Law of the Father, where reality is discursive.

Indeed, he is horribly punished for his one attempt to speak, when he supposedly attacks the girl at the fence. "I was trying to say, and I caught her, trying to say, and she screamed and I was trying to say" (60). Benjy's attempt "to say" is interpreted as—and may very well be—attempted rape. Jason immediately has him castrated, a fact of which Benjy is well aware. "*I got undressed and I looked at myself, and I began to cry. Hush, Luster said. Looking for them aint going to do no good. They're gone*" (84). Benjy here recognizes and mourns his fate; he realizes he can never enter into manhood and an autonomous identity, and his only response—crying—further grounds him in semiotic discourse. Language, which should subsume this phase according to Lacan, leading Benjy to the realm of the Father, instead relegates him to the prediscursive sphere of the mother and keeps him there, mute and castrated.

Yet Benjy comes closer than either Quentin or Jason to recovering Caddy in his semiotic discourse, precisely because he does not rely on an attempted verbal reconstitution. He does not use the language of the Father to return to the sister/mother, but rather evokes her through objects. By refusing to accept symbolic discourse in lieu of Caddy he may perpetuate her loss, but he also maintains a constant sense of her physical presence because he never displaces her. In addition, he perceives time not as linear but as a mode of repetition and eternity, which Kristeva identifies as women's time (*Reader* 191). Caddy is both always lost and always present. Thus it is only through techniques associated with femininity that Benjy can re-evoke Caddy. But lest we be too ready to construe this as a triumph on his part, it is important to remember that his "success" leaves him emmeshed in an eternal stasis. The inability to get beyond the semiotic leads to psychosis. Benjy needs not to dissolve into Caddy but to achieve a psychological separation from her, a move he never accomplishes. Without access to voice, he cannot construct an autonomous self and remains, despite Caddy's claim to the contrary, a "poor baby" (9).

Quentin, unlike Benjy, does attempt to take refuge in symbolic discourse, but the maternal semiotic constantly threatens to engulf him. Though his father claims that virginity is just a word, Quentin cannot be comforted by language, for he expects both too much and too little of it. While Quentin can use language with considerable facility, it does not grant him masculine power, for he cannot assert himself as a man and a brother. He fails sexually in that he finds himself unable to make love to Caddy and unable to use the knife as a substitute: in a sexually charged scene he holds the knife to Caddy's throat but can't push it in. Neither can his language accomplish what his penis and phallus cannot, for after shakily ordering Dalton Ames to get out of town by sundown, he faints "like a girl" (186). Betrayed by his lack of masculinity, he also tries femininity, imagining himself as Dalton Ames's mother: "If I could have been his mother lying with open body lifted laughing, holding his father with my hand refraining, seeing, watching him die before he lived" (91). It is significant that only mothers have this power of life and death in Quentin's world. Not only does he want to be a mother, he imagines himself as woman resisting the temptation to which Caddy succumbs: holding off the man, denying procreation and thus motherhood. However, only as an imaginative fantasy can this possibility exist. The body of the mother is too powerful for Quentin.

Despite all his lengthy conversations with his father, some real, some apparently imagined, Quentin faces a constant threat of re-engulfment in the mother. His almost frenzied focus on words marks the degree of desperation in his struggle to control experience through language rather than bodies. He wants to erase Caddy's literal motherhood, so he can restore her to a male-constructed linguistic state: virginity. When he tries to force Caddy to articulate specifically her reasons for marrying, she replies, "*Do you want me to say it do you think that if I say it wont be*" (140). Caddy recognizes that pregnancy is beyond language, something that need not be said. She also knows her brother well enough to realize that he wants to be able to contain experience in language, because language is just words—like virginity—and thus not physically real. Quentin's hope—that if Caddy can say it, "it wont be"—can be viewed as an attempt to widen the gap between the semiotic and the symbolic, to define reality symbolically rather than physically. Her language will replace the condition of her body. In order to protect himself from becoming engulfed by the feminine, he tries to shore up the foundations of symbolic discourse, knowing all the while that his attempt will be in vain.

His desperate need to confess to his father that he has committed incest, which probably occurs only in his imagination, can be read in similar terms:

> and he did you try to make her do it and i i was afraid to i was
> afraid she might and then it wouldnt have done any good but if
> i could tell you we did it would have been so and then the others
> wouldnt be so and then the world would roar away. (203)

While this passage reflects Quentin's fear that his impotence has caused Caddy's problems—"if I could tell you we did it would have been so and then the others wouldnt be so"—it also illustrates his further attempts to block out literal reality with language. If he could *say* we did it, then his problems would disappear, not necessarily because he did it, but because it would then become a linguistic rather than a sexual act, and language, Quentin hopes, triumphs over the body.

Unfortunately for him, he can neither say it nor do it. Unable to leave the semiotic behind and to establish himself firmly within the symbolic, he makes literal his non-being through suicide, a choice which aligns him even more closely to the mother, both in its literalization and in the method he selects. He chooses to drown, to return to the symbolic womb and thus transform it into a literal tomb. As Marsha Warren points out, he "attempts to (re)create himself by rejecting the Law of the Father (time) as the regulating agency of discourse, and entering the Body of the Mother (space), thereby recovering the maternal semiotic flux" (101). In the final pages of his narrative his language comes more and more to resemble Benjy's semiotic discourse, as grammar and punctuation vanish, revealing the fragile line between semiotic and symbolic. Symbolic discourse fails him, stripping him of the emblem of separation from the mother. Since he cannot "say Mother" and escape into language, he cannot differentiate himself from her.

Jason, however, can say a great deal. He appears to heed the warnings of his brothers' struggles to master language and opens his narrative with an aggressive verbal stance. "Once a bitch always a bitch, what I say. I says you're lucky if her playing out of school is all that worries you. I says she ought to be down there in that kitchen right now" (206). Every time Jason speaks, he reaffirms that act with an "I says." Often, he even breaks up a paragraph of his own voice to inject an additional "I says." Unlike Benjy, Jason does indeed say, or rather, says. He didn't go to Harvard, so he learns neither "how to go for a swim at night without knowing how to swim" (224–25) nor grammar, thereby undercutting some of the authority of his speech. Indeed, his constant reiteration of both his speech act and his own control over it—"*I says*"—bear considerable similarity to Quentin's attempts to find refuge in language, the extent of the effort revealing the anxiety behind it.

One of the more obvious ways Jason seeks to control the power of the mother is by assuming an overtly protective relation to his own mother. He constantly reminds himself of the need to protect her, almost reveling in her helplessness. Jason's concerns lie with "my Mother's name" rather than the name of the Father (269). In claiming to defend his mother's position, he is, of course, primarily defending his own, revealing his selfishness and his lack of separation from his mother. Her battles are his because his identity is hers. Despite his mother's contention that he is not a real Compson, a remark that probably does little to soothe his concern over his family status, Jason displays great concern over the behavior of his niece due to his pride in the family he constantly disparages, a family defined by blood. "I haven't got much pride, I cant afford it with a kitchen full of niggers to feed and robbing the state asylum of its star freshman. Blood, I says, governers and generals" (265). Just as Jason defines himself through the family blood, so does he define Miss Quentin: "Like I say blood always tells. If you've got blood like that in you, you'll do anything" (275). The power of blood continues to haunt him when he encounters the old man from the circus and falls down (similar to Quentin's fainting in front of Dalton Ames), terrified that he might be bleeding.

> "Am I bleeding much?" he said. "The back of my head. Am I bleeding?" He was still saying that while he felt himself being propelled rapidly away ... "Look at my head," he said. (359)

This excessive concern over blood, both as an actuality and as a metaphor, suggests a concern with the body, particularly with the female body and its bloody functions of menstruation and childbirth. Quentin displays a similar obsession in his attempts to clean the bloodstains off his tie before committing suicide. In identifying blood as a source of trouble, both implicitly recognize the threat of women's bodies.

But Jason's response goes beyond his brothers' efforts to construct a linguistic refuge from the mother. Jason employs a combination of language and robbery. He robs his own mother of the thousand dollars she gives him to invest in Earl's store, and he robs Caddy of the child support she sends each month. Not content with simply robbing the mother, Jason also steals from his niece and surrogate daughter, Miss Quentin. For Jason, who has a more literal mind than Faulkner, robbing women means appropriating not their creativity but their cash. His first attempt to rob Caddy is linguistic, when he gives her a momentary glance of her daughter in exchange for one hundred dollars. Observing his own word to the letter—"I said see her a minute, didn't I?"—he is outraged when Caddy manages to circumvent his strategies: "I didn't have any more sense than to believe what they said" (236). In relying on literal meaning, he fails to consider that Caddy may have greater imaginative powers. Ever the tattletale, Jason resorts to telling mother. Only a mother has the power of interdiction needed to defeat a mother, and with Caroline's words behind him, he defies both Dilsey and Caddy: "I know you wont pay me any mind, but I reckon you'll do what Mother says" (238). Ironically, robbing the mother teaches him the value of the mother's voice. After this questionable victory, he moves from verbal tricks to simple robbery, tacitly admitting linguistic defeat.

Forced to recognize the vulnerability of his verbal aggression, Jason learns to rely more heavily on money than language. Just as losing the job at the bank costs him his manhood, in that it makes him a victim of his sister's sexuality, accumulating money—especially by robbing his niece—gives him a sense of potency and power. His one sexual relationship is conducted largely on a cash basis, and he has "every respect for a good honest whore" (269). Consequently, when Jason reads Lorraine's letter, he rather naïvely assumes she's telling the truth when she says she misses him because, as he notes, "Last time I gave her forty dollars" (222). Having established his potency and worth through his money, he cannot doubt her regard. Significantly, after Miss Quentin's theft, he again thinks of Lorraine, this time in very different terms: "He imagined himself in bed with her, only he was just lying beside her, pleading with her to help him, then he thought of the money again, and that he had been outwitted by a woman, a girl. If he could just believe it was the man who had robbed him" (355). Having already been defeated in the battle of language, he now loses the battle of money—both to a woman. Thus he also loses his belief in his sexual virility and is driven home, unable even to operate the car for which he robbed his mother.

Jason, like his brothers, is rendered impotent in the face of feminine power and, like them, discovers that language provides no refuge. Thus it makes sense that Jason should be the one to calm Benjy in the final paragraph, when he rushes over to send the buggy the right way around the square. Jason, forced to confront his final defeat at the hands of women, may recognize a stronger bond with his brothers than he has ever felt before. "Cornice and façade flowed smoothly once more from left to right; post and tree, window and doorway and signboard each in its ordered place" (371). The flowing from left to right, possibly an emblem of the reading process but of a literal rather than written text, imposes the only order possible in a world where men can neither master symbolic discourse nor escape the semiotic. Language cannot control the maternal presence because if one accepts the feminist premise that the maternal, with its inherent division, gives rise, requoting Jacobus, to both the subject and language, then the mother is not ruled by language but actually controls it. As Minrose Gwin points out, Caddy is a "text which speaks multiplicity, maternity, sexuality, and as such she retains not just one voice but many" (46). The many voices of woman overwhelm the Compson brothers who find in their own lack of differentiation from the feminine the true threat of Caddy's transgression—we have looked on the female outlaw and she is us. The body of the mother/sister, the "very site of the uncanny," according to Sprengnether, denies masculine authority the power to order the world. The uncanny, a reminder of castration fears, quite literally fulfills its threat in this novel, as all three brothers are rendered impotent, unable to vanquish the spectral presence of a sister who represents home and not-home, self and not-self.

But what about the primary mother in the novel, Caroline Compson, the character everyone loves to hate?[2] How much responsibility does she bear for the disruptions within her family? A cold, selfish, complaining woman, she neglects all of her children, including her later favorite, Jason, who cries every night when he can no longer sleep with his grandmother. Her maternal absence is largely filled by Caddy, but Caddy has no maternal model, for her own mother has only indicated how to be a lady. She orders Caddy not to carry Benjy because it will ruin her back. "All of our women have prided themselves on their carriage. Do you want to look like a washerwoman" (72). Caddy should not spoil—love—Benjy; "Damuddy spoiled Jason that way and it took him two years to outgrow it" (73). No wonder Jason cries himself to sleep when his grandmother dies. Finally, when her daughter emerges into womanhood, Caroline wears black and goes into mourning after she sees Caddy kissing a boy. For a woman to express sexual desire is for her to be denied status as lady, and thus, as living entity: "I was taught that there is no halfway ground that a woman is either a lady or not" (118). By accepting no halfway ground, Caroline Compson denies the grounding of motherhood itself, which is predicated upon an essential duality. Having challenged and defied maternity, it comes as no surprise to discover that she refuses to let her motherhood get in the way of her ladyhood. "I'm a lady. You might not believe that from my offspring, but I am" (346).

After Caddy's transgression it is Caroline who judges her. It is Caroline who refuses to allow her to return home, and Caroline who will not permit her name to be spoken, thus reversing the strategy of her husband and son, who invent labels—virginity—in an attempt to control female sexuality. Mrs. Compson erases Caddy by refusing to name or label her; Caddy exists only through what she is not: a lady. If she is not a lady, she cannot be named. Names have great significance for Caroline Compson who insisted that Maury's name be changed to Benjamin when his mental disabilities became known. She strenuously objects to both "Caddy" and "Benjy" as names because "nicknames are vulgar. Only common people use them" (73). Jason, she repeatedly states, is the only one of her children who is a "real Bascomb"; the others are all Compson, that being the mark of their difference from her.

Caroline, the strongest proponent of the lady, who marries Caddy off in an attempt to prevent scandal, nonetheless resists the traditional expectations of how a married woman should behave: that she will take on her husband's name and define herself through him. Just as Rosa Coldfield will refuse to become an incubator for Sutpen sons, Caroline rejects the Compson identity. She may have married a Compson, but she has not become a Compson, insisting to the end that she is a lady and a Bascomb. While far from being a protofeminist, Mrs. Compson nevertheless undermines the patriarchal structure of marriage and motherhood somewhat differently, but no less significantly, than Caddy, who turns out to inherit more from her mother than the ability to procreate.

Addie Bundren displays what may seem a similar interest in names, particularly those of her husband and sons. "And when I would think Cash and Darl that way until their names would die and solidify into a shape and then fade away, I would say, All right. It doesn't matter. It doesn't matter what they call them" (*AILD* 159). Addie, a more complex character and mother, recognizes that names and labels cannot define, that "words are no good." But Caroline Compson, having thoroughly internalized the cult of southern gentility, clings to such labels—emblems of masculine discourse— as a means of separating herself from her family. She puts great faith in the power of language; by changing her son's name she denies his association with her brother and thus erases any equation of the Bascombs with idiocy. And by refusing to allow her daughter's name to be spoken she denies Caddy's identity as both mother and daughter.

In this focus on the power of the name, the label, Caroline achieves the kind of power for which her sons seek in vain. Despite her repeated claims that she'll soon be dead, she outlives both husband and eldest son. While Quentin cannot live in a world where virginity is just a word and Benjy is castrated for "trying to say," Caroline successfully "masters" a language which imposes limits and boundaries, interestingly enough, the language of the Father. Critics have long castigated Mrs. Compson for being unmotherly, but maybe she simply plays the wrong parental role. She takes over the position of the father, redefining the Compson family as the Bascombs. She is left with Jason, a "real" Bascomb, Benjy, whom she renamed, and young Quentin, nameless. If it is generally the father, as Bleikasten asserts, "who names, places, marks," Caroline Compson is a father par excellence (*Light* 87). While Mr. Compson wallows in alcoholic verbiage, unable to impose order or even to oppose his wife's interdiction against speaking Caddy's name, Mrs. Compson is redefining her family and her world. If Quentin wants someone to say "Mother Mother" to, maybe he should turn to his father.[3] In this novel, mothers are, above all else, survivors, certainly a feature that would attract the artist/robber. One robs the mother because she will always be there, controlling both procreation and language.

There is, of course, one other significant mother in this novel. Dilsey, identified by Sally Page as Faulkner's "ideal woman" (70), by David Williams and more recently Philip M. Weinstein as a madonna, has long been hailed as the novel's savior, the only truly admirable character in the book (Williams 11; Weinstein 7). Her warmth and endurance have endeared her to generations of readers, and, apparently, to Faulkner himself. But Faulkner and his readers tend to overlook the problematic issue of race in deifying the stereotype of the black mammy. The suggestion that African American women make the best mothers—especially to white children— reflects not an idealization of the mother or the black woman but a cultural disdain for both. Mothers are only "good" when socially powerless, when controlled by those they "mother," when selflessly dedicated to selfish undeserving children. A close examination of Dilsey's maternal halo reveals the inadequacy of white cultural assessments of mothering when applied to African American women.

Whence comes this halo? Certainly Dilsey appears to feel more compassion for the Compson children than any of their biological parents. She cares for Benjy, defies Jason in giving Caddy a chance to see her daughter, and protects Miss Quentin from physical abuse. Yet she cannot function as a mother to these children, not because she didn't give birth to them but because she lacks selfhood and power in a white racist world. "You damn old nigger," says Miss Quentin after Dilsey saves her from a beating (213). In calling attention to her race, and thus to her cultural powerlessness, Miss Quentin denies Dilsey maternal control. While Dilsey stands up to Jason, who seems to live in some fear of her, she makes no attempt to defy Mrs. Compson's selfish and inconsiderate demands, dedicating her life to the people who oppress her. In fact, she favors her white employers above her own family, granting Luster no hearing or compassion in his monumental task of caring for Benjy. Her selflessness confers sainthood upon her in the eyes of her white creator and a large portion of predominantly white readers. As Myra Jehlen points out, Dilsey's virtues "recall the traditional Mammy virtues Faulkner extolled in his own Mammy" (76). However, the novel Faulkner dedicated to his mammy, Caroline Barr, is not *Sound and the Fury* but *Go Down, Moses*, where Mollie Beachamp at least exerts herself for her own children and grandchildren, and where Lucas challenges white expectations of black mammies in his confrontation with Zach Edmonds. Faulkner pays Caroline Barr the compliment not only of the dedication but of the presentation of a black woman who comes across as less idealized and, ironically, less of a mammy than Dilsey.

On the other hand, Dilsey's idealized status as a madonna/mammy denies her both subjectivity and sexuality, and thus robs her of the mother's pervasive power, her control over being and language. The descriptions of her body focus on its decay, not its feminine appeal or procreative potential. She has a "collapsed face that gave the impression of the bones themselves being outside the flesh" (307). Dilsey's "indomitable skeleton" evokes only the body's framework, the mother's potential worn away by the oppressive demands of a racist culture.

The narrative strategy of the fourth section of the novel, sometimes called Dilsey's section, reconfirms her questionable status. If this is Dilsey's section, why does she not get a voice? If Caddy was too beautiful and too moving, is Dilsey too much of a madonna and not enough of a mother to speak? Thadious Davis suggests that the use of the third-person narrator here establishes "the perspective of time. Faulkner creates a sense of the passing of an era, and within that perspective he presents the destruction of one family and the endurance of another." Dilsey, Davis says, "exists as a kind of sacred vessel, suggesting an experience that is both visionary and tragic" (106). She may be a "visionary and tragic" vessel, but she is not a maternal vessel. Her lack of direct voice highlights her symbolic rather than her bodily role. Not until *Light in August* does Faulkner make his first serious attempt to deal with black subjectivity. And mothers, above all else, are subjects in Faulkner's work. Dilsey, possibly more a wish-fulfillment than a real character, more symbolic than human, may endure, but as an idealized image, not as a source of being and not-being, of language and separation—not, in other words, as a mother.

Faulkner said that his feeling on beginning to write *The Sound and the Fury* was, "Now I can make myself a vase like that which the old Roman kept at his bedside and wore the rim slowly away with kissing it" ("Intro." 710). Minter points out that this urn takes on multiple meanings: a haven, a feminine ideal, a work of art, and a burial urn. "If it is a mouth he may freely kiss, it is also a world in which he may find shelter; if it is a womb he may enter, it is also an urn in which his troubled spirit now finds temporary shelter and hopes to find lasting expression" (102). Re-entering the womb, however, may not be as benign as Minter suggests, particularly when we consider the experiences of the Compson brothers. But urn or womb, shelter or art, this vase clearly represents the novel Faulkner loved so much, a vessel which, the rim having worn down, disgorges its contents and overflows its boundaries. In short, it behaves like a woman and a mother.

In speaking of the feminine, Luce Irigaray cautions that while it is often defined as "lack, deficiency, or as imitation and negative image of the subject," it can also be characterized as "*disruptive excess*" capable of "jamming the theoretical machinery" (78). Certainly the maternal feminine presence fits this description. Caddy's disruptive excess jams the machinery of language and masculinity, neither able to hold off the feminine. Shoshana Felman observes that the feminine "is not *outside* the masculine, its reassuring canny *opposite*, it is *inside* the masculine, its *uncanny difference from itself*" (41). The Compson men find that the feminine within themselves leads to their own destruction. Wounded both physically and psychically, they lose life, language, and masculinity. Caddy may be doomed and her mother damned, but Quentin is killed off, Jason robbed (and thus figuratively castrated), and Benjy literally castrated in a text where the mother controls both literal being and figurative identity. Maternal power thus forges a novel of separation and loss out of the story of "a woman that cant name the father of her own child" (303). In this book, the name of the father gives way to the body of the mother.

> When he was born I knew that motherhood was invented
>   by someone who had to have a word for it because the
>   ones that had the children didn't care whether there was
>   a word for it or not.
>   (*AILD* 157)

Motherhood—invented by men, who use words, and accomplished by women, who use bodies—lies at the core of *As I Lay Dying*, highlighting the tension between literal and linguistic creativity. Both *The Sound and the Fury* and *As I Lay Dying* deal with absent mothers, but the absences have differing causes and implications. While *Sound* grows out of Caddy's maternity, *As I Lay Dying* is born out of Addie's death. A maternal corpse replaces maternal absence. Faulkner sets up two creative paradigms in the novel: mothering and speaking. What he does not do, however, is to set them in opposition to each other, with women as literal and men as figurative creators. After all, Addie's voice is strong enough to be heard through her coffin, and her son Darl achieves, at times, a kind of nonlinguistic "feminine" intuition.

The two dominant motifs in the book—corpse and voice—twist slightly the kind of dichotomy between the semiotic and symbolic presented in *Sound*, for by placing the mother's literal dead body rather than the mother's absence in the center of the text, Faulkner grants greater power to the physical, while at the same time erasing its boundaries as the decaying corpse disperses its odor and its influence throughout the novel. Then, after finally getting the mother into the ground, returning her to the earth, the Bundrens are still left with Dewey Dell, defeated in her attempts to end her pregnancy, and presented with a second Mrs. Bundren. The mother's body, ultimately, cannot be vanquished. Neither does that body, a speaking corpse, give up control over language, thus reducing even further the division between physical and linguistic power. In fact, language in the novel is strongly tied to maternity. Just as the Compson brothers find symbolic discourse an inadequate replacement for the mother, so the Bundrens struggle in vain to fill her place with words and symbols. The mother's body and the mother's voice are vividly present, as Faulkner constructs a tale where even killing the mother does not silence her.[4]

Warwick Wadlington, examining the role of voice in Faulknerian tragedy, argues that voice "says No to death primordially: voice is the breath of life transformed through sound into communication, communion" (105). Certainly voice serves as one of—if not the—most important empowering forces in Faulkner's work. In this novel in particular, even the dead speak. Yet not only is that voice often disembodied, it is also often unspoken in a text which highlights the close connections between voice and silence. The "dark voicelessness" Addie experiences "in which the words are the deeds" (160) transforms language into action, taking it out of the realm of the spoken voice and into a prediscursive semiotic sphere. Thus the blurred boundaries between voice and silence resemble the collapsing distinction between paternal and maternal discourse, between body and language. Does voice also say no to maternity, the primordial reality which precedes language, or does it emanate from the mother's body?

This novel, even more than *The Sound and the Fury*, focuses on voice; created out of its many speakers, *As I Lay Dying* attests to the power of spoken language but also insists, through its title, on the centrality of the body. The mother may die, but her body remains. Voice, however, proves a bit more evanescent, for the book frequently documents the characters' reluctance to employ verbal discourse. Darl and Dewey Dell communicate without words; Addie realizes that "words are no good" (157); Vardaman finds he "couldn't say it" when he understands that his mother is about to be placed in a coffin (59); Whitfield "frames" rather than speaks his confession. In order for voice to say no to death, one must use it as a vehicle for linguistic expression, a feat often left unaccomplished in this book.

But those who do place faith in language often find themselves deluded by their misguided beliefs in language's controlling power. Anse repeatedly announces, "I give her my promised word" (111), to justify a journey which costs Jewel a horse, Cash a leg, and Darl his freedom. Cora worries about losing the cost of the eggs that went into the cakes, for it was on her "say-so" that they bought the hens (5). Her daughter Kate resents the lady who changes her mind about buying them, insisting, "She ought to taken those cakes when she same as gave you her word" (6). This comic undercutting of the power of the word reveals Faulkner's skepticism regarding language's ability to represent "truth" and delineate human experience, reflecting his modernist agenda and tying him to another great modernist practitioner, Robert Frost. Whitfield's attempt to "frame" the words of his confession conjures up the final lines of Frost "Oven Bird": "The question that he frames in all but words / Is what to make of a diminished thing."

To frame is not to speak, but to circumscribe, limit, and define a shape; in this novel, however, words, as Addie says, are "just a shape to fill a lack" (158). While filling and framing would seem to be antithetical operations, they do have a common element—both present language as a physical form, a characteristic, Irigaray claims, of women's language. "This 'style,' or 'writing,' of women . . . does not privilege sight; instead, it takes each figure back to its source, which is among other things *tactile*" (79). By conceiving words as "tactile," Faulkner ties language to the literal, to the body. Because words are cast as physical they cannot function as a replacement or substitution *for* the physical. Thus Faulkner's recognition of the limitations of language reflects the pervasive power of the mother both to enable and to inhibit symbolic discourse, to transform words into shapes and so to deny their purely symbolic nature.

When presented as abstract concepts, words, to Addie, only get in the way because they dangle like spiders, "swinging and twisting and never touching" (158), a mode which prevents true knowledge and intimacy. This can only be achieved through blood—when she whips her students or when she gives birth to Cash. Initially, she is exhilarated by the bloodletting of motherhood, believing that she has found an escape from symbolic discourse. Next to the experience of maternity, "words dont ever fit even what they are trying to say at" (157). Her blissful union with Cash exists beyond language: "Cash did not need to say it [love] to me nor I to him" (158). But her second pregnancy destroys her belief that motherhood's prediscursive communion heals the gap which words, "never touching," inscribe. Having once been "made whole again by the violation" (158) of childbirth, an additional childbirth re-violates her. She now recognizes that motherhood is as great a trick as language. "I realized that I had been tricked by words older than Anse or love" (158–59)—the word *motherhood*, invented by men but referring to an experience which predates language, the presence of prediscursive reality.

Betrayed by both the figurative word and the literal experience, Addie finds no comfort in maternity once it becomes repetitious. Where the initial act liberates her, the repetition entraps her. She seems to recognize the problem inherent in the feminist privileging of the maternal metaphor. As Domna Stanton explains, while this paradigm does value the female experience, it also reinforces the essential Law of the Father. The privileging of wombs over words still restricts women to their roles as wombs. Once, for Addie, motherhood provides a haven from symbolic discourse; twice, however, forces her to realize, Constance Pierce says, "the power of what has been as persistent an enemy as language: her own biology and her inevitable place in the biological scheme of things" (297). Despite her powerful control over the process of figurative thought, her body now defines her identity. She takes a final stand against maternal definition by returning to her own father, both symbolically in her realization that he "had been right," and literally in her insistence on being buried next to him (159).

But if Addie thinks she has abjured mothering by realigning herself with her father and his belief that "the reason for living is getting ready to stay dead," she is wrong (162). Her tie to her mother is even more compelling. Doreen Fowler points out, "If Addie's father 'planted' her, then Addie's mother is the land, in which the seed grows. But the mother herself is never named. She is the repressed referent, the origin that imbues all symbols with meaning, but is herself absent" ("Matricide" 116). This description could refer to the state which the Bundrens hope to impose on Addie: returned to the land, repressed, and, most of all, absent. But while Addie's mother may be the repressed unspoken referent, Addie herself is far more difficult to deny, at once mother and earth, present and absent. Not only does she live on as corpse rather than staying dead, but her maternal influence lives on in her children, further denying the finality of death. Thus though T. H. Adamowski has called Addie a "woman with a penis" (225), her womb exerts a far more powerful force over her life and the lives of those around her.

Rather than becoming a phallic mother, Addie rebels against both the language of the father and that of the mother. Not only do words take on physical shapes, they take on the feminine of the vessel: "I could see the word as a shape, a vessel." Gendering words as feminine, Addie uses them to transform abstract concepts into physical reality, then collapses the reality back into the abstract concept. "I would watch him [Anse] liquify and flow into it like cold molasses flowing out of the darkness into the vessel, until the jar stood full and motionless: a significant shape profoundly without life" (159). Words neither protect nor contain life; they, like the physical body, are subject to disintegration, as she repeats the names of her husband and sons "until their names would die and solidify into a shape and then fade away" (159). Words, as either figurative names or literal shapes, cannot cohere to their referents. As Addie phrases it, "I would think how words go straight up in a thin line, quick and harmless, and how terribly doing goes along the earth, clinging to it, so that after a while the two lines are too far apart for the same person to straddle from one to the other" (160). Though she sets up an opposition between the figurative and literal, her analysis is not quite accurate, for these two forms of discourse do intersect within her own body. Both die, and both share the same shape: the word, "a significant shape profoundly without life like an empty door frame" and the "shape of my body where I used to be a virgin" are empty vessels. Neither words nor virgin bodies produce life.

That the mother's body literally subsumes life and language, collapses literal and figurative, is absolutely appropriate for a novel in which the mother is both figured and embodied as a corpse. Emblemizing the dissolution of both bodies and language, Addie's corpse stands beyond the control of either literal or symbolic discourse, presenting a formidable challenge to the family that must repudiate it. Thus while the Compson brothers attempt to fill the gap Caddy leaves behind with language, in *As I Lay Dying*, where words, "profoundly without life," are too much a part of the mother's body to replace it, the Bundrens try to lessen the impact of Addie's death more through deeds and symbols. They must combine doing and language to deal with a body which has transcended both. Their struggles reflect the broader concerns of the novel which, says André Bleikasten, "interrogates the relationship—or lack of relationship—between world and language" (*Ink* 202). This problematic connection intensifies the dilemma of Addie's children, who attempt to use a language that is "no good" in achieving their separation from a mother's body which is all too vividly present. The corpse, both origin and end, refuses to die. As Julia Kristeva explains in *Powers of Horror*, "the corpse, the most sickening of wastes, is a border that has encroached upon everything" (3).

Addie's corpse, which encroaches upon the family, the community, and the novel, seems to encroach even upon the laws of physical dissolution by refusing to go away. In fact, its prolonged existence is largely enabled by the Bundrens' reluctance to consign it to the earth too quickly, despite Samson's remark that "a woman that's been dead in a box four days, the best way to respect her is to get her into the ground as quick as you can" (102). Addie's extended existence as corpse denies the divisions between life and death and impedes the literal and symbolic transformation of mother to earth. The family's resistance to completing the process, to consigning the body to the land, is illustrated by Vardaman's boring holes in the coffin and Cash's care in removing the mud splashed on it, as he "scours at the stain with the wet leaves" (96). While Vardaman attempts to erase the coffin's boundaries and Cash to keep them proper, both act in a way that reflects a denial of the mother's death; Vardaman wants to make sure she can breathe, and Cash seems to feel that she would be disturbed by a dirty coffin. Unable to articulate their feelings, to transform their doing into language, they cannot yet understand that the mother now has a figurative rather than a literal presence. Thus it is not just through Addie that Faulkner illustrates the connections between bodies and language, between maternal and patriarchal discourse. Her sons need to construct a discourse of separation which is both literal and symbolic. They rely on symbols which are physical objects rather than words. For Cash, the coffin that he so carefully constructs becomes the emblem of the mother, while Jewel's horse functions as a clear mother substitute. Even young Vardaman, struggling with metaphor in his famous line, "My mother is a fish" (74), chooses a figure which is literal and which he himself has killed.

As Fowler suggests, each of these symbolic substitutions "reenacts the original separation from the mother, the cutting of the umbilical cord" ("Matricide" 117). But none of the separations seem to work, possibly because these substitutions, rather than moving into language, remain grounded in the realm of the physical. In fact, the objects are themselves replaced, while the body of the mother remains present. Thus Jewel must sacrifice his horse, and the work Cash puts into the coffin is largely undone by Vardaman's drilling and by the wetting it receives in the river. Even Vardaman's fish disappears into "not-fish" (49), which is "cooked and et" (52). They must lose these symbols of the mother and reconnect themselves literally to the mother's body before the final burial of the mother can be achieved. Cash, with his broken leg, lies on the coffin itself for several days, Jewel carries the coffin out of the burning barn singlehandedly, and Vardaman moves from denial—"*My mother is not in the box. My mother does not smell like that*" (182)—to acceptance that the coffin does contain the body of his mother for he "can hear her" (197) through the wood and "can smell her" (199). The failure of their symbolic substitutions forces them to realize that the process of figuration—even using literal objects—will not displace the mother. Only a literal burial can accomplish that, and that burial cannot occur until they have sacrificed their symbolic replacements and carried out the mother's final law: that she be buried in Jefferson.

The daughter, however, has a different experience. Not only does Dewey Dell have no time "to let her die" (106), she heals the separation at the moment of death, as "she flings herself across Addie Bundren's knees, clutching her, shaking her with the furious strength of the young before sprawling suddenly across the handful of rotten bones that Addie Bundren left" (44). Gabriele Schwab points out that Dewey Dell "literally buries that body under her own sensual corporeality. In this image mother and daughter melt into a dark version of a grotesque 'pregnant death'" (213). Having buried the mother well before the epic journey begins, Dewey Dell has no need to replace the mother figuratively, for she literally replicates the mother in her own pregnancy. In both burying and reproducing the mother with her own body, she eschews language, and rather than speaking "begins to keen," expressing herself not in symbolic discourse but through a prediscursive semiotic non-language (44).

In fact, Dewey Dell communicates without needing verbal discourse, saying of Darl's knowledge of her pregnancy: "He said he knew without the words . . . and I knew he knew because if he had said he knew with the words I would not have believed that he had been there and saw us" (24). The wording foreshadows Faulkner's later experiments with what, in *Absalom, Absalom!*, he would term "notlanguage." By the time of *Absalom*, Faulkner had become much more daring and sophisticated in his representation of nonlinguistic communication, for there the characters never do learn the actual truth in words; the best approximation to what might be the truth is an unverified intuitive leap by Quentin. But in *As I Lay Dying* this unspoken discourse is confirmed: we know from Dewey Dell that she is pregnant and from Darl that he knows it. Why, then, would Faulkner choose this "notlanguage" if he is not, as in *Absalom*, challenging the possibility of ever truly knowing?

The answer lies in the nature of the subject at hand. Pregnancy, like motherhood, cannot be "invented" with words, can be established only through experience, that is, through the body. If Faulkner is not yet ready to launch a full-scale attack on the power of symbolic discourse, he does recognize that there may be conditions, such as pregnancy, in which such discourse is rendered obsolete. Body language and symbolic discourse compete for dominance in a book which, Eric Sundquist writes, "is obsessively concerned with problems of disembodiment" (29), and in which "acts of speech" should be interpreted "as partially or wholly detached from the bodily selves that appear to utter them" (30). By separating speech from body, Faulkner allows for multiple permutations of the relations between them. It is women, however, who seem most aware of the choices inherent in such a division.

Dewey Dell, though she lacks her mother's more philosophic recognition of language's limitations, views it with suspicion and takes every opportunity to avoid using it. In a conversation which strongly recalls that between Caddy and Quentin, Darl says to her,

> The reason you will not say it is, when you say it, even to yourself, you will know it is true: is that it? But you know it is true now. I can almost tell you the day when you knew it is true. Why wont you say it, even to yourself. (35)

While Quentin hoped that if Caddy could "say it," it wouldn't be true, Dewey Dell seems to recognize that once she says it, she will know that it is true. Contrary to Quentin, who wants to replace the physical pregnancy with words, Dewey Dell recognizes that language has no such power to eradicate the body. Language merely verifies what she already knows "is true now." Her feeble hope to stave off knowledge of her condition lacks the almost insane force with which Quentin makes a similar demand. Dewey Dell, as Darl understands, is simply refusing to articulate what her body has already told her. Though by this silence she fails to ask Dr. Peabody for an abortion and thereby loses what may be her only chance to avert maternity, she does go to considerable lengths—short of literally saying it—in her quest to end her pregnancy.

Dewey Dell's response, then, to both impending motherhood and the death of the mother, is to refuse to put her thoughts and feelings into words. She keens or she stays quiet, in each case resisting the movement into symbolic discourse, the movement away from the mother. Instead, she throws herself upon the mother and finds herself unable to pronounce the words which might get her an abortion, thus ensuring that she will replicate rather than replace the body of the mother. Trapped by the physical, she feels, "It's like everything in the world for me is inside a tub full of guts" (53). Women's lives, as she realizes, are literally shaped by their bodies.

"For the same reason that women are identified with nature and matter in any traditional thematics of gender," writes Margaret Homans, "women are also identified with the literal, the absent referent in our predominant myth of language. From the point of view of this myth, the literal both makes possible and endangers the figurative structures of literature" (4). Addie's procreation, her doing, has engendered the need for her sons to find words to gain autonomy from her, and her death, another doing, reconfronts them with what they are trying to separate from: quite literally, the earth. Likewise, we see in Dewey Dell the literal which both births and threatens the figurative. By re-embodying the mother she reinvents motherhood and yet also confirms the fear that one can never escape the mother's body; like Hydra's heads, it replicates itself unendingly in the face of death.

Despite Dewey Dell's strong identification with the natural world, she does, of course, speak as well. Yet her language, even when she appears to speak metaphorically, is language of the body, the literal: "He is a big tub of guts and I am a little tub of guts" (53); "I am my guts. And I am Lafe's guts" (54). Dewey Dell expresses her pregnancy both literally and metaphorically in these remarks. To say that she is now both her "guts" and "Lafe's guts" is, of course, quite accurate. Her words display significant facility with language, challenging her exclusion from the figurative. Yet Dewey Dell does have difficulty with simple expression; she never once articulates her condition directly and, in fact, displaces her own fertility onto the natural world: "I feel like a wet seed wild in the hot blind earth" (58). Thus while she clearly has been identified with the physical, with nature, her association with literal discourse seems problematic; she is unable to speak the literal truth and expresses herself, despite her language of the physical, figuratively. Dewey Dell, the creation of a male author, both displays and challenges modes of discourse associated with women. She uses language which is both figurative and tactile, trying to see Vardaman's face, to "feel it with my eyes" (57). Her transformation of vision into touch recalls the prediscursive relation between mother and child, linking her to the maternal even in her language.

Dewey Dell's facility with language, however, exists only as unspoken. More than her brothers, who frequently express themselves aloud as well as within their own minds, she has great difficulty speaking. Even Vardaman, struggling to find the words to deal with his mother's death, has several conversations about it with Darl. Dewey Dell's silence, as much as her tactile and physical diction, defines her feminine status. Only Darl can read her mind, though she vainly hopes that Dr. Peabody will cross the language barrier and answer her unspoken request. "He could do everything for me if he just knowed it" (53). Because she cannot "master" speech and persuade someone to give her an abortion, she is relegated to silence and thus to pregnancy and motherhood. Indeed, she finds herself in this predicament precisely due to her decision to allow a physical circumstance—whether or not her cotton sack is full at the end of the row—to determine her sexual actions. She communicates with Lafe primarily sensually and physically: "our eyes would drown together touching on his hands and my hands and I didn't say anything" (23–24). Her silent acquiescence to Lafe's determination to beat chance by picking into her sack seals her fate. Dewey Dell's nonverbal communication, a kind of semiotic discourse, restricts her to her maternal function. One needs oral expression to challenge, and possibly hold off, maternity. Even her desperation to find an abortion-inducing drug does not facilitate her speech. The druggist Moseley first sees her "just standing there with her head turned this way and her eyes full on me and kind of blank too, like she was waiting for a sign" (183). However, signs—the symbolic—will not erase her physical condition.

It is tempting to read Dewey Dell's pregnancy, like Lena Grove's, as an emblem of hope. Moseley rebukes her search for an abortion, telling her,

> You get that notion out of your head. The Lord gave you what you have, even if He did use the devil to do it; you let Him take it away from you if it's His will to do so. You go on back to Lafe and you and him take that ten dollars and get married with it. (188)

Amid all this pro-life and pro-Lafe rhetoric, one can forget that for Dewey,
Dell, this pregnancy is a violation. She has been violated by Lafe, by
MacGowen, and by Darl, when he sees her and thus invades her privacy.

Pregnancy, rather than confirming her abilities to procreate life, denies
her control over her own life and her own body. Her pregnancy results from
her acquiescence in removing herself from her identity, in allowing her own
disembodiment. "I said if the sack is full when we get to the woods it wont
be me" (23). She refuses to accept responsibility for her decision and to
participate in her own sexuality: "it wont be me." By denying her body she
denies her identity, for if she is not Dewey Dell, she becomes simply sexuality
embodied, as, indeed, many scholars have labeled her.[5] Yet once again, there
is more to her language than denial; she eerily foreshadows her own position
as expectant mother by realizing that once her "sack" is full, it won't be her.
Once pregnant, Dewey Dell loses human identity, and is described by Darl
as a "leg coming long from beneath her tightening dress: that lever which
moves the world; one of that caliper which measures the length and breadth
of life" (91). He later comments that one can see, shaped by her wet dress,
"those mammalian ludicrosities which are the horizons and the valleys of the
earth" (150).

But to accept this reading, however persuasive, that she represents
the life of the physical earth, the literal, is to ignore her recognition of
how it denies her very being. She feels that if Dr. Peabody could give her
an abortion, "then I would not be alone. Then I could be all right alone"
(53). She would not be alone because Peabody would share her trouble.
But, more importantly, she would not be alone because she would regain
her self, her identity; then, she would be "all right alone," having healed
the lack within herself. Far from granting life, pregnancy robs her of being:
"I feel my body, my bones and flesh beginning to part and open upon the
alone, and the process of coming unalone is terrible" (56). No wonder she
displays such animosity towards Darl, whose thoughts she seems to be very
well able to read, for his rhetoric inscribes pregnancy as life-embodying
rather than self-denying.

Darl's reading of pregnancy as a force beyond the body, as an embodiment
of life itself, is understandable given his own problematic relationship with
his mother, which causes him to doubt the existence of literal mothers. He
reads motherhood figuratively rather than literally, realizing that he never had
a mother, but "Jewel's mother is a horse" (89). While Dewey Dell never fully
separates from the mother due to her gender, Darl never breaks away because
he was never mothered, was never really a part of her. Thus Darl takes on a
kind of feminine identity, one which may contribute to his growing insanity.
He is capable of nonverbal communication, which sets him apart from the
other men in the novel. Darl sees and understands things that others do

not. As Tull says, "It's like he had got into the inside of you, someway. Like somehow you was looking at yourself and your doings outen his eyes" (111). Not only does his body lack clear boundaries, but it is also associated with the "land [which] runs out of Darl's eyes" (106).

His ability to overflow his physical boundaries and his weakening grasp on his own identity, which deteriorates to the point of speaking of himself in the third person, in some ways mirror Dewey Dell's denial of herself when she removes herself from the sexual act. The fluid ego boundary, Nancy Chodorow has argued, is a feature of women, whose identities are not constructed on difference from the mother but on similarity. When applied to Darl, however, the effect is devastating. Dewey Dell's ability to step outside herself reinforces her sexual identity as it facilitates the act which results in her pregnancy. Dewey Dell is driven into her body, but Darl is out of his mind by this division of self. His intrusion into the minds of both Dewey Dell and Jewel proves so serious a threat that they conspire to commit him. Women often suffer drastic fates when forced to live in a male-oriented system. Darl demonstrates how a man's participation in a female experience may be equally dangerous. Time and again, Faulkner demonstrates the problems of categorizing gender roles, though focusing less often on the women than on the men driven mad by the need to be manly men.

Darl, who seems to float through a world of words, passing into people's minds and crossing vast spaces at will—such as when he narrates the scene of Addie's death from miles away—lacks the stability to fix an identity. The one who produced him failed to mother him; as he says, "I cannot love my mother because I have no mother" (84). Because Darl lacks a stable ego, he lacks stable ego boundaries, leaving him with the fluidity of the mother without her prediscursive power. He uses figurative discourse with great facility but never attempts to construct a figurative replacement for the mother, possibly because he never had a mother to replace. He simply wants to destroy her remains. Thus his poetic and metaphoric language lacks purpose and definition, undermining his position within the realm of the father; he has nothing against which to define himself.

Both Fowler and Bleikasten grant Darl honorary maternal status. Fowler claims "he is like the mother" ("Matricide" 122), while Bleikasten notes "in many ways he is his mother. His gaze is hers—not reembodied, but disembodied, excarnated" (*Ink* 188). Darl's disembodiment is critical, however, for it marks his lack of procreative power. He may be like the mother, but he is producing no babies, no life. To be identified with the mother is deadly in this book. Just as his gaze becomes "excarnated," so too does his identity, leaving him only with insane laughter, "our brother Darl in a cage in Jackson" (236). When Darl tries to substitute doing for words, when he burns down Gillespie's barn in order literally to destroy the body of the mother, he reveals his inability to function within the literal world; for Darl, to do is to threaten both symbolic law and cultural law. Committed to the asylum for his doing, he is expelled from family and from sanity. That Darl, the most articulate and perceptive character in the book, cannot survive illustrates the limitations of disembodied language, of functioning linguistically rather than physically.

Though Darl vanishes with a burst of insane laughter, Cash remains behind, realizing that "this world is not his world" (242), yet still wondering whether "ere a man has the right to say what is crazy and what aint" (221). Cash, the careful craftsman who seems to replace Darl as the artist/narrator by the end of the novel, shares some of Darl's mind-reading capabilities. As he and Darl watch Jewel ride his horse across the river, Darl thinks, "When he was born, he had a bad time of it. Ma would sit in the lamplight, holding him on a pillow on her lap." Cash immediately responds to this thought by saying, "That pillow was longer than him" (130). But while this interchange reveals some fluid ego boundaries, it primarily reflects the intimacy between the two brothers (as Cash says, "It's because me and him was born close together" (217)) more than it suggests an intrusion into another's thoughts; each simply understands what the other may be thinking. Unlike Darl, Cash remains grounded in his body, undergoing considerable physical pain to complete the journey. Though tempted, at the river, to feel relief at the possibility of getting rid of the corpse, he recognizes the function of the ritual, of putting the mother's body to rest physically and symbolically.

If completing the ceremony grants Cash autonomy and artistic power, Jewel the satisfaction of honoring his mother's last request, Vardaman and Dewey Dell some bananas, and Anse a new wife, it would appear that the mother has finally been vanquished, that she ceases to control and order the family. But if the mother's body no longer grounds the family, neither does symbolic discourse, for with the loss of Addie and Darl, we lose the two characters most able to use language with grace and facility. What remains is Dewey Dell's pregnancy, suggesting that, despite the burial of the mother, maternity seems to triumph over language. Yet Faulkner is far from reducing the creative tension between the literal and linguistic to a simple victory for motherhood. Motherhood breeds isolation rather than communion, and, for Dewey Dell, it represents her failure to employ symbolic discourse as a means of averting maternity. She is a mother by default, not by choice. The juxtapositioning of the corpse of the mother with the mother-to-be further undercuts privileging of motherhood. On one hand, we can say that the cycle continues: the mother is dead, long live the mother. But the continuation reinforces women's subjection, both to words, such as love and motherhood, and to wombs.

Both figurative and literal conspire to entrap women in motherhood. Yet in revealing his awareness of the problematic nature of both modes of discourse, Faulkner aligns himself with women writers through his manipulation of this dichotomy. One of the several ways that Homans identifies through which women writers express ambivalence about myths of language which separate and privilege the figurative is the literalization of the figurative. If figurative discourse is essentially masculine, literalizing it makes it more feminine. "Such literalizations of figures," Homans writes, "especially when connected to female themes, articulate a woman writer's ambivalent turning toward female linguistic practices and yet at the same time associating such a choice with danger and death" (30). One reproduces the figurative but recognizes its cost to women. Addie's statement, "He is my cross and he will be my salvation. He will save me from the water and from the fire" (154), becomes literalized when Jewel rescues the coffin from the river and the burning barn. Yet the statement, as Cora realizes, is perilous; "out of the vanity of her heart she had spoken sacrilege." Addie's literalization rewrites the Word of God, and thus constitutes a serious challenge to patriarchal discourse.

The challenge, however, is limited, for the literalization of this figure depends on Addie being in her coffin. In literalizing the word of God the Father, making Jewel her savior, Addie also literalizes herself from soul to corpse. The decaying body is as literal and natural as one can get: the person gone beyond language to what we might call a post-discursive reality. But that corpse also becomes an emblem; each family member displaces onto the dead mother the true meaning for his or her journey. The ostensible motive—to bury the mother in town—gives way to many not-so-hidden agendas: Anse wants new teeth and a new wife, Cash a phonograph, Dewey Dell her abortion, Vardaman to see the train in the store window and to eat bananas. Even Jewel has a deeper motive in his need to bury his mother figuratively as well as literally. This transformation of corpse into symbol allows the family to construct a discourse for the journey and to put up with physical hardships ranging from floods to the sickening odor of the decaying body.

The two who fail to construct a symbolic substitute for the mother, Dewey Dell and Darl, pay the highest price. For Dewey Dell, this trip does not even bury the mother; rather, it ensures the survival of motherhood in her failure to abort her fetus. Darl, who not only fails to construct a discourse for the journey but who does his best to prevent it by taking Jewel and the team away just before Addie's death, by not trying to save the coffin from the river, and by burning down the barn, pays even more dearly, sacrificed to the family's need to re-establish its identity as grounded in culture rather than corpse. "It wasn't nothing else to do. It was either send him to Jackson, or have Gillespie sue us" (215). Significantly, this situation results from the one time Dewey Dell does use verbal expression and tells Gillespie of Darl's guilt, despite her warning to Vardaman to say nothing. In this move into symbolic discourse she sacrifices not just her brother but a part of herself: "I always kind of had a idea that him and Dewey Dell kind of knowed things betwixt them. If I'd a said it was ere a one of us she liked better than ere a other, I'd a said it was Darl" (220). But in expelling Darl, who knows of and in some ways shares her pregnancy, Dewey Dell succeeds in ridding herself only of the figurative emblem of her violation, not the fetus—and thus not the maternity.

Finally, despite all the linguistic anguish in the novel, all the words which "go straight up in a thin line, quick and harmless," it is maternity that cannot be vanquished. The mother's body—the crossing between literal and figurative, patriarchal and maternal discourse, controls the journey and the text. Ultimately, the power of this novel lies in the ways these two creative paradigms both challenge and reinforce each other. The reliance on words and wombs highlights their intersection, a possibility which only women can fulfill. Men may invent motherhood, but women, who embody it, also encroach upon the invented word.

Women's bodies, whether present or absent, exert considerable power in both of these novels, mocking male impotence and challenging male control of figurative expression. If excluded—until after death—from symbolic language, they at least ensure that language will provide no refuge from maternal engulfment. The absent maternal presence collapses the distinctions between presence and absence, literal and figurative, bodies and language, transgressing upon individual identity and, ultimately, being itself. Dead, violated, or exiled, these women embody the tensions out of which art is made, as the mother exacts the price for the "Ode on a Grecian Urn."

NOTES

1. David Minter, one of the exceptions, points to a failure of both parents and links that failure to Faulkner's mixed emotions toward his own parents, especially his supportive but domineering mother. He asserts that Faulkner's sympathy lies with children in both this novel and *As I Lay Dying* (97). For condemnations of Mrs. Compson see Cleanth Brooks, *The Yoknapatawpha Country* (333–34); Mark Spilka, "Quentin Compson's Universal Grief" (456); Jackson J. Benson, "Quentin Compson: Self-Portrait of a Young Artist's Emotions" (148); Elizabeth Kerr, "The Women of Yoknapatawpha" (94). Brooks offers one of the more sympathetic treatments of Mr. Compson. While Mrs. Compson has been the subject of fewer diatribes in recent criticism, in general the critical tendency seems to be to judge her while analyzing her husband, thus implicitly granting him a more privileged position.

2. Philip Weinstein also discusses Caroline Compson in a fine essay, "'If I could Say Mother," which I first saw after this chapter was written. While we come to many of the same conclusions, he focuses more on her failure and lack of power.

3. Weinstein also makes this point (5).

4. Doreen Fowler's excellent article, "Matricide and the Mother's Revenge," appeared while I was revising this chapter after presenting it at the California State Symposium on American Literature in May 1989. Fowler and I have independently reached many similar conclusions and employed similar methodology, relying on feminist revisions of Lacanian models and Margaret Homans's treatment of the literal and figurative. But Fowler's treatment focuses more on the Lacanian move from the Imaginary to the Symbolic, while I emphasize creativity as an interplay between the physical and linguistic.

5. André Bleikasten, for example, ties Dewey Dell to the "Cosmic Mothers of mythology." She is equated with "mother-earth" as the "mysterious life forces that send tremors through her womb are no different from the ones that make the crops grow" (*Ink* 170–71).

JUDITH BRYANT WITTENBERG

Go Down, Moses *and the* Discourse *of* Environmentalism

Go Down, Moses is one of the more remarkable fictions created by William Faulkner in his long and distinguished career. Technically complex, the work's method—the intricate interweaving of previously published short stories with added material designed both to connect the segments and to increase their thematic range—has over the years elicited arguments among critics as to whether it is a collection of short stories, a "composite" (Creighton), or a cohesive novel; recent judgments essentially concur that it is a novel unified by its compelling portrayal of an abusive social and economic system and that its somewhat fragmented method and varied tone echo central thematic elements and intentionally deconstruct the very notion of facile aesthetic closure (Morris 123). The novel depicts a large number of distinctive characters, more perhaps than any other Faulkner novel, many of them connected by blood through several generations of a complicated family that includes individuals of both Caucasian and African heritage. The portrayal of its central figure, Isaac McCaslin, is sufficiently ambiguous that commentators continue to disagree as to the implications of his rhetoric and his behavior (Wall summarizes much of the controversy). The conceptual scope of *Go Down, Moses* is impressive, because its rich and provocative treatment of racial, class, and gender issues is splendidly amplified by its consideration of the interrelationship

From *New Essays on Go Down, Moses*, pp. 49–71 © 1996 by Cambridge University Press.

of the human problems with basic questions concerning not only land ownership—most vividly apparent in Isaac McCaslin's radical gesture of repudiation—but also the very essence of the connections between human beings and the natural environment.

Some years after the publication of *Go Down, Moses*, Faulkner spoke on several occasions about the European colonizers' effect on the American landscape over the centuries, sometimes doing so in a general way, sometimes making particular reference to that portion of wilderness exemplified in the Mississippi Delta region often referred to as "The Big Bottom." During a question and answer period at the University of Virginia, Faulkner described the tragedy inherent in the moment of origin when land ownership in the United States essentially began, when it was first taken by white settlers from the indigenous inhabitants, who "held the land communally." There is a "ghost of ravishment that lingers in the land," said Faulkner, "the land is inimical to the white man because of the unjust way in which it was taken from [the Indians]" (*Faulkner in the University*, hereafter FIU:43). In another moment, he lamented the widespread destruction of the wilderness, reflecting that it is "a change that's going on everywhere; man spends more time ruining the wilderness than he does finding something to replace it" (FIU 68). On other occasions, he spoke somewhat more equivocally. Asked, for example, whether "The Bear" portion of the novel was about a conflict between man and the wilderness, Faulkner said that he was not asking anyone to choose sides, that we need rather "to compassionate the good splendid things which change must destroy." He went on to say that process of change in the landscape must be judged by its outcome: "to clear wilderness just to make cotton land, to raise cotton in an agrarian economy of peonage, slavery, is base because it's not as good as the wilderness which it replaces. If the destruction of the wilderness means more education for more people and more food, then it was worth destroying" (FIU 277). Some of Faulkner's willingness to accept certain alterations in the environment may be attributable to his participation in the "ravishment" represented by land ownership and cultivation: At the time he wrote *Go Down, Moses* he was, says his biographer, the largest landholder in Oxford, Mississippi, owning, in addition to the land on which his house Rowan Oak stood, the single largest tract of land inside the town—the twenty-four acre Bailey's Woods— and a three-hundred-and-twenty-acre farm outside Oxford, complete with tenant farmers and even a commissary (Blotner 986–1069). In at least one instance, Faulkner evinced pride in his land acquisitions, telling someone that "I own a larger parcel of it than anybody in town" (*Selected Letters* 128). Nevertheless, in his 1942 novel, as in other fictions such as *The Hamlet* and *Big Woods*, and in his public statements, Faulkner thoughtfully explores the tragic implications of land ownership and the depredation of the wilderness, although he does so in a manner sufficiently ambiguous as to suggest the complexity of the issues.

Because of this, *Go Down, Moses* is often cited as one of the most significant American novels—if not *the* most—that deals with wilderness and environmental themes. Leonard Lutwack describes the work as the "most eloquent statement on behalf of the wilderness" (169), and John Elder calls it one of the works "which most profoundly depicts the shifting balance between man and nature in American history" (44–45). Annette Kolodny says that the portrait of Isaac McCaslin and his ameliorative response to the contemplation of the land which man has "deswamped and denuded and derivered in two generations" should be read not merely as a story of the South but as a comment on the course of an entire nation's pastoral impulse, and that Ike's characterization is Faulkner's attempt to introduce a vocabulary that will do away with the notion of the land as something to be either possessed or preyed upon and to suggest a human–land relationship based on reciprocity and communality (Kolodny 140, 145).

To say that *Go Down, Moses* is a protoecological work of fiction which, in significant ways, anticipates the outpouring of environmental concern that occurred about twenty years later would be, perhaps, to overstate the case. Nor is it primarily focused on what has been called "the biotic community." It is a distinctly anthropocentric novel whose conceptual fulcrum is the complicated interracial dramas that constitute its various segments and whose overarching thematic focus is the destructive long-term impact of the colonizing white settlers on those from whom they took the land—in Northern Mississippi, the Chickasaw and Choctaw Indians—and on those whom they brought to work the land—the slaves forcibly transported from Africa—and their descendants. As depicted in *Go Down, Moses*, the inmixing of these three groups over the generations ironically complicates and amplifies the destructiveness rather than in any way ameliorating it. At least one critic asserts that, for Faulkner, behind these tragic human dramas of the nineteenth and twentieth centuries depicted in the novel lies the shadow of the larger tragedy in which they all originated, the seizing of the land centuries before and its subsequent clearing for cultivation. This, says Leonard Lutwack, is "the original Southern sin," "the guilt of the past," in which all the subsequent social and economic failures dramatized by Faulkner have their source (Lutwack 163; see also Breaden).

Faulkner's compelling depiction in *Go Down, Moses* of various attitudes toward the Mississippi landscape and its function as background for a series of morally problematic and frequently destructive human relationships not only gives the work a breadth and resonance found only in a handful of his greatest fictions, it also connects the novel with a significant aspect of the cultural context, the growing discussion of environmentalism and ecology that was taking place during the 1930s and the 1940s even as Faulkner was completing the various segments of his 1942 novel and undertaking the process of integrating them into a cohesive whole. This discussion, so splendidly articulated in differing ways by major figures of the era like Faulkner and Aldo Leopold, author of the landmark environmental work, *Sand County Almanac*, would intensify in ensuing decades and eventuate in statutory reforms such as the Endangered Species Act of 1973. It might seem less than appropriate to compare Faulkner's great novel, so clearly centered on complex familial and other human interrelationships, to a series of nonfiction works that include nature journals, autobiographies, and hortative essays and almost exclusively focus on environmental issues, but the linkages between them are compelling and important. *Go Down, Moses* and texts by Aldo Leopold and other environmental thinkers of the period not only reveal their authors as grappling conceptually with many of the same ideas, they also evolved from a more general and increasingly well articulated discussion of environmental issues.

* * * * *

The thematic nexus of such works as *Go Down, Moses* and some of the environmental texts—the delicate and crucial interconnection of all things on and of this earth, and the alarming human capacity for violent disruption—makes it productive to approach them via an intertextual reading. In "The Bounded Text," Julia Kristeva speaks of any text as "a permutation of texts, an intertextuality," in which discourses from other texts "intersect" one another (Kristeva 36). This vision of discursive intersection suggests the notion of "network," which, in some sense, is the dominant trope not only of *Go Down, Moses* but of ecological thinking generally, which views the entire earth as a single community that functions as an intricate web. Relevant to this intertextual exploration is SueEllen Campbell's identification, in her discussion of the shared premises of deep ecology and post-structuralism, of "the network" as the most important of the fundamental parallels between the two theoretical positions. Both ecologists and poststructuralists, says Campbell, critique the dominant structures of Western culture such as the idea of an authoritative locus of hierarchical meaning or of the human being as either central or centered, substituting instead the notion of "the network." She notes the presence of this trope in work by Derrida, Lacan, and Foucault, the latter of whom asserted, for example, that any individual is merely a "node within a network" (quoted in Campbell, 207). Similarly, ecologists believe that all elements on earth are interconnected, that any organism is simply a "knot" in the biospherical field. Although Faulkner's 1942 novel is certainly not explicit about this viewpoint, traces of it are evident, and the environmentalist critics speak quite pointedly about the biotic community. Thus, as both thematic focus and critical strategy, the network metaphor is not only appropriate for approaching such texts but for placing their ideas in a conceptual context.

The richness of this context is striking. The works of the 1940s by William Faulkner and the environmentalists had deep historical roots. To say that Faulkner was not the first American writer to use a regional wilderness as both backdrop and "character" in his work is to state the obvious; any student in an American literature survey course quickly notes the extensive role played by "nature" in the literature of the past two centuries. Although the concept of nature itself has been revealed as problematic in recent discussions by Lawrence Buell, Myra Jehlen, and others, who have critiqued it as a hegemonic formation, it has long been acknowledged as a, perhaps *the*, formative influence in traditional American writing (see Buell). The sense of an unspoiled landscape—the "fresh, green breast of the new world," in Fitzgerald's memorable phrase from *The Great Gatsby* (Fitzgerald 182)—capable of inspiring and restoring the human spirit "corrupted" by civilization has, says Leo Marx, never lost its powerful hold on the American imagination (Marx 3, passim).

For novelists, poets, and essayists from Cooper, Emerson, and Thoreau to Jeffers and Faulkner, the imaginative influence of nature has been of major significance. Their work has, as we know, affected both literary successors and environmental activists; although the relationship of the former to their predecessors may perhaps be marked by subconscious anxiety, that of the latter has frequently been characterized by enthusiastic admiration. Thoreau, for example, whose classic work *Walden* (1854) had a limited impact beyond a small group of literary admirers, became an environmental hero in both the United States and Great Britain in the later twentieth century, inspiring both those who supported ecological activism and those in favor of animal rights. Thoreau was, it has been pointed out, an ecologist before we called it "ecology" (Nash, *Rights* 35–36). It also seems worthy of note that central elements of *Walden* recur, mutatis mutandis, in *Go Down, Moses*: the concepts that in the wilderness one confronts "only the essential facts of life" and is thus able to respond simply and meaningfully; that ownership of property is deleterious, an "imprison[ing]" state; that hunting is a stage of "education" for a youth, one to be outgrown, superseded by the recognition that he is profoundly connected to his fellow creatures; and the presence of the ledgers whose objective records of expenditures function in counterpoint with Thoreau's philosophical ruminations.

More geographically relevant to Faulkner's work, if less significant in a literary sense, are the "pen pictures" of the vanishing Mississippi wilderness of the 1840s published at the beginning of the twentieth century in a Tupelo newspaper by W. F. Clayton. Seeming to anticipate aspects of *Go Down, Moses* with their description of the "vast forests" of the past as they were when inhabited only by Indians, teeming with wild game and "covered with great upstretching trees" (13–14), Clayton's sketches lament the way in which, by the beginning of the twentieth century, the landscape had been adversely affected by loggers and planters, who destroyed "nature's handiwork," felling the great trees for lumber and replacing them with fields of corn and cotton. In passages that sound almost like source material for portions of "Fire and the Hearth," Clayton also assails the distractions of a capitalist economy that occupies men with pecuniary gain and expresses sentimental affection for figures of the past such as the "old black mammy" whom children of white households often regarded as "almost a savior" (Clayton 22, 27).

Writers such as these were part of the ongoing literary celebration of the vanishing wilderness and its salutary challenges to those individuals who encountered it in its pristine state. Their voices also contributed to a more general discussion about environmental issues that grew in strength in the United States during the 1930s and 1940s. The environmental crisis was not new, however, and some have suggested that it had its roots in early Judeo-Christian thought, originating in God's reported command to mankind to "be fruitful, and multiply, and replenish the earth, and subdue it: and have dominion over the fish of the sea, and over the fowl of the air, and over every living thing that moveth upon the earth" (Genesis 1:28; see White). In the United States, the myth of the West as a "vacant continent" awaiting the "civilizing" impact of European settlers encouraged development in a westerly direction in a process championed most vociferously in Congress by Thomas Hart Benton and celebrated in literary works like Whitman's "O Pioneers," which, says Henry Nash Smith, "gave final imaginative expression to the theme of manifest destiny" (Smith 47–48). This process accelerated after the Civil War with the manipulations of land speculators and the efforts of the railroad builders, whose new form of transportation delivered eager settlers into the "empty" landscape at a rapid pace. Nevertheless, awareness of the problems created by such incursions, formerly confined to an enlightened few, increased as a result of the cataclysm of World War I, which revealed that an increasingly industrialized and urbanized world had also become prey to international power struggles, thus raising further doubts about the effects of so-called "civilization" on human beings and the natural environment (Nash, *Wilderness* 160).

Although the environmental crisis in the United States was deep-rooted and increasing with each decade, the public perception that it was fast assuming disastrous proportions grew during the 1930s and 1940s as a result of some consciousness-raising events and the publication or rediscovery of several influential texts. One such event was the terrible "dust bowl" phenomenon of the 1930s, when thousands of farmers were dispossessed from the plains region as a consequence of both an extended drought and their destructive land-use methods of previous years. Those ultimately responsible were the "sodbusters" of an earlier era, who had tilled the soil with wanton disregard for the impact of their techniques; the dust bowl expulsions of the 1930s, pervasively tragic in human terms, might also be seen as the revenge of the land. As Donald Worster notes, the farmers' attitude toward the environment—their disregard for the land as a permanent home and their heedless depletion of the soil—ironically resulted in their own poverty and dislocation (Worster 226). The incremental effects of such human behavior were analyzed in an influential work of the mid-1930s, Paul Sears's *Deserts on the March*, which criticized prevailing land-use practices like those that eventuated in the dust bowl. Such occurrences contributed to the increasing awareness that the commodity approach of an earlier conservation figure like Gifford Pinchot was based on concern for the nation's economy rather than nature's and that it had negative implications for the environment. The gradual tipping of the conceptual scales from nature-as-commodity to nature-as-community was an important development in the environmental thinking of this era, and vestiges of both viewpoints can be seen in *Go Down, Moses*.

* * * * *

The impact of significant environmental events such as the dust bowl was augmented by the publication or rediscovery of some crucial texts in the field, which both increased the public awareness of the basic issues and brought the discussion forward in meaningful ways. Max Horkheimer and Theodor Adorno, in their *Dialectic of Enlightenment* (1944), argued that, since the eighteenth century, Western thought had confronted two contradictory stances: the first, a dedication to the search for intrinsic value and ultimate purpose—"the mythic imagination," or "the mythological," in which reason is devoted to transcendence—and, the second, a desacralized view of the world that makes reason instrumental in the drive for the domination of nature—"enlightenment." In this dialectic, individuals believe either in human subjection to nature or nature's subjection to the self (Horkheimer and Adorno 32, and passim; see also Worster); one can see the operation of a comparable dialectic in *Go Down, Moses*, particularly in the commissary discussion between Ike and his cousin Cass. Cass asserts the value of their ancestor's efforts that overcame nature, that "cleared" the "wilderness of wild beasts and wilder man" and "translated it into something to bequeath to his children," whereas Ike refutes him with statements grounded in a more sacral view of nature and a sense that the relationship of human beings to the land must be one of mutuality and community (245–246). Faulkner critics have often faulted Ike for his reliance on such "weak" arguments; indeed, the rationalist "man over nature" thought characterized by Horkheimer and Adorno as "enlightenment" has often informed critical assessments of *Go Down, Moses* (Wall 153). In the environmental writing of this period, however, one sees a certain trend toward the side of the dialectic termed by Horkheimer and Adorno "the mythological," as some influential texts began to question the ascendancy of the human over the natural world. Works which appeared—or re-appeared—during the 1930s and 1940s and to varying degrees had an effect on the public discussion, included George Perkins Marsh's *Man and Nature*, Albert Schweitzer's *My Life and Thought: An Autobiography*, John Muir's journals, and Aldo Leopold's *Sand County Almanac*.

Marsh's *Man and Nature*, first published in 1864, was rediscovered in the 1930s, in large measure because of the growing evidence during that era that the "hostile influence of man" on the environment of which Marsh had warned his readers seventy years before was now coming to some sort of destructive fruition. Marsh raised the "great question," later explored by Horkheimer and Adorno, as to "whether man is of nature or above her" and anticipated the ecological perspective of the twentieth century with his concern about the hazards of human interference "with the spontaneous arrangements of the organic or the inorganic world" (Marsh 3, 36, 186–187, 465). One of Marsh's dedicated readers was John Muir, founder of the Sierra Club; Muir's journals, published in 1938, evinced a reverential view of nature very much like "the mythological" as later defined by Horkheimer and Adorno. Muir described Yosemite Valley as a "temple," a place of "divine beauty," where "God's glory is . . . written upon every field and sky" (Muir 39, 47). Like the Mississippians W. F. Clayton and William Faulkner, whose devout regard for the majestic southern wilderness of earlier years informed their work, Muir also described the forests of the American South in awed terms, as a place of "noble trees," many of them as tall as one hundred feet (Muir 365). Albert Schweitzer, known more for his humanitarian efforts than for his ecological ideas, revealed in his 1933 autobiography, *My Life and Thought*, a concern for an ethics grounded in "Reverence for Life," asserting that a human being can be ethical "only when life, as such, is sacred to him, that of plants and animals as much as that of his fellow man" (Schweitzer 185, 188).

All these individuals and their texts contributed to the growing discourse on environmental issues, but Aldo Leopold is in many ways the pivotal figure of the period, despite the fact that he and his work were little known to the wider public until after his death. Not only is Leopold's posthumously published *Sand County Almanac* regarded by many as the "bible of the ecology movement" of the latter twentieth century, but in his own intellectual development Leopold also mirrors the changes occurring during the 1930s and 1940s. At the start of his career in forestry, Leopold was a utilitarian in the Gifford Pinchot mold and dedicated to the extermination of predatory animals. He was, however, profoundly influenced by two events and evolved into the figure we know today, an environmental ethicist of the first order. The first of these events was a meeting in 1931 with Charles Elton, author of the 1927 landmark work *Animal Ecology*, which posited the notion of the food chain and the close linkages between the plant and animal "communities." Elton noted the interdependence of all of earth's inhabitants and asserted that when human beings attempt to exploit nature's resources, they disturb its balance (Elton 9, 16, 52–54). It has been suggested that discussions with Elton during this meeting essentially "converted" Leopold to a more ecological view of nature (Worster 300); his founding of the Wilderness Society in 1935 revealed his dedication to the preservation of areas where natural communities could continue without further human disruption. A second event that visibly contributed to the evolution of Leopold's thinking about the environment was his 1936 camping trip in the Sierra Madre region of Mexico, when he experienced what might be called an epiphany, dramatically responding to the realization that this area of Mexico represented the wilderness at its most pristine and that the wild areas of the United States had already been adversely affected by human efforts.

In subsequent years, he began the process of preparing the volume known as *Sand County Almanac*, which may be productively read against *Go Down, Moses*. Although Leopold's work is undramatized nonfiction prose and Faulkner's is a complex and ambiguous narrative, the two texts have important conceptual parallels and carry on a fruitful intertextual dialogue. Somewhat comparable in their methods, the two texts are also parallel in their consideration of certain basic environmental themes. Their techniques—the weaving together of interconnected fragments—are appropriate for their topic, the complicated linkages between the discrete but interrelated members of the earthly community. *Sand County Almanac* has an unusual three-segment structure, each portion of which is composed of smaller pieces: The first part is a series of short prose poems and anecdotes, seasonally arranged for continuity; the second, a group of topical essays inspired by a variety of geographical locales; and the third, several long and issue-oriented essays that elucidate points of ecological doctrine and rise to hortatory eloquence. The seven-part structure of *Go Down, Moses* comprises distinct narratives connected by genealogical ties among their principal characters, recurrent thematic elements, and a chronological movement generally forward in time. Despite a degree of unity and some sense of "progression," if you will, in each text, there is an equally strong counter-pull away from the center; this methodological tension is clearly suitable to the subject, a community paradoxically at once interconnected and atomized.

Faulkner's and Leopold's texts are most closely affiliated in the comparability of their central concepts. In his 1948 foreword, Leopold identifies himself as one of that minority which sees "a law of diminishing returns of progress" (Leopold xvii)—a group to which Faulkner, with his increasingly explicit criticisms of everything from radios to government regulations, obviously also belongs—and makes his central point, that human beings are capable of abusing the land "because we regard it as a commodity belonging to us." He writes that when we instead "see land as a community to which we belong, we may begin to use it with love and respect. There is no other way for land to survive" (Leopold xviii–xix). Throughout the book, Leopold assails the "profit-motive," "economic self-interest," and the view of land as a commodity, proposing instead an ethic based in the "community concept." Some of these ideas had been put forth in somewhat different terms but with equal fervor a hundred years before by Karl Marx, who assailed the notion of private property, seeing land ownership as originating in "robbery" and inevitably involving exploitation of other human beings as well as of the land itself. In his early writings, Marx asserted the close interdependency of human beings and nature and proposed, in place of land ownership, something he called "association," which would restore the intimate relationship between man and the land (Marx 116).

Echoes of both Leopold and Marx can be found in Faulkner's portrayal of Isaac McCaslin, who repudiates the large land holdings that he inherits, becoming one "who owned no property and never desired to since the earth was no man's but all men's" (4). The portrait of Ike stands in dramatic apposition to that of his cousin Cass, whose view is that land can not only be owned, but should be developed and cultivated, in order to make it "worthy of bequeathment," a "legacy and monument" (245). That the adumbration of Ike's viewpoint frames the text of Go Down, Moses and recurs in many of the segments obviously accords it greater conceptual weight than that of the property owner Cass. Ike even provides his own exegesis of the passage from Genesis that has troubled ecologists, asserting that God "created man to be His overseer on the earth and to hold suzerainty over the earth and the animals on it in His name, not to hold for himself and his descendants inviolable title forever, . . . but to hold the earth mutual and intact in the communal anonymity of brotherhood" (246). Moreover, in assailing the plantation economy toward which land-use was directed in the South—an "edifice intricate and complex and founded upon injustice and erected by ruthless rapacity and carried on even yet with at times downright savagery not only to the human beings but the valuable animals too" (285)—Ike provides an implicit critique of capitalism itself.

* * * * *

In many of its other portrayals, *Go Down, Moses* offers either direct or subtle evidence of a skeptical view of a commodified approach either to land or to the methods of production. In the fictive northern region of Mississippi, the "original sin" was committed by the Chickasaw Indian Ikkemotubbe. As well as proving himself capable of murder and the appalling sale of his own family into slavery, Ikkemotubbe also, in profound violation of Indian belief, sells some of his people's land. The confluence of complicity in murder, slavery, and land conveyance in the brief portrait of Ikkemotubbe is, however exaggerated, telling. As Faulkner himself said some years after the publication of *Go Down, Moses*, the acceptance by white settlers of property signed over to them by indigenous peoples unleashed a "ghost of ravishment that lingers in the land" (FIU 43).

As the 1942 novel makes clear, this ravishment has tainted all those who participated in it, however indirectly. Even Lucas Beauchamp, consigned to the economic margins by his part-African ancestry, appears in "Fire and the Hearth" as a greedy would-be landowner who regards the field he cultivates as "his own" and believes he "would own the land if his just rights were only known," if Cass had not "beat him out of his patrimony" (36); Lucas accordingly regards Ike as "apostate to his name and lineage" for "weakly relinquishing the land which was rightfully his" (39). Lucas is also a striving entrepreneur whose musings on the threats to his illegal but profitable manufacture of alcohol by a new "competitor" turn him into a comical caricature of capitalist obsession. He is anxious about the "interruption of business" and "loss of revenue" created by the need to move his still and fears the incursion into "his established trade, his old regular clientele," longing for the recent days in which he held a virtual monopoly on the local trade (33–36). Lucas's preoccupation with his economic ambitions makes him heedless toward the landscape, even the Indian mound, which he is prepared to desecrate in his quest for gold. The prospect of digging it up "did not bother him" (42). One of the more memorable aspects of *Go Down, Moses* is the portrait of Lucas Beauchamp, who is, like Ike McCaslin, a figure at once sympathetic and problematic.

Although Lucas himself has been profoundly and adversely affected by the white colonizers' attitudes toward property—both land and, under slavery, human beings—he appears to have internalized them and to have unwittingly accepted other attitudes with which they are closely linked. These are evident not only in his obsession with material gain, but also in his patriarchal assumption that male lineage is superior, his nostalgia for the days in which he believed that "men . . . were men," and his possessive attitude toward the women in his family, whom he often treats as if they were objects of exchange. A product of slavery, Lucas has become himself enslaved to the sort of thinking that initially made it conceivable. In this instance, Faulkner's critique is subtle and rather humorous. More pointed and earnest is Leopold's invocation of "god-like Odysseus" as an example of ethical blindness when he hangs a dozen slave girls whom he suspected of misbehavior. Even an heroic figure such as Odysseus, says Leopold, proves capable of egregious behavior when it involves "disposal of property." Leopold then asserts that ethical treatment must be extended not only to all human beings but to the environment itself; this is his "land ethic." He calls for a repudiation of the notion of "land [as] the slave and servant" and its replacement with the idea of "land the collective organism" (Leopold 237, 261). Leopold's vivid example of the extension of destructive attitudes toward property into the human sphere and his subsequent plea for a much more communo-ethical stance toward land and human beings are reflected in Faulkner's character portrayals. In *Go Down, Moses*, the region and its peoples all seem to have been contaminated to a greater or lesser degree by the concepts that flow from the notion that land can be dominated and possessed. Belief in the ownership of land is part of what Marc Baldwin describes as a "culture of domination" and is causally linked to claims to the ownership of blacks and women (Baldwin 200).

In addition to questioning the very concept of land ownership, *Go Down, Moses*, like *Sand County Almanac*, places high value on wilderness; indeed, the word itself is the most frequently used uncommon term in the novel, recurring fifty times in the second half (Capps). Wilderness is valuable not only in and of itself but also for the sort of enriching experiences it offers to responsive human beings. Faulkner's novel is, among other things, a bildungsroman in which the natural environment plays a crucial role in the development of the central character. For Ike McCaslin, the wilderness has both educational and spiritual significance; it is "his college," the place where he "entered his novitiate," as if "witnessing his own birth" (202, 187). The moment in which Ike discards the items which are the last vestiges and "taints" of "civilization" and "relinquishes" to the wilderness is the one in which he fully discovers the profundity of his connection to his natural surroundings and is rewarded by the sight, first, of a fresh paw print and, next, of the bear itself, "as big as he had expected, bigger, dimensionless against the dappled obscurity" (200). Leopold also discusses the way in which a woodland can provide an individual with a "liberal education," referring to the "many lessons" he himself learned there (Leopold 77); again, observing two youths canoeing, he reflects on the educational merits of wilderness travel, which allows one the "complete freedom to make mistakes" and teaches the "rewards and penalties for wise and foolish acts" (Leopold 120).

For Faulkner's Ike, as well as for Leopold, hunting proves to be a crucial element in this "education." Although it might seem paradoxical that those with a reverence for nature and its creatures would be willing to kill any of them—and Thoreau certainly saw hunting as a questionable "phase" of moral development, a phase which must be outgrown by any "humane being"—it is the case that many of the environmentalists, even those most fervent about conserving wild areas, saw hunting as integral to the wilderness experience. Leopold, say his editors, considered hunting as "important to the building of character" (Brown and Carmony 67), and he wrote an essay (1925) entitled "A Plea for Wilderness Hunting Grounds." In it, he argued for hunters' access to wilderness areas and discussed the merits of the pursuit. Faulkner, too, spoke in more or less positive terms about hunting, also with reference to its function as a symbol of the "pursuit" which he described as fundamental to human life—"the pursuit is the thing, not the reward, not the gain"; and he asserted that one should "slay the animals with the nearest approach you can to dignity and decency" (FIU 272, 54). Pursuit is a central motif in *Go Down, Moses*, from the comical, if unnerving, chase of Tomey's Turl in "Was," where the slave is treated as if he were an animal quarry, through the various wilderness segments, to the quest by Mollie Beauchamp, in the final portion of the novel, to retrieve the body of her grandson. Ike's accession to manhood is clearly signified by his brave and sometimes solitary tracking of the old bear; though he does not participate in this culminating kill, his shooting of a deer and his willing involvement in the pursuit and final confrontation with Old Ben indicate the range and strength of his courage. As a youth, Ike feels "alien" to the woods "until he had drawn honorably blood worthy of being drawn," and the tutelary figure Sam Fathers tells him that, once he has killed a deer, "You'll be a hunter. You'll be a man" (169–170). When he succeeds and is ritualistically marked with the hot blood of the felled deer, Ike becomes "one with the wilderness which had accepted him" and "ceased to be a child and became a hunter and a man" (171).

Still, as both Faulkner and some of the environmental writers made clear, in some memorable moments, a hunter's awed response to a game animal he has been avidly pursuing precludes the possibility of killing it. John Muir records an instance when he was part of a group hunting the wild sheep of Shasta, whose leader was a huge ram, "a noble old fellow." During the pursuit the ram stopped for a moment, "his form and noble horns . . . clearly outlined against the sky." Muir experiences guilt, feeling wolflike in his "savage exhilaration" at the hunt, and another member of the party simply gazes at the ram until he disappears into a thicket (Muir 199–200). Similarly, in *Go Down, Moses*, when Sam Fathers, who equates hunting with manhood, sees an impressive buck "full and wild and unafraid," walking "tremendous" and "unhurried," he simply salutes him, saying, "Oleh, Chief. Grandfather" (177). In thus paying awed tribute to the majesty of one manifestation of nature's grandeur, Sam reveals that such moments of reverence for the splendor of a single wild animal can overcome the will to slay of even a dedicated hunter.

Intriguingly, in both *Sand County Almanac* and *Go Down, Moses*, the most compelling symbol of the wilderness that is at once magnificent, threatening, and threatened is an immense and fearsome, yet ultimately vulnerable, bear. Much of Leopold's work reveals his special reverence for the grizzly bears that once inhabited portions of the American West in substantial numbers. In a 1936 article on "Threatened Species," Leopold warned that all conservation projects in or near locations inhabited by grizzlies must be judged "in the light of whether they help or hinder the perpetuation of the noblest of American mammals" (Brown and Carmony 195), and in *Sand County Almanac*, he memorializes a single specimen, the huge bear known as Old Bigfoot. This bear lived on the Arizona mountain called Escudilla, from which he descended each spring to kill and feast on one of a local rancher's cows; the force of Old Bigfoot's murderous assault was such that in one recorded instance the dead cow looked as if "she had collided with a fast freight [train]." Old Bigfoot's predatory habits, along with his size, made evident by his "incredible tracks," and his elusiveness—"no one ever saw the old bear"—imbue him with an extraordinary mystique; all those living in the area are frightened of and fascinated by him. Although he "claimed for his own only a cow a year, and a few square miles of useless rocks," nonetheless "his personality pervaded the [surrounding] county" (Leopold 142–143). With bleak and sarcastic brevity, Leopold records the arrival in the area around Escudilla of a government trapper looking to exterminate "destructive animals," who finally, after several vain attempts, manages to slay Old Bigfoot only by ambushing him with a set-gun in a defile. "The last grizzly walked into the string and shot himself" (144). Fearsome in life yet pathetically reduced by the nature of his death and the patchy pelt he leaves behind, Old Bigfoot becomes an emblem not only of the ultimately pointless assaults on predatory animals but also of the very wilderness itself, venerable and splendid yet vulnerable to destruction by ill conceived human efforts.

Faulkner's Old Ben, who occupies a similar emblematic position in *Go Down, Moses*, evinces many of the same characteristics as Old Bigfoot; he is simultaneously menacing and awe-inspiring, a creature known to and feared by all who venture into the region he inhabits. The moment in which Ike McCaslin first sees Old Ben has quasi-religious overtones—the bear appears almost as if by magic in a sunlit glade—and recalls, says Susan

Donaldson, Mircea Eliade's definition of the mystical encounter with the sacred (Donaldson 39). Like Old Bigfoot, the bear is terrifying to human beings as a result of his size, his elusiveness, and his predatory habits; he is even compared to a locomotive, that darkly ambiguous emblem of human incursion and "progress." The moment in which Old Ben "breaks the rules" established by his human admirers, who have hitherto pursued him regularly but without fully murderous intent, and kills one of Major de Spain's colts, proves to be the moment in which his doom is sealed. Although Old Ben's animal antagonist, the yellow-eyed and fierce dog Lion, is in many ways a more worthy opponent than Leopold's government trapper, Faulkner's bear is also compromised at the moment of death, brought down in a wild encounter with the less-than-admirable Boon Hogganbeck. Symbolically, the bear "crashed down . . . as a tree falls" (231).

Fittingly for its genre, Faulkner's narrative of the death of the majestic bear is enriched by several memorable human characterizations; thus, although, as in Leopold's text, the demise of a single animal signifies the loss of something splendid and unreplaceable, as well as the ultimate decay of the surrounding wilderness, it also resonates throughout the rest of that segment of the novel and beyond. The impact on the part-Chickasaw Sam Fathers is devastating; not long after Old Ben dies, Sam follows him, having fallen insensate to the ground in the very moment the bear is fatally stricken. Ike knows instinctively "that Sam too was going to die" (236). In both Leopold's and Faulkner's texts the death of an awe-inspiring creature at the hands of unworthy human beings heralds the decline of the wild areas he inhabits.

* * * * *

Even as the Leopold and Faulkner texts evince reverential regard for the wilderness and its enriching effects on those who respect it and respond to it, they serve finally as elegiac witnesses to the ways in which it is being destructively altered, moving gradually and perhaps irrevocably beyond the point of reclamation. In the penultimate essay of *Sand County Almanac*, Leopold says that wilderness is, for the philosophical observer, "something to be loved and cherished," the more so because "many of the diverse wildernesses out of which we have hammered America are already gone" (Leopold 265). He appraises the "value of wilderness" in humanistic terms, asserting that in its "raw" form it "gives definition and meaning to the human enterprise" (Leopold 279). In this same passage, Leopold also comments on the "humility" required to see the fundamental worth of the wilderness.

Although Leopold here refers to intellectual humility, of which he believes "only the scholar" is capable, the response he describes is something akin to the emotions experienced by Faulkner's young Ike McCaslin. In revising the material from which he created *Go Down, Moses*, Faulkner was careful to amplify the reverential aspect of the boy's attitude toward the wilderness (Creighton 122). As Ike confronts the big woods and their quality, "profound, sentient, gigantic and brooding," he feels "dwarfed" (169). Ike experiences "an abjectness, a sense of his own fragility and impotence against the timeless woods, yet without doubt or dread" (192). During his last trip into the Big Bottom as a youth, Ike is shocked at the sight of the changes wrought by further development of the area, responding with "grieved amazement" to the changes in the "doomed wilderness" (303, 306). The train now looks like a "snake" bearing with it into the landscape "the shadow and portent of the new [planing] mill" (306). This segment—which follows the all-important passages in which Ike expresses his deeply held belief that the land he has relinquished was "never mine to repudiate" (246) and makes his horrifying discovery of the human "crimes" recorded in the family ledgers—ends with further haunting images of decline: a visit to the graves of Lion and Sam Fathers, Boon's demented hammering of his dismembered gun, and Ike's saluting of the enormous rattlesnake, "ancient and accursed," evocative "of pariah-hood and of death" (314).

In the penultimate segment of *Go Down, Moses*, "Delta Autumn," which is also the bleakest portion of the novel, the darkness of the human story has its parallels in the depredations visited upon the landscape. Now the aged Ike sees himself and the wilderness "as coevals," the "two spans running out together" (337), connected in such fundamental ways that the decay of the wilderness mirrors his. He reflects sadly on how dramatically it has diminished, retreated, been beaten back by loggers, planters, developers, and automobiles until only a small portion of the splendid vastness remains. It has been "deswamped and denuded and derivered in two generations" (347). Ike, too, is in decline, descending into the last moments of old age and impending death. Worse, physical decay is imaged in ethical inadequacy; Ike McCaslin displays in these passages a haunting failure of moral imagination and a revelation of racist attitudes, as he tries desperately to buy off the part-black granddaughter of Tennie's Jim, who has come looking for Roth Edmonds, and tells her to marry a man of her own race. He also pointlessly offers her, for her son, the hunting horn that once belonged to General Compson. It is as if the "ruined woods" have visited their "retribution" even on an individual who has always evinced only profound respect and admiration for them. The tale ends with a telling description of Ike lying alone and corpselike, barely protected from "the constant and grieving rain" (347–348). The hunt, too, has been degraded, in the formerly taboo killing of a doe.

The final section of *Go Down, Moses*, although not directly concerned with the environmental issues so central to other portions of the novel, nevertheless focuses on some of the indirect and unfortunate consequences of the original mistreatment of the land—the fatal deracination of a member of the youngest generation of Beauchamps, who has been expelled from the land by an Edmonds and executed in a northern prison for killing a policeman, and, in the ultimate manifestation of the racial divide, the complete failure of one well-meaning white person, Gavin Stevens, to comprehend the powerful grief of the elderly black woman he is trying to help. The downward emotional trajectory of Faulkner's novel conforms to its moving portrayal of a complicated and ultimately tragic array of interracial and intergenerational relationships and its evocation of a vanishing natural splendor that has been destroyed by the same attitudes that, extended into the human sphere, result in misunderstanding and exploitive treatment. Like Aldo Leopold's landmark work *Sand County Almanac*, which a Secretary of the Interior called "a noble elegy for the American earth" (quoted in Sessions 34), *Go Down, Moses* explores with elegiac eloquence essential questions about the interconnections between human beings and their environment. That these two texts, which represent in differing ways culminating moments in their own genres and in the emerging discourse of environmentalism of an earlier era, continue to engage a wide public with their memorable descriptions of the natural world and with their provocative considerations of ethical questions, bears plangent witness to their timeless significance.

Works Cited

Baldwin, Marc D. "Faulkner's Cartographic Method." *Faulkner Journal* 7:1–2 (1991–92), 193–214.

Blotner, Joseph. *Faulkner: A Biography*. New York: Random House, 1974.

Breaden, Dale G. "William Faulkner and the Land." *American Quarterly* 10:3 (Fall 1958), 344–357.

Brown, David E. and Neil B. Carmony, eds. *Aldo Leopold's Wilderness*. Harrisburg, PA: Stackpole, 1990.

Buell, Lawrence. "American Pastoral Ideology Reappraised." *American Literary History* 1:1 (Spring 1989), 1–29.

Campbell, SueEllen. "The Land and Language of Desire: Where Deep Ecology and Post-Structuralism Meet." *Western American Literature* 24:3 (Fall 1989), 199–211.

Capps, Jack L., ed. *Go Down, Moses: A Concordance to the Novel*. Ann Arbor: University Microfilms, 1977.

Clayton, W. L. *Olden Times Revisited*, ed. Minrose Gwin. Jackson: University Press of Mississippi, 1982.

Creighton, Joanne V. *William Faulkner's Craft of Revision*. Detroit: Wayne State University Press, 1977.

Donaldson, Susan. "Isaac McCaslin and the Possibilities of Vision." *Southern Review* 22:1 (Winter 1986), 37–50.

Elder, John. *Imagining the Earth: Poetry and the Vision of Nature*. Champaign: University of Illinois Press, 1985.

Elton, Charles. *Animal Ecology*. London: Sidgwick & Jackson, 1927.

Faulkner, William. *Go Down, Moses*. New York: Vintage, 1990.

———. *Faulkner in the University*, eds. Frederick Gwynn and Joseph Blotner. Charlottesville: University Press of Virginia, 1959.

———. *Selected Letters of William Faulkner*, ed. Joseph Blotner. New York: Random House, 1977.

Fitzgerald, F. Scott. *The Great Gatsby*. New York: Scribner, 1953.

Horkheimer, Max, and Theodor Adorno. *Dialectic of Enlightenment*. Trans. John Cumming. New York: Continuum, 1987.

Kolodny, Annette. *The Lay of the Land*. Chapel Hill: University of North Carolina Press, 1975.

Kristeva, Julia. "The Bounded Text," in *Desire in Language*, ed. Leon Roudiez. New York: Columbia University Press, 1980, pp. 36–63.

Leopold, Aldo. *A Sand County Almanac*. New York: Ballantine, 1966.

Lutwack, Leonard. *The Role of Place in Literature*. Syracuse: Syracuse University Press, 1984.

Marsh, George Perkins. *Man and Nature* [1864]. Cambridge, MA: Belknap Press of Harvard, 1965.

Marx, Karl. *Early Writings*. Trans. and ed. T. B. Bottomore. New York: McGraw-Hill, 1964.

Marx, Leo. *The Machine in the Garden*. New York: Oxford University Press, 1964.

Morris, Wesley and Barbara. *Reading Faulkner*. Madison: University of Wisconsin Press, 1989.

Muir, John. *John of the Mountains: The Unpublished Journals of John Muir*, ed. Linnie Marsh Wolfe. Boston: Houghton Mifflin, 1938.

Nash, Roderick. *The Rights of Nature*. Madison: University of Wisconsin Press, 1989.

———. *Wilderness and the American Mind*, rev. ed. New Haven: Yale University Press, 1973.

Schweitzer, Albert. *My Life and Thought: An Autobiography*. Trans. C. T. Campion. London: George Allen & Unwin, 1933.

Sears, Paul B. *Deserts on the March* [1935]. 3d. ed., rev. Norman: University of Oklahoma Press, 1959.

Sessions, George. "Ecological Consciousness and Paradigm Change." In *Deep Ecology*, ed. Michael Tobias. San Marcos, CA: Avant Books, 1988.

Smith, Henry Nash. *The Virgin Land*. New York: Vintage, 1950.

Wall, Carey. "*Go Down, Moses*: The Collective Action of Redress." *Faulkner Journal* 7:1–2 (1991–92), 151–174.

White, Lynn, Jr. "The Historical Roots of Our Ecologic Crisis." *Science* 10 (March 1967), 1203–1207.

Worster, Donald. *Nature's Economy: A History of Ecological Ideas*. New York: Cambridge University Press, 1985.

OWEN ROBINSON

Interested Parties and Theorems to Prove: Narrative and Identity in Faulkner's Snopes Trilogy

As readers of William Faulkner's Snopes trilogy, we find ourselves considering both the life of Flem Snopes, and the comparable attempts of readers within the narratives to similarly interpret him, these interpretations having crucial effects on the respective positions of both Flem and Faulkner's reader with regard to the texts. Each of these books takes a different narrative approach. *The Hamlet* (1940) is delivered by an authorial voice, though it is one that is frequently inhabited by the eager contributions of others, most notably V. K. Ratliff. As ever with Faulkner's use of such a voice, its own position can never be taken for granted—it would be a mistake, for instance, to assume omniscience in any Faulkner narrative, however external the voice may seem. *The Town* (1957) apparently goes to the other extreme, being entirely constructed of the first-person accounts of Ratliff, Charles Mallison, and Gavin Stevens. These three also figure prominently in the narration of *The Mansion* (1959), but are joined here by an authorial voice in certain sections of the story—prominently those featuring two of Flem's most directly constructive (or, perhaps, *de*structive) observers, Mink and Linda Snopes, who themselves are never given narrative voices of their own. These general, novel-wide narrative set-ups each have very distinct effects on the material that they deal with, even before we consider subtleties within them.

From *The Southern Literary Journal,* pp. 58–73. © 2003 by the Department of English of the University of North Carolina at Chapel Hill.

It might almost be tempting, for instance, to liken the narrative basis
of *The Hamlet* to that of *Absalom, Absalom!* (1936), in that it is a story told
by an authorial voice that is frequently invaded or even usurped by the
voices of other narrators or characters. But we are prevented from doing
so by the crucial point that, whereas Thomas Sutpen's interpreters in the
earlier book work in terms of a historical and interpretive network that
works through time at the business of constructing the story of a man from
the past, Flem's readers are contemporaneous with him. They are not, like
Quentin and Shreve, attempting to piece together a text from "the rag-tag
and bob-ends of old tales and talking" (*Absalom, Absalom!* 303), but rather
trying to understand and come to terms with a man they live and develop
with, in whose story they can become involved at the level of action as well
as interpretation. Whereas Quentin and Shreve create through narrative
the circumstances in which the Sutpen drama can unfold, Gavin Stevens,
for instance, can try through money and warning to prevent the murder of
his long-time foe, Flem Snopes, thereby becoming an important part of
the events described as well as of their description. This, as we shall see, is
vital to the nature of the understanding and construction of Flem, as a text,
that develops across the trilogy, and implies important questions about the
closeness of a text to its readership.

In the early stages of *The Hamlet*, Ratliff takes over the narrative to tell
the tall tale of Ab Snopes and Pat Stamper. After many pages of the story,
we suddenly and briefly leave Ratliff's voice and swing out to see the scene of
its telling:

> "Sho now," Stamper says. "That horse will surprise you."
>
> "And it did," Ratliff said. He laughed, for the first time, quietly,
> invisible to his hearers though they knew exactly how he would
> look at the moment as well as if they could see him, easy and
> relaxed in his chair, with his lean brown pleasant shrewd face,
> in his faded clean blue shirt, with that same air of perpetual
> bachelorhood which Jody Varner had, although there was no
> other resemblance between them and not much here, since in
> Varner it was a quality of shabby and fustian gallantry where in
> Ratliff it was that hearty celibacy as of a lay brother in a twelfth-
> century monastery—a gardener, a pruner of vines, say. "That
> horse surprised us." (48–49)

Ratliff is talking here to the apparently ever-present group of poor white
Frenchman's Bend men assembled on the porch of Varner's store, a chorus
with whom he is frequently seen and, more importantly, heard throughout
the novel. Part of the effect of this passage is to make us newly aware of

this: it is important that we do not treat his rambling account in isolation, but rather as part of the scene in which its teller is present. Ratliff's tale, his telling of it, is necessarily full of his readings, and this authorial step back in the middle of the narrative reminds us of its contingency. More than this, though, Faulkner carefully contextualises Ratliff himself here: he is presented in terms of his intimates, largely through that familiar Faulknerian technique of describing in the negative—they can't see him, but we are treated to their understanding of how he looks despite this. This also represents a prime example of one of the great achievements of the narrative voice in *The Hamlet*, as well as sections of *The Mansion*, in that it subtly but inextricably combines the thoughts and interpretation of the chorus with the diction and broader worldview of the authorial voice. Factual description is tinged with slight value judgments, (Ratliff's "lean brown pleasant shrewd face") and wilfully speculative analogy ("a gardener, a pruner of vines, say") that serve to accommodate the views of Ratliff's audience at the same time as allowing authorial freedom to suggest. This in turn reminds us that the interactivity between Ratliff as narrator and his audience, and between Faulkner and ourselves, are essentially engagements in the same process.[1]

This passage is typical of much the handling of material in *The Hamlet*, and is itself contextualised and qualified a little later when we are told of Will Varner's first encounter with Flem:

> Then at last, on Friday afternoon, Will Varner himself appeared. Perhaps it was for this Ratliff and his companions had been waiting. But if it was, it was doubtless not Ratliff but the others who even hoped that anything would divulge here. So it was very likely Ratliff alone who was not surprised, since what did divulge was the obverse of what they might have hoped for; it was not the clerk who now discovered at last whom he was working for, but Will Varner who discovered who was working for him. (61)

Again, what could be a simple description of a meeting of two people is turned into a multi-levelled analysis of the scene in all its narrative relevance. Everything is couched in uncertainty here—even the uncertainty. The authorial voice gives us a detailed and indeed plausible account of the thinking of the porch-chorus, while at the same time registering Ratliff's at least partial distinction from them, and even goes further to posit probable ramifications of the meeting of expectation and event. But despite the description of the scene through fine psychological detail, it is undercut throughout by acknowledgement of the portrait's own basis in supposition. We observe Ratliff and the chorus reading Flem Snopes, but our own necessary uncertainty with regard to reading *them* reminds us of the doubt at every level from writer to character to narrator to reader.

This represents a double-edged narrative approach, with the use of free indirect discourse with characters or groups, most poignantly and parodically used in the astonishing romance of Ike and the cow, interspersed with wider-angled meditations upon problems of social and personal readership. Adding to this the heady element of conversation, *The Hamlet* is steeped in what Richard Gray has called "narrative plenitude" (254). "The talking of the people of Frenchman's Bend," Gray continues, is

> a system of verbal collusion that implies its own gaps and omissions ... The talking that incorporates and surrounds these people—that is, the talking of *The Hamlet* as a whole—is something quite different: an exchange of voices which challenges the idea that any relationship is fixed and stable, and invites us to see all relationships—between, say, character and narrator and reader, or personality and environment—as existing in a medium of change. (268–269)

This presence within the text of different levels of "talking" brings to mind certain dynamics of *The Sound and the Fury* (1929), wherein voices form and are formed by personal conceptions of truth, while our privileged position as reader allows us to witness and partake of the instability of the relationships between them. The perspective is different here, however, this relationship existing within the text itself between the varying levels of voice, while we constitute another stage. And while the voices in the earlier novel were striking for their painful isolation, their intermingling rather a process of invasion only realised at the level of our readership, here they form a kind of linguistic foundation for such fragile social cohesion as exists in the village. Seen in this light, Frenchman's Bend's "verbal collusion" represents a dramatisation of Stanley E. Fish's idea of an "interpretive community." Fish introduces this concept to attempt to explain how anyone ever manages to agree about a text, or how one reader can adopt such different approaches in relation to different texts, given the degree of interpretive individualism he posits as intrinsic to the reading/writing process. An interpretive community is essentially temporary and unstable, and consists of "those who share interpretive strategies not for reading (in the conventional sense) but for writing texts, for constituting their properties and assigning their intentions" (182). Of course, the incessant talkers of Frenchman's Bend have no conception of themselves as an interpretive community—as Gray points out, their problem is that "they see their world as set firm and authorized" (269), that they view the world in a particular way because that is the way it is. The "exchange of voices" that constitutes the narrative as a whole enables us to see the fallacy of this, to experience all relationships as part of a "medium of change" (269). And perhaps the biggest effect of Flem Snopes's entire rise is that he exposes the contrived and transient nature of any such community, making clear the arrogance, however unconscious, of such prescriptive assumption. Whereas the narrative framework clearly contextualizes this interpretive community for us, juxtaposing its conception of itself with its position in the wider scheme of things, Flem effectively forces such a realisation upon the talkers themselves. Consequently, *The Hamlet* consists not just of the early rise of Flem Snopes, but also a study of the "gaps and omissions" (Gray 268) that exist and develop between a readership that would assume none such to exist, and the crises that arise when acknowledgement is forced.

If the Frenchman's Bend interpretive community's lack of self-awareness, their apparently unquestioning acquiescence with what they take the world to be, renders them pliable components in the dominating power of Will Varner, then the shock that Flem represents and the crises that accompany it at least serve to make them aware of this, regardless of the turmoil caused. If, as Fish states, such a community's interpretive strategies "exist prior to the act of reading and therefore determine the shape of what is read rather than, as is usually assumed, the other way around" (182), then Flem effectively challenges their right to be so paradoxically deterministic and unaware of being so. The broader conception of *The Hamlet*, as it develops, allows us to see the chorus both as a mass and as a collection of individuals with individual concerns, but the degree to which this distinction is recognised varies through the text.[2]

If the shift in narrative tone upon beginning *The Town* seems extreme at first, with its use of three narrators to deliver the whole novel, then Charles Mallison immediately makes an issue of the kind of responsibilities of the audience alluded to in the apparent omniscience of *The Hamlet*. In a text that frequently seems to offer an overly prescriptive account of "Snopesism," Charles's accounts to some extent serve to reflect the novel's consideration of its own practices, to show that the text is far from ignorant of its contingencies. Indeed, Charles starts the novel by discussing the potential "narrative plenitude" (Gray 254) that exists in the background to his and his co-narrators' readings of Flem, an active consideration of the means by which information reaches its source:

> I wasn't born yet so it was Cousin Gowan who was there and big
> enough to see and remember and tell me afterward when I was
> big enough for it to make sense. That is, it was Cousin Gowan
> plus Uncle Gavin or maybe Uncle Gavin plus Cousin Gowan....
> / "Us" was Grandfather and Mother and Father and Uncle Gavin

then. So this is what Gowan knew about it until I got born and big enough to know about it too. So when I say "we" and "we thought" what I mean is Jefferson and what Jefferson thought. (*The Town* 3)

Charles here undermines the authority of the storyteller from the outset: he will tell his side of the story, but he will not assume the godlike status that his uncle frequently does. Both his apparent humility as a narrator and his awareness of the difficulties inherent in the enterprise are apparent here, though he also asserts that despite his own absence from the early scenes, there necessarily *had* to be someone there to fill the narrative role, in this case his cousin. Immediately, however, Charles qualifies even this opening qualification with the consideration that readership of this stage of Flem's career perhaps belongs in greater or lesser part to his uncle as well, presumably both as a major character in the drama and as somebody who has related the events to him through his childhood. Already, we have a conscious undermining of narrative authority, as marked as that in *The Hamlet*, with both the story's origins and its telling subject to the blurring effect of being undefined and a process of amalgamation. Similarly, Charles's use of "we" to describe the town's reactions and actions is not the assumption of some sort of divine right over their collective consciousness, but rather his recognition of himself as a mutually constitutive product of the environment of which he is speaking. Rather than speaking as a universal voice, Charles posits himself as part of a collective one; nevertheless, the awareness that this is a construct, a creation of Jefferson, is there from the start. This amounts, effectively, to an explicit recognition of an interpretive community, of which he is a member, directed toward the life of Flem Snopes. But, unlike *The Hamlet*'s porch-chorus, Charles seems fully alert to the ambiguities of his and his community's position: inherent in his opening disclaimers is an admission of Jefferson's authorial input, but also of its essentially unstable and transient nature in itself. If *The Hamlet* shows us from a relatively external position the shifting relationships between, for instance, character and narrator, then *The Town* takes this one stage further by having its very narrators, the readers within the text, actively consider what they are doing and lay that consideration before us.

Perhaps even more disarming, in this fashion, is that these first-person speakers directly address the reader, such as when Gavin Stevens delivers an aside such as "You see?" (202). Paradoxically, this acknowledgement of the reader's existence, and the at least superficial appeal to his or her cognitive abilities, actually distances us from the events being shown. We are on the exterior, not only of the narrators but of everything they describe. The narrators of *The Town*, and Gavin Stevens in particular, seem determined to keep us at arm's length: to provide us with a surplus of information, certainly, but to ensure that it is information given rather than discovered independently. For their own part, the narrators actively consider *themselves* as readers of Flem Snopes, but our fate, it would seem, is to be readers only of the book in which he appears.

Gavin Stevens's narratives assert this most forcefully. As a reader, he is perpetually analysing his own role along with those of his subjects, but as regards his audience (us) he will allow no deviation from his own authorial interests. When he considers the possibilities surrounding Eula Varner's reaction to his ordering of college catalogues for her daughter Linda, he posits as an aside, "(Oh yes, it had already occurred to me also that she had no reason whatever to assume I knew she had the catalogues, let alone had instigated them. But I dismissed that as immediately as you will too if we are to get on with this)" (211). Stevens not only acknowledges us, but anticipates our thoughts and reactions, here answering our assumed unspoken interjection. He then tells us what to think: if "this" is to work, you had better follow my version of it. "This," of course, is a story, and such devices remind us of the necessarily fictive nature of what we are reading. True, Stevens's use of "we" does imply a collaborative effort, but nonetheless the boundaries are established between speaker, subject and audience. Involved though the narrators are in the action, both narrator and reader are outside the arena of the story, outside Jefferson and Yoknapatawpha County.

This principle is illustrated most dramatically by the most well-known passage in the novel, wherein Gavin Stevens surveys "all Yoknapatawpha in the dying last of day beneath you":

> First is Jefferson, the center, radiating weakly its puny glow into space; beyond it, enclosing it, spreads the County, tied by the diverging roads to that center as is the rim to the hub by its spokes, yourself detached as God Himself for this moment above the cradle of your nativity and of the men and women who made you, the ripple and chronicle of your native land proffered for your perusal in ring by concentric ring like the ripples on living water above the dreamless slumber of your past; you to preside unanguished and immune above this miniature of man's passions and hopes and disasters. (315–316)

And so the world of the novel, the trilogy, and the Yoknapatawpha series is set out before us. No harm will come to the teller of this tale, the Godlike detachment protecting him from the travails of the players in this "miniature" through which "you" can consider the lot of mankind. Creative power is absolute here: as "God," the storyteller is writing what he relays.

Importantly, however, the awareness of readership within that writing is still paramount: "you" "peruse" as much as "preside" in "your" immunity. But for all Stevens's use of "you," this is rather a consideration of what it is to tell than an opportunity to join in the telling: the entire description of the scene is couched in his terms as an assumption, to the point of implied command, that we see things as he does, making this a view even more singular than that of an "I." He is using the audience to assert his writings as universal, even merging them together verbally as "you, the old man" (317).

Stevens does not go unchecked, of course, and it would be a mistake to identify his aims too closely with those of Faulkner himself. Ratliff and Charles Mallison frequently challenged his authority, and the interplay between the three allows the novel the space in which to investigate more sensitively the processes of storytelling. As with Stevens's first appearance in the Yoknapatawpha series, where he replays part of Joe Christmas's story to a friend in *Light in August* (1932) (333–338), his view is one among many. Faulkner plays the narrators off against each other, but in an almost exclusively linear fashion. Unlike the starkly clashing accounts juxtaposed in *The Sound and the Fury*, these narratives lead on from each other, often correcting each other as they go along. Sometimes they directly respond to each other: after Gavin's authorial-seeming rendering of Flem, Ratliff begins the following chapter with "No no, no no, no no. He was wrong" (*The Town* 296), effectively dismissing the lengthy portrait and displaying awareness of both his audience and his fellow narrators. Ratliff delivers quite a few of these rejoinders: "Because he missed it. He missed it completely" forms the whole of Chapter Nine (153). As well as undermining the tendencies of any of them to assume absolute authority over the text of Flem Snopes, these interjections reinforce the sense of a story-telling session around the hearth that pervades the whole book.

The Mansion represents a merging of the approaches of the previous two volumes of the trilogy, combining sections delivered by an authorial voice similar to that in *The Hamlet* with first-person narratives from *The Town*'s speakers, as well as one by Montgomery Ward Snopes—the only time a Snopes actually gets to speak for himself. But while this does provide a balance of sorts to the trilogy as a whole, it more importantly develops some of the possibilities suggested by the narrative considerations I have discussed. It is perhaps in reading this final instalment of the trilogy that we are most strongly forced to consider the relationship between narrator-reader and material, and to re-evaluate what has come before in this light. Indeed, the novel itself does this, frequently revisiting previously covered events, such as Mink's killing of Jack Houston and the resulting lifetime of imprisonment and pent-up resentment against Flem, but putting a different spin on them or even changing the details of what "happened." Faulkner adds a caveat to this novel, letting us know that he is aware of the discrepancies between the various books of his series, putting them down to his writing a "living literature," work to which his own attitudes will necessarily change, as well as those of his characters (*The Mansion* 6). We might put the apparently more sympathetic portrayal of Mink by *The Mansion*'s authorial voice down to such changes in Faulkner himself, but even were this not the case we are surely identifying a technique that has been fundamental to much of the Yoknapatawpha series: the presentation of an event or individual from a variety of viewpoints resulting in a kaleidoscopic and myriad portrayal. In *The Hamlet*, the murder of Houston is primarily presented, to dramatic effect, from the perspective of the slain man himself, with the resulting social view of Mink's behavior coming across as generally negative. Here, however, the authorial voice follows Mink himself, much as it follows Ratliff or Ike in *The Hamlet*, for instance, and we thereby get a picture of him as an Everyman hero against the intimidating and all-pervading forces of "*Them*," personified in such men as Houston and Flem (*The Mansion* 11 and *passim*). I would suggest, therefore, that despite Faulkner's defensiveness and the apparent similarity of voice, we have no more cause to expect or desire "consistency" in the presentation of Mink than in, for instance, that of Benjy in the four sections of *The Sound and the Fury*. Where this *does* represent an appropriate consistency with *The Hamlet* is in again forcing consideration of the spaces between character, event, and perspective: if *The Hamlet* shows the authorial voice as a reader of readers and readings, then this reminds us that even such views as these are contingent, that the view we have of Mink from *The Hamlet* can in no way be considered definitive but rather the product of a series of interpretations at various stages.

The sections of *The Mansion* that are delivered in the first person also continue themes considered previously in *The Town*. Here, however, Ratliff is the most vocal theorist of reader-writer processes, and in discussing his own machinations as a creative reader of the ongoing Snopes scenarios he also offers candid observations upon the writerly presumptions of, for instance, Gavin Stevens and Faulkner. In giving his version of the humiliation and jealousy of the village boys over the union of Eula Varner and Hoake McCarron—a situation already familiar to us from *The Hamlet*—Ratliff considers one of the injured:

> it was Theron Quick; for a week after it you could still see the print of that loaded buggy whip across the back of his skull; not the first time naming him Quick turned out to be what the feller calls jest a humorous allusion—laying cold in the weeds beside the road. And that's when I believe it happened. I don't even insist or argue that it happened that way. I jest simply decline

to have it any other way except that one because there ain't no
acceptable degrees between what has got to be right and what
jest can possibly be. (*The Mansion* 120)

This passage is full not only of loaded references to recognisable scenes from
the trilogy, but of slyly self-referential jokes about Faulkner's meditations
upon readership throughout his career. In the fictive terms of Yoknapatawpha
County itself, Quick is a family name like any other, and Ratliff is free to
laugh about its inaptitude on these grounds alone. But in the wider sphere in
which the county is a construct of the writers and readers of books, it is, of
course, Faulkner who has decided both to name a particular character Quick,
and to make it that character who ends up in the ditch—at least as far as we
can gather from Ratliff. Ratliff himself, of course, is unaware of Faulkner,
but is keenly alert to the humour in such an apparent half-wit being "named
Quick"—the remark works both as the sort of literary in-joke we might
encounter in *Absalom, Absalom!*, for instance, and as a Ratliffian aside on the
spuriousness of creation. This would be rich enough in itself, but the creation
motif is continued into Ratliff's analysis of his own interpretive actions.
Having, in effect, referred to a godlike writerly force dictating events—a
figure not unlike Gavin Stevens's conception of himself in *The Town*—he
then goes on to identify just such a trait in his own readership of the situation.
It happened like this, he says, simply because he "decline[s] to have it any
other way." This is a multiple-reference, in the Faulknerian context. It is
exactly this kind of absolutism of thought that has been highlighted in, for
instance, *The Hamlet*: the kind of intractability displayed by the interpretive
community of Frenchman's Bend that is so challenged by Flem Snopes. It is,
of course, profoundly un-Faulknerian, in that if the best of Faulkner's work
shows us anything, it is those very "degrees" that Ratliff so blithely dismisses
here. Again, this works both as a joke and as a more serious reflection upon
fictive creation on Faulkner's part, but also on Ratliff's. For Ratliff himself is
self-deprecating and somewhat sardonic here, freely admitting his own wilful
creative bigotry by declining to argue his point and telling us this. Ratliff, as
well as Faulkner, is pointing to the constructive power of readership and, in
effect, of interpretive communities. The implication of this passage as a whole
is that the authorial, godlike figure sensed in the "humorous" naming of Quick
is in fact those who interpret him, his readers both within Yoknapatawpha
and outside it, thereby implicating Ratliff, Faulkner, ourselves, and so on. In
fact, just before this passage, Ratliff offers another observation by which to
contextualise his apparent assumption of absolutism:

Naturally they never brought no bystanders with them and after
the first two or three minutes there wasn't no witness a-tall

left, since he was already laying out cold in the ditch. So my
conjecture is as good as yourn, maybe better since I'm a interested
party, being as I got what a feller calls a theorem to prove. (*The
Mansion* 119)

Again, here, Ratliff undercuts his own reading, and its professed "truth,"
by admitting its conjectural premise. He also, however, points to one of the
most important dynamics of the phenomenon of "Snopeswatching": that
those engaging in it are "interested parties," and this has a crucial effect on
the nature of their writerly construction of character and event.

A fundamental difference between this situation and that in, say,
Absalom, Absalom! is this contemporaneousness of Flem and his readers.
True, Thomas Sutpen had plenty of contemporary readers as well, but the
narrative framework of that novel is his construction through the creative
space afforded by time and its related interpretive ambiguity. While the
conclusions arrived at regarding Sutpen and his career are shown to be of
painful importance to his readers' regional and self-identity, not least that of
Quentin Compson, here we are faced with a collection of interpreters who
are practically as well as theoretically involved in their subject. This degree of
direct, personal involvement in the very story that the narrators tell gives a
very particular aspect to their relationship to it.

Wolfgang Iser discusses the degree to which the reader's personal role
in the creation of text involves a certain relinquishing of control over one's
own position in order to partake in the process:

As the literary text involves the reader in the formation of
illusion and the simultaneous formation of the means whereby
the illusion is punctured, reading reflects the process by which
we gain experience. Once the reader is entangled, his own
preconceptions are continually overtaken, so that the text
becomes his "present" while his own ideas fade into the "past";
as soon as this happens he is open to the immediate experience
of the text, which was impossible so long as his preconceptions
were his "present." (64)

We see this phenomenon developing throughout the trilogy, as various
readers become so "entangled" in the affairs of Flem Snopes—or rather in
the attempt to understand them—that their individual existences are, to a
large extent, compromised. Of course, there is a certain amount of editorial
responsibility on the part of Faulkner here—for the most part, we only see
Ratliff and company when they are involved in Snopeswatching—but this
does seem to be their primary motivation, nonetheless. The various members

of the porch-chorus, for instance, are only gradually given individual identity for us as they become further and further involved in the Snopes text, down to their names only being divulged long after the group as a whole is shown in operation. Especially in the earlier stages of *The Hamlet*, Ratliff's dependence upon Snopesism for personal identity seems extreme. When illness has forced his absence from Frenchman's Bend for a year, his first questions to Bookwright and Tull are about Flem's activities, as though the man is a page-turner of which no episode can be missed (*The Hamlet* 79).

But more than simply wanting to know about Flem, Ratliff becomes actively involved in his development. The complicated dealings over the goats, in which Ratliff attempts to outdo Flem in terms of economic cunning through an application of moral rectitude, represent an active engagement in Flem's role in Frenchman's Bend. Ratliff does win a moral victory in some ways here, in that he donates his earnings to Ike—the real loser, having been used by Flem as everybody is—but he wholly fails either to put Flem in his place or, perhaps more importantly, to raise his own game to an appropriate Snopesian level:

> I just never went far enough, he thought. I quit too soon. I went as far as one Snopes will set fire to another Snopeses barn and both Snopeses know it, and that was all right. But I stopped there. I never went on to where that first Snopes will turn around and stomp the fire out so that he can sue that second Snopes for the reward and both Snopeses know that too. (*The Hamlet* 64)[3]

Ratliff recognises, all too late, that his reading of Flem has not been deep enough, or that his capacity for readership is not sufficient to cope with the extent to which Flem will go. Nonetheless, this is an attempt to apply such reading as he has to its subject, to use it to affect Flem—to use interpretation actively to mould the Snopes text. And indeed, this he does, though not in the manner he had hoped, for Flem's Snopesism is given ever more strength through this episode.

Toward the end of *The Hamlet*, Ratliff displays a rare lack of self-control that stems from his increasing crisis of readership. Having made himself so involved in the continuing saga of Flem Snopes and Frenchman's Bend, and faced with cutting insinuations as to his culpability from Odum Bookwright, Ratliff eventually exclaims, "I never made them Snopeses and I never made the folk that cant wait to bare their backsides to them. I could do more, but I wont. I wont, I tell you!" (367). This is a denial of authorial responsibility, and is somewhat disingenuous in itself—partly because, in such scenes as the goat-transactions, he has to an extent contributed to the growth of Snopesism, at least in mythic terms, and partly because soon after this moment of crisis Ratliff himself will allow himself to become one of those "baring their backsides" to Flem in the Old Frenchman's place fiasco. It is as though such abilities as he displayed in such episodes as the goats affair are eventually worn away through overuse, and he, Bookwright and the apparently possessed Henry Armstid sacrifice money and concerns they can ill afford unwittingly to enable Flem to pull off the greatest coup of his early career and propel himself toward the richer pastures of Jefferson. Ratliff's readership of Flem both actively contributes to the latter's rise, and has a profound effect on Ratliff himself—following his crisis and ultimate Snopesian defeat in the closing pages of *The Hamlet*—the remaining two volumes of the trilogy see the more interventionist responsibilities of Snopeswatching mostly assumed by the lawyer Gavin Stevens, though this does not indicate a lessening of Ratliff's more theoretical, narrative interest.

Gavin Stevens's assumed narrative detachment from the scenes he describes in *The Town* and *The Mansion* is juxtaposed with his apparently unstoppable impulse to take part in them, from his obsession first with Flem's wife Eula, and then in trying to free her daughter Linda from the restrictive hold of her supposed father's influence, to his eventual culpability, through his failure properly to read Linda's actions, in Flem's murder even as he tries to prevent it. His intervention is the most extreme of any of the direct narrators of the trilogy, and has the greatest effect, through his incessant meddling in the affairs of others. But, as already suggested, his separation of his duties as narrator and as protagonist is often equally extreme, and on occasion virtually absolute. In his long discussion of Flem's motives, which constitutes Chapter Seventeen of *The Town* (262–295), Stevens assumes a similar position of omniscient authority over his subject as he does over the reader in the scene I discussed earlier, giving the whole account as though with perfect understanding of Flem's mind, and as though from Flem's perspective. These are scenes, of course, in which Stevens himself is directly involved, personally and professionally, but as a narrator he completely separates himself from the action. So closely does he presume authorially to follow Flem, "the bachelor lawyer" is introduced as an external, wholly separate entity (285). That this is all deflated by Ratliff's dismissal of Gavin's long reading in the very next chapter effectively serves to show how impossible this attempt is: that his participation in events, and the effect that this has, cannot be so separated from their narration as the lawyer would have us believe, and perhaps even believes himself. This aspect of the narrator's art in the trilogy is fundamental to its effect, to creating the figures both of Flem himself and of his readers and co-creators. It is an effect that Stevens seems only intermittently aware of himself, and the chief importance of Chapter Seventeen lies in its construction both of an "alternative" Flem and of Stevens himself. Despite his apparent lack of self-knowledge here, Gavin is actually brilliantly realised through narrative device, Faulkner allowing—or requiring—us to see what this narrator-protagonist cannot and witness his failure to do what he believes he succeeds at: separating his two roles.

But for all this contemporaneous relationship between reader and subject, do we gain any further insight than in the time-distended structures of, say, *Absalom, Absalom!*? What effect does all this have on Flem himself, or rather, perhaps, on our understanding of him? If anything, the situation is shown to be remarkably similar, at least in terms of his narrative presence. Flem remains an enigma whom we can never firmly say we "know," much as we can speculate—and see others speculate—about the inner workings of Sutpen without ever being able to lay claim to his psyche. Flem himself remains tight-lipped throughout his life: for a man so studied, we hear incredibly little from him. The narrators, his own contemporaries, spend so much time trying to work him out because they cannot find a way to do so, and this renders his relation to them analogous to Sutpen's readers with their temporal distance. Paradoxically, this makes him highly subject to the machinations of readership, for the necessary gaps in the narrators' and our knowledge require us to invent and create for ourselves.

However, there are two Snopeswatchers who have gone largely undiscussed, and they are perhaps the two most important, at least in terms of Flem's practical presence: Mink Snopes and Linda Snopes Kohl. Just as Thomas Sutpen is eventually toppled by his arrogant disregard for the critical feelings of his killer, so Flem falls prey to those figures whose lives, along with Eula's, are most damagingly affected by his actions and attitudes. Like Wash Jones, neither Mink nor Linda has a narrative voice of their own, but they similarly have the final say upon whether their subject lives or dies. Their readership of Flem lacks the vocality of a Stevens or a Ratliff, and they are never given the opportunity to turn interpretation into creation in narrative terms; instead, their life-long, brooding obsession with him creates the monster in more horrific ways than those given voice can imagine. Linda and Mink, in their different ways, create a Flem Snopes that can meet only one end, an end that they work actively to bring into being, despite the efforts of those more vocal but less definite in their readings to prevent it. Ultimately, Flem Snopes dies because the text he quietly but devastatingly writes over so many years is subject to the negative but heartfelt interpretations of two very "interested parties." In the single-mindedness of Mink and the quiet determination of Linda, Flem loses the ambiguity afforded by his more "literary" readers, and becomes a text that requires closure, a man who must die in order that they might shake off the roles he has written for them.

NOTES

1. For further discussion of the relationship between the authorial voice and characters' consciousness, but with more emphasis on *The Mansion*, see Warren Beck. *Man in Motion: Faulkner's Trilogy*. Madison: U of Wisconsin P, 1961: 44–47.

2. Beck points out that "Faulkner's choruses ... are not in the classical mode; they are more personalized dramatically, subordinating the voice of the poet, enfranchising the speaker as *persona*. Whether the comment is from any single character or in the dialogue of two or three, there are subtle but persistent variations to accord with different minds and temperaments" (48).

3. Richard Godden has recently discussed how Ratliff himself should not be automatically considered as *The Hamlet*'s ultimate anti-Snopes, as a pure authorial mouthpiece, but rather as someone with somewhat common interests: "Ratliff's perception of Flem needs to be recognised as partial, interested and class based. Despite posing as Flem's arch-rival, and seeming to exist as his antithesis ... Ratliff shares much with Flem, not least that both quit rented fields for versions of the store. Indeed, it might be argued that similarity of class origin might partially validate Ratliff's judgments on Flem, were it not that Ratliff's own stepping from the agricultural ladder leads him to depoliticize his own antecedents ..." (Richard Godden. "Earthing *The Hamlet*, an Anti-Ratliffian Reading." *The Faulkner Journal*, 14–2 [1999]: 86–87.)

WORKS CITED

Faulkner, William. *Absalom, Absalom!* London: Chatto and Windus, 1969.

———. *The Hamlet*. New York: Random House, 1940.

———. *Light in August*. London: Penguin, 1964.

———. *The Mansion*. London: Reprint Society, 1962.

———. *The Sound and the Fury*. London: Penguin, 1967.

———. *The Town*. New York: Vintage, 1961.

Fish, Stanley. "Interpreting the *Variorum*." *Reader-Response Criticism: From Formalism to Post-Structuralism*. Ed. Jane P. Tompkins. Baltimore: Johns Hopkins UP, 1980. 164–184.

Gray, Richard. *The Life of William Faulkner: A Critical Biography*. Oxford: Blackwell, 1994.

Iser, Wolfgang. "The Reading Process: A Phenomenological Approach." *Reader-Response Criticism: From Formalism to Post-Structuralism*. Ed. Jane P. Tompkins. Baltimore: Johns Hopkins UP, 1980. 50–69.

JAY PARINI

As I Lay Dying

> I took this family and subjected them to the greatest catastrophes which
> man can suffer—flood and fire, that's all.
> —FAULKNER, *Lion in the Garden*

The great mythic journey is the journey home, from the Trojan wars to
Ithaca or, in Joyce's version, through the night streets of Dublin to Molly
Bloom. For modernist authors, the journey from one place to another is a
form of dislocation, even though the goal might be home. It might be argued
that modern life, with its serial uprootings and the demand for mobility,
created an existential crisis that literature simply reflected. These instabilities
also meant that class status became fluid, and one could no longer depend
on being able to cling to a particular station in life. This volatility works
to unhinge the characters in *The Sound and the Fury*, especially Jason and
Quentin, who cannot depend on an inheritance or their inherited status as
Compsons to give them a perch in life. In *Sanctuary*, the "modern girl" is
Temple Drake, a perpetually destablizing force who thrusts herself in the
face of paternalism of various kinds. The journey itself becomes the focal
symbol in *As I Lay Dying*, a bleak and black comedy about a family coming
unhinged as it moves homeward.

The journey "home" belongs to Addie Bundren, who is dying as the
novel opens, with her son Cash working on her wooden coffin with care

From *One Matchless Time: A Life of William Faulkner*, pp. 143–150, 442–443, New York:
HarperCollins. © 2004 by Jay Parini.

and calculation, measuring each board and holding it up for his mother to see before he nails it into place. Addie is a stoic, noting (as her father once suggested) that the main reason for living was to get "ready to be dead a long time." She certainly gets little sympathy in dying from her husband, Anse, who takes a second wife on the same day he buries Addie. A lazy hypochondriac who thinks that if he sweats he will expire, Anse has managed to get others to do his bidding through much of his life; he is deformed (hunchbacked) and hapless. Though driven by his promise to his wife to get her in the earth beside her folks in Jefferson, he is also propelled by a wish to acquire some "storebought teeth." Indeed, as soon as his wife dies, he says: "Now I can get them teeth." Yet he is not, as Cleanth Brooks argues rather narrowly, "one of Faulkner's most accomplished villains."[23] He is just a slaggard who wants to keep a promise to a dying wife: "villainous" is not the word for him. Indeed, there is something remarkable about a man who can talk about himself in these terms: "I have heard men cuss their luck, and right, for they were sinful men. But I do not say it's a curse on me, because I have done no wrong to be cussed by. I am not religious, I reckon. But peace is my heart: I know it is. I have done things but neither better nor worse than them that pretend otherlike, and I know that Old Marster will care for me ere a sparrow that falls."[24]

Jefferson was perhaps fifteen miles away (no specifics are given), but given the intense heat, the flood, and the blazing incompetence of this clan, it takes ten full days on the road to achieve their destination. With the Bundrens, Faulkner looks closely at the poor white country folks of Yoknapatawpha County (called by this name for the first time in his fiction here). Faulkner's imagination was more powerfully drawn to other families—Sartoris, Compson, McCaslin, Snopes. But the Bundrens opened fresh possibilities for the novelist to examine the value system of these country people. As Kevin Railey observes, the Bundrens (excepting Darl and Addie) "reveal their acceptance of middle-class values throughout the book. What this acceptance means for them as Mississippi dirt farmers is an identification with the values of the Protestant middle class—independence, individuality, and reward based on merit—which were buttressed by religious beliefs."[25]

The novel is wonderfully centered, following a single action over a limited number of days. It opens at twilight as Addie dies and concludes just after her burial. Addie was for most of the Bundren family a stabilizing force, and her death pulls the existential rug out from under her children and husband, who must tumble in the sharp air of absurdity as they search to reconnect to the ground, moving through time and space with an eerie compulsion. But the story here isn't everything; indeed, the genius of Faulkner's narrative inheres in the monologues: fifty-nine in all, each of varying length and consistency. Seven of the fifteen speakers are Bundrens, and they take up most of the narrative space, though monologues by eight "outsiders" add to the layering of voices. In addition to Addie and Anse, the speakers include the Bundren children: Cash, Darl, Jewel, Dewey Dell (the only daughter in the family), and Vardaman.

Like the Compsons, the Bundrens seem bound to the family circle by invisible but relentless ties. Cash and Darl have no life beyond their parents. Cash is cool-headed and practical, not terribly unlike Jason Compson in his attention to the world's surfaces. He hopes to obtain a "graphophone" in Jefferson. As the novel progresses, he seems to become more rooted in an independent sense of self. Dewey Dell is no Caddy Compson, but she is just as willful and becomes pregnant by a man called Lafe. What she wants in Jefferson is a medicine that will induce an abortion. Darl, the second son of Anse and Addie, is unnaturally close to his mother (like Faulkner and Miss Maud?), despite Addie's rejection of him on some deep level, which nearly drives him insane. With his fragile ego, Darl recalls Quentin Compson, though he is not educated like Quentin, and so his meditations grope uncertainly for abstractions. His painful debates with himself recall Hamlet as well: "I must be, or I could not empty myself for sleep in a strange room. And so if I am not emptied yet, I am *is*." He is also fiercely jealous of Jewel, the child of an adulterous affair his mother had with a preacher named Whitfield. Addie loves Jewel above the others, in part because he has none of Anse's genes in his body. He is the son of a man from a higher caste. For his part, Jewel is selfish and cruel. He believes that the others have driven his mother to her grave, and he cannot forgive them. Vardaman, the youngest, plays a role vaguely similar to that of Benjy in *The Sound and the Fury*, that is, he sees more than he can say or understand. He is both young and delusional. Afraid that his mother will suffocate in her coffin, he drills holes into the lid, which tear into her face. What he wishes for at the end of the journey into Jefferson is nothing more than a toy train.

Disasters in the form of flood and fire befall the Bundrens as they slog their way through frantic heat and rain with their mother's corpse in her handmade coffin loaded on a mule-drawn wagon. Flooding of the Yoknapatawpha River has swept away two bridges, so the family opts to ford the river. This attempt goes badly, however, and the wagon overturns; in the upset, Cash rebreaks a leg that was previously broken in a fall from a church steeple. The mules drown, forcing the family to trade Jewel's much prized horse for another span of mules. Meanwhile, the coffin reeks of decay, and buzzards swarm. Another night, the beleaguered family stores the wagon and the coffin in a barn at a farm owned by Gillespie, who takes pity on the Bundrens and allows them to stay overnight. Mysteriously, the barn erupts into flames, a fire described in haunting terms by Vardaman: "The barn was still red, but it wasn't a barn now. It was sunk down, and the red went swirling up. The barn went swirling up in little red pieces, against the sky and the stars so that the stars moved backward."[26] The rotting corpse of Addie Bundren is barely saved from this conflagration, which Darl in fact set in the vain hope of cutting short this ridiculous journey.

Dewey Dell has learned from Vardaman that Darl set the barn on fire, and she conspires with Jewel to bring their wayward, difficult brother to justice. Cash himself is convinced that Darl must be sent away, although his reasoning is convoluted: "It was either send him to Jackson, or have Gillespie sue us, because he knowed some way that Darl set fire to it. I dont know how he knowed, but he did. Vardaman seen him do it, but he swore he never told nobody but Dewey Dell and she told him not to tell nobody. But Gillespie knowed it. But he would a suspicioned it sooner or later. *He could have done it that night just watching the way Darl acted.*"[27] So Darl is arrested and taken away.

In a mad monologue at the end, Darl stands aside from himself, observing his own demise as they take him away to Jackson to an institution for the criminally insane: "Darl has gone to Jackson. They put him on the train, laughing, down the long car laughing, the heads turning like the heads of owls when he passed." And at the end of this monologue: "Darl is our brother, our brother Darl. Our brother Darl in a cage in Jackson where, his grimed hand lying light in the quiet interstices, looking out he foams." In the meantime, Dewey Dell's frantic search for an abortion drug only gets her swindled and seduced by Skeets MacGowan, a slimy soda jerk who pretends that he is a druggist (Skeets is a minor character who makes several later appearances in Faulkner's work, including *Intruder in the Dust* and *The Mansion*).

As I Lay Dying is among Faulkner's most unified and satisfying novels; it hovers among the several peaks of his achievement, less self-consciously modernist than, say, *The Sound and the Fury* or *Absalom, Absalom!* and less concerned than many of his books with values that Cleanth Brooks and others would identify as residually Christian. Faulkner—like Robert Frost, with whom he has something in common as a universal writer who worked a small geographical patch—preferred the Old Testament to the New. The morality in his fiction is starkly perceived, unrelenting, cutting to the quick of human nature, propelled by raw but natural drives. In Frost's poetry, people occupy their ground for habitual reasons, going mad like the hill wife in his eponymous poem, their communities dwindling into cellar holes. In Faulkner's fiction, communities and the families within them survive through habit as well. But families and community become a prison, exacting duties and pieties that they do not earn by giving sympathy and support. The madness of Quentin Compson and Darl Bundren follows naturally from these broken circles, from the countless invisible ties of love and thought that have been severed.

The strength of this novel also has much to do with its unique language, with metaphors creating a web of correspondences, weaving a systematic world, a world wherein journeys—like metaphorical language— lead toward certain ultimacies of desire, purpose, and expression," as Patrick O'Donnell argues in a seminal essay.[28] The most obvious example is the metaphor of the road. The Jefferson road carries the coffin along, a vehicle in itself, that which carries meaning or fails to do so. O'Donnell comments: "From the perspective that the novel's metaphor network is revelatory of a structured world of significances tending toward some final end, the road would represent a sign of linkage and connection, a metaphor for the act of metaphor as it joins and binds."

For Anse, the road is a tangle of possibilities, a metaphor that confounds him as he searches for clues to the nature of his own life: "I told Addie it want [*sic*] any luck living on a road when it come by here, and she said, for the world like a woman, 'get up and move, then.' But I told her it want no luck in it, because the Lord puts roads for travelling: why He laid them down flat on the earth. When He aims for something to be always a-moving, He makes it longways, like a road or a horse or a wagon, but when He aims for something to stay put, He makes it up-and-down ways, like a tree or a man. And so he never aimed for folks to live on a road, because which gets there first, I says, the road or the house?"[29]

The chief monologist in the novel, Darl, has a mind whose roadways are marked by blockages and evasions, floods and fires. Darl notes that the road runs parallel to telephone lines, which carry messages as the filaments of the brain carry signals and create significations. Contradictory images for the road occur in his distorting mind, as when he describes it as being "like a spoke of which Addie Bundren is the rim." This tortuous road ends in the public square, "where the square opens and the monument stands before the courthouse." This image represents law and order, which are just the forces that Darl rubs against with rough consequences. Yet he evinces the road, a literal and figurative image, repeatedly in his sixteen monologues. In one famous passage, he suggests (by implication) that knowledge is only obtainable by friction and motion, as when he describes the disastrous fording of the river, where men and animals only touch bottom occasionally: "*I felt the current take us and I knew we were on the ford by that reason, since it was only by means of that slipping contact that we were in motion at all.*" Thus meaning itself seems to occur only in slips and scrapes, in chance contacts between signifiers and those objects in the world to which they attach themselves.

The journey of the narrative underscores the increasing madness of Darl and the disintegration of the Bundren family itself, which "never aimed to bother nobody," as Anse puts it in his pathetic way. This is a darkly comic journey, however. The absurdities and cruelties that befall the Bundrens make one wince. Even the apparent gesture of restitution in the end, where a new Mrs. Bundren replaces the dead one, is absurd, filled with the dark laughter of a distant, even cruel, God who finds human beings utterly foolish. The family situation dramatized here, so representative of family dynamics in Faulkner, is nothing short of frightening. As Harold Bloom notes: "The Bundrens manifestly constitute one of the most terrifying visions of the family romance in the history of literature."[30]

The layered subjectivities of this novel, already used to good effect in *The Sound and the Fury*, are another aspect of its greatness. Faulkner vividly distinguished the voices and visions of his speakers, with Darl as the central and disintegrating consciousness. Nevertheless, it is the madman who sees truly. He understands that Addie has preferred Jewel to the others; he sees into Dewey Dell's deepest thoughts; he seems to have a finger on everyone, intuiting their motives. He alone realizes that the entire project of conducting the coffin to Jefferson by wagon is absurd, and he tries to stop it. His supposedly warped vision of reality is, in the inverse logic of the novel, "sane." And he must pay for his sanity by being sent to a mental asylum.

Everyone, of course, has access to the same reality, but the mode of language and perception alters this reality, splinters it, subjects it to refreshments, revisions, moral complexities, and whims. Anse is evasive, self-justifying, eager to displace blame, ineffectual. Jewel is high-strung, impulsive, overbearing, heedless. Vardaman, as the naïve and simple-minded child, responds intuitively to life, nearly free of interpretive lenses. "My mother is a fish," he famously says, even before Addie has begun to smell. His perception reflects his agony, a jumble of sounds and sights, tastes and smells, redolent of its own fierce logic. Cora Tull, a friend who visits Addie at her deathbed, is mired in her own religiosity, blinkered by dogma. Cash (whose name symbolizes cool transaction) sees the world as a carpenter, hammering chaos into order, with the requisite sacrifices of openness and flexibility. A basic decency shimmers through his monologues. Dewey Dell sinks helplessly into her own sensuousness, her own reproductive nature, the world of repetition that William Blake calls Generation: "I feel like a wet seed wild in the hot blind earth," Dewey Dell says.[31] And so Faulkner's characters speak in their own metaphors and within a tonal and linguistic range unique to each sensibility, which governs their worldviews and limits their range of moral options.

Faulkner was not the first author to use the technique of layering subjectivities. As precursors, one thinks of Robert Browning in *The Ring and the Book* as well as more modern authors, such as Joyce, Woolf, and Conrad, who turned to similar strategies of narration. But Faulkner's mastery of so many distinct points of view—with each being a version of the same story and each filtering the data at hand in ways that become vivid distortions or misreadings—conveys an overwhelming sense of epistemological slip and slide. In the end, his novel is all performance, a play with different voices, a blistering and darkly comic summoning of decay.

As I Lay Dying also stands out for the complex variety of tones that, quite ingeniously, mingle and cohere. The grotesque arises in many instances, from Anse's wish for "storebought teeth" to Cash's broken leg, which his family decides to set in cement. The rotting corpse of Addie Bundren is, of course, the most grotesque image of all, a primary form of sacrilege: the body of one's mother should, of all things, remain sacrosanct. But Faulkner adds a wry touch to these grotesqueries, making one smile as well as cringe. The absurdity of the essential situation mingles with a heroic aspect that verges on the mock-heroic; nevertheless, one inevitably admires the animal persistence of the Bundren clan in their preposterous journey to Jefferson. Faulkner at once underscores and deconstructs the male drive to adhere to a code of honor, to fulfill the need to bury the mother even though the journey itself puts the family at risk of life and limb. The Bundrens certainly risk ridicule, as when a passerby shrieks: "Great God, what they got in that wagon?" The response from Jewel is telling. "Son of a bitches," he spits, then takes a swing at the man, who draws a knife in response.

This strange, hilarious, terrifying novel presents the drama of a damaged family, with each character searching for a wholeness that cannot be restored, and that probably never was.

NOTES

23. Cleanth Brooks, *The Yoknapatawpha Country* (New Haven: Yale University Press, 1963), 154–55.

24. William Faulkner, *As I Lay Dying* (New York: Random House, 1957 edition), 24. Originally published in 1930 by Cape and Smith.

25. Kevin Railey, *Natural Aristocracy: History, Ideology, and the Production of William Faulkner* (Tuscaloosa: University of Alabama Press, 1999), 89.

26. Faulkner, *As I Lay Dying*, 154.

27. Ibid., 160.

28. See Patrick O'Donnell, "The Spectral Road; Metaphors of Transference in Faulkner's As I Lay Dying." *Papers on Language and Literature* 20, 1 (winter 1984), passim.

29. Faulkner, *As I Lay Dying*, 22.

30. Harold Bloom, ed., *American Fiction 1914–1945* (New York: Chelsea House, 1987), 10. This quotation is from Bloom's introduction.

31. Faulkner, *As I Lay Dying*, 41.

Chronology

1897	Born William Cuthbert Faulkner in New Albany, Mississippi, on September 25; first child of Murry Faulkner and Maud Butler.
1898–1899	Family moves to Ripley, Mississippi.
1899	Brother Murry C. (Jack) Faulkner Jr. born on June 26.
1901	Brother John Wesley Thompson Faulkner III born on September 24. William falls ill with scarlet fever.
1902	Family moves to Oxford, Mississippi.
1905	William enters first grade at Oxford Graded School.
1906	Skips to third grade. Grandmother Sallie Murry Faulkner dies on December 21.
1907	Grandmother Lelia Dean Swift Butler dies on June 1. Brother Dean Swift Faulkner born on August 15.
1908	May have witnessed the lynching of a black man, Nelse Patton, on the square in Oxford.
1909	Works in father's livery stable.
1911	Enters eighth grade where he is increasingly truant.
1914	Takes poetry to lawyer Phil Stone, which marks the beginning of a long friendship between the two. Faulkner enters eleventh and final grade of Oxford High School and drops out in December.
1915	Returns to school to play football. Quits school for good that fall. Goes bear hunting at "General" James Stone's camp.

1916	Holds a brief position as a clerk at grandfather's First National Bank and begins to frequent the University of Mississippi campus where he writes verse under the influence of Algernon Charles Swinburne and A.E. Housman.
1917	Begins supplying drawings for yearbook *Ole Miss*.
1918	Tries to enlist in U.S. Army but is turned down. Joins Phil Stone in New Haven, Cnnecticut, where he begins work as a ledger clerk for Winchester Repeating Arms Co. Accepted by the Canadian Royal Air Force as cadet. Discharged in December and returns to Oxford.
1919	Poem "*L'Apres-Midi d'un Faune*" appears in *The New Republic*. Enters the University of Mississippi and begins publishing poems in *The Mississippian* and the Oxford *Eagle*.
1920	Wins $10 poetry prize offered by Professor Calvin S. Brown. Commission arrives as honorable second lieutenant, RAF. Withdraws from the university.
1921	Presents a gift volume of poetry to Estelle Franklin. Visits New York and works as a bookstore clerk. Returns to Oxford to work as postmaster at the University of Mississippi post office.
1922	Grandfather J.W.T. Faulkner Jr. dies. Poem "Portrait" published in *The Double- Dealer*.
1924	Publishes *The Marble Faun*.
1925	Leaves Oxford for New Orleans, where he spends time with Sherwood Anderson. Contributes to the *Times-Picayune*. Sails for Europe with William Spratling.
1926	Moves to New Orleans and publishes *Soldier's Pay*. Collaborates with Spratling on *Sherwood Anderson & Other Famous Creoles*.
1927	*Mosquitoes* published.
1928	*Sartoris* accepted by Harcourt, Brace.
1929	*Sartoris* published. *The Sound and the Fury* published. Marries Estelle Franklin.
1930	Purchases house and land and names it Rowan Oak. *As I Lay Dying* published.
1931	Birth and death of daughter Alabama. Publishes *Sanctuary* and *These 13*.

1932	Begins writing for MGM as a screenwriter. His father Murry Faulkner dies August 7. *Light in August* published.
1933	*A Green Bough* published, daughter Jill Faulkner is born on June 24.
1934	Publishes *Doctor Martino and Other Stories*.
1935	Publishes *Pylon*. Brother Dean killed in a plane crash on November 10. Meets Meta Dougherty Carpenter and begins intimate relationship that would last intermittently for fifteen years.
1936	Publishes *Absalom, Absalom!*
1938	*The Unvanquished* published; screen rights are sold to MGM.
1939	Elected to National Institute of Arts and Letters. Publishes *The Wild Palms*.
1940	Mammy Caroline (Callie) Barr dies on January 31. Publishes *The Hamlet*.
1942	*Go Down, Moses* published.
1946	Viking Press publishes *The Portable Faulkner*, edited by Malcolm Cowley.
1948	*Intruder in the Dust* published. Elected to American Academy of Arts and Letters.
1949	Meets Joan Williams. *Knight's Gambit* published. Wins Nobel Prize for Literature.
1950	*Collected Stories* of William Faulkner published.
1951	Publishes *Notes on a Horsethief*. Receives National Book Award for Fiction for *Collected Stories*. *Requiem for a Nun* published. Begins relationship with Joan Williams.
1952–1954	Travels throughout Europe and works on *A Fable* and *Land of the Pharaohs*.
1954	Publishes *A Fable*, begins relationship with Jean Stein.
1955	Accepts National Book Award for Fiction for *A Fable*, travels to Japan for the State Department. Publishes *Big Woods*.
1957	Travels to Athens on two-week mission for State Department, accepts Silver Medal of Greek Academy, publishes *The Town*.
1959	American debut of *Requiem for a Nun* on Broadway; publishes *The Mansion*.
1960	Mother, Maud Butler Faulkner, dies October 16.

1962   Publishes *The Reivers*. Dies of heart attack on July 6 and is
                buried in Saint Peter's Cemetery in Oxford, Mississippi.

Contributors

HAROLD BLOOM is Sterling Professor of the Humanities at Yale University. He is the author of thirty books, including *Shelley's Mythmaking, The Visionary Company, Blake's Apocalypse, Yeats, A Map of Misreading, Kabbalah and Criticism, Agon: Toward a Theory of Revisionism, The American Religion, The Western Canon,* and *Omens of Millennium: The Gnosis of Angels, Dreams, and Resurrection. The Anxiety of Influence* sets forth Professor Bloom's provocative theory of the literary relationships between the great writers and their predecessors. His most recent books include *Shakespeare: The Invention of the Human,* a 1998 National Book Award finalist, *How to Read and Why, Genius: A Mosaic of One Hundred Exemplary Creative Minds, Hamlet: Poem Unlimited, Where Shall Wisdom Be Found?,* and *Jesus and Yahweh: The Names Divine.* In 1999 Professor Bloom received the prestigious American Academy of Arts and Letters Gold Medal for Criticism. He has also received the International Prize of Catalonia, the Alfonso Reyes Prize of Mexico, and the Hans Christian Andersen Bicentennial Prize of Denmark.

IRVING HOWE was known for his literary criticism as well as his social and political activism. He helped found the intellectual quarterly *Dissent,* which he edited until his death in 1993. Howe wrote seminal studies on Thomas Hardy, William Faulkner, and politics and the novel.

CLEANTH BROOKS, who died in 1994, was an influential American literary critic and professor. His books included *The Well Wrought Urn* and *Modern Poetry and the Tradition.* He was also the author of *William Faulkner:*

The Yoknapatawpha Country and *William Faulkner: Toward Yoknapatawpha and Beyond.*

MICHAEL MILLGATE, professor of English, University of Toronto (emeritus), is the author of the biographies *The Achievement of William Faulkner* and *Thomas Hardy.*

DAVID MINTER is the Bruce and Elizabeth Dunlevie Professor Emeritus of English at Rice University. He is the author *of William Faulkner: His Life and Work* and *Faulkner's Questioning Narratives.*

ERIC J. SUNDQUIST is a UCLA Foundation Professor of Literature and a member of the Department of English. He is the author of *Strangers in the Land: Blacks, Jews, Post-Holocaust America; To Wake the Nations: Race in the Making of American Literature; Faulkner: The House Divided;* and *The Hammers of Creation: Folk Culture in Modern African-American Fiction.*

THADIOUS DAVIS is the Geraldine R. Segal Professor of American Social Thought and Professor of English at the University of Pennsylvania. She is the author of *Games of Property: Law, Race, Gender, and Faulkner's Go Down, Moses; Nella Larsen, Novelist of the Harlem Renaissance;* and *Faulkner's "Negro": Art and the Southern Context.*

DIANNE LUCE COX is a professor at Midlands Technical College in Columbia, South Carolina. She has published articles on Cormac McCarthy and William Faulkner. She is coeditor of books on McCarthy and co-author of *As I Lay Dying*, with James B. Meriwether.

DEBORAH CLARKE is an associate professor of English and women's studies at Penn State. Her primary field is twentieth-century American fiction, with particular emphasis on Faulkner and women writers. She is the author of *Robbing the Mother: Women in Faulkner.*

JUDITH BRYANT WITTENBERG is a co-editor of the book *Unflinching Gaze: Morrison and Faulkner Re-Envisioned*, and the author of *Faulkner: The Transfiguration of Biography.*

OWEN ROBINSON teaches at the University of Essex. His main research interests are in the writing of the U.S. South, having published articles on William Faulkner in the *Southern Literary Journal, The Faulkner Journal*, the *European Journal of American Culture*, and the *Journal of American Studies.*

JAY PARINI teaches at Middlebury College. He is the author of many books, including *Robert Frost: A Life; John Steinbeck;* and *One Matchless Time: A Life of William Faulkner.*

Bibliography

BOOKS AND ARTICLES

Adams, Richard P. "Faulkner's Use of Nation as Metaphor." In *Readings on William Faulkner*. Ed. Clarice Swisher. San Diego: Greenhaven, 1998. 54–63.

Baker, Charles. *William Faulkner's Postcolonial South*. New York: Peter Lang, 2000.

Blotner, Joseph. *Faulkner: A Biography*. New York: Random House, 1984.

Brooks, Cleanth. *William Faulkner: The Yoknapatawpha Country*. Baton Rouge: Louisiana State University Press, 1963.

Clarke, Deborah. *Robbing the Mother: Women in Faulkner*. Jackson: University Press of Mississippi, 1994.

Cowley, Malcolm. *The Faulkner-Cowley File: Letters and Memories, 1944–1962*. London: Chatto & Windus, 1966.

Davis, Thadious M. *Faulkner's "Negro": Art and the Southern Context*. Baton Rouge: Louisiana State University Press, 1983.

Davis, Todd. "A Loss of Innocence: The Act of Reading William Faulkner in a Postmodern World." *Mississippi Quarterly* 49.3 (1996): 619–32.

Dussere, Erik. *Balancing the Books: Faulkner, Morrison and the Economies of Slavery*. New York: Routledge, 2003.

Duvall, John N. *Faulkner's Marginal Couple: Invisible, Outlaw, and Unspeakable Communities*. Austin: University of Texas Press, 1990.

Duvall, John N., and Ann Abadie, eds. *Faulkner and Postmodernism: Faulkner and Yoknapatawpha*, 1999. Jackson: University Press of Mississippi, 2002.

Fayen, Tanya T. *In Search of the Latin American Faulkner.* Lanham, Md.: University Press of America, 1995.

Fowler, Doreen, and Ann J. Abadie, eds. *Faulkner and Race. Faulkner and Yoknapatawpha, 1986.* Jackson: University Press of Mississippi, 1987.

———. *Faulkner and Religion.* Faulkner and Yoknapatawpha 1989. Jackson: University Press of Mississippi, 1991.

Hobson, Fred. *William Faulkner's Absalom, Absalom: A Casebook.* Oxford: Oxford University Press, 2003.

Inge, M. Thomas, ed. *The Achievement of William Faulkner: A Centennial Tribute.* Ashland, VA: Randolph-Macon College, 1998.

Karl, Frederick Robert. *William Faulkner, American Writer: A Biography.* New York: Weidenfeld & Nicolson, 1989.

Kartiganer, Donald M., and Ann J. Abadie, eds. *Faulkner and Gender.* Jackson: University Press of Mississippi, 1996.

———. *Faulkner and the Natural World: Faulkner and Yoknapatawhpa, 1996.* Jackson: University Press of Mississippi, 1999.

———. *Faulkner at 100: Retrospect and Prospect. Faulkner and Yoknapatawhpa, 1997.* Jackson: University Press of Mississippi, 2000.

Marquez, Antonio C. "Faulkner in Latin America." *Faulkner Journal* 11.1–2 (Fall 1995–Spring 1996): 83–100.

Millgate, Michael, ed. *New Essays on Light in August.* Cambridge: Cambridge University Press, 1987.

———. *Achievement of William Faulkner.* Athens: University of Georgia Press, 1989.

———. *Faulkner's Place.* Athens: The University of Georgia Press, 1997.

Minrose, Gwin. *The Feminine and Faulkner: Reading Beyond Sexual Difference.* Knoxville: University of Tennessee Press, 1990.

Mortimer, Gail L. *Faulkner's Rhetoric of Loss: A Study of Perception and Meaning.* Austin: University of Texas Press, 1983.

Polk, Noel. *Children of the Dark House: Text and Context in Faulkner.* Jackson: University Press of Mississippi, 1996.

Parini, Jay, *One Matchless Time: A Life of William Faulkner.* New York: HarperCollins Publishers, 2004.

Sundquist, Eric J. *Faulkner: The House Divided.* Baltimore: Johns Hopkins University Press, 1983.

Towner, Theresa M. *Faulkner on the Color Line: The Later Novels.* Jackson: University Press of Mississippi, 2000.

Urgo, Joseph R., and Ann J. Abadie, eds. *Faulkner and the Ecology of the South: Faulkner and Yoknapatawpha, 2003.* Jackson: University Press of Mississippi, 2005.

Vickery, Olga W., ed. *The Novels of William Faulkner: A Critical Interpretation.* Baton Rouge: Louisiana State University Press, 1964.

Volpe, Edmond L. *A Reader's Guide to William Faulkner: The Novels.* Syracuse: Syracuse University Press, 2004.

Wagner-Martin, Linda, ed. *New Essays on Go Down, Moses.* Cambridge: Cambridge University Press, 1996.

Warren, Robert Penn, ed. *Faulkner: A Collection of Critical Essays.* Englewood Cliffs, NJ: Prentice-Hall, 1966.

Weinstein, Philip M., ed. *The Cambridge Companion to William Faulkner.* Cambridge: Cambridge Univ. Press, 1995.

———. *What Else but Love?: The Ordeal of Race in Faulkner and Morrison.* Jackson: University Press of Mississippi, 1996.

Wittenberg, Judith Bryant. *Faulkner: The Transfiguration of Biography.* Lincoln: University of Nebraska Press, 1979.

Zender, Karl F. *The Crossing of the Ways: William Faulkner, the South, and the Modern World.* New Brunswick: Rutgers University Press, 1989.

———. *Faulkner and the Politics of Reading.* Baton Rouge: Louisiana State University Press, 2002.

WEB SITES

William Faulkner on the Web
http://www.mcsr.olemiss.edu/~egjbp/faulkner/faulkner.html

Wikipedia: William Faulkner
http://en.wikipedia.org/wiki/William_Faulkner

The Mississippi Writers Page: William Faulkner
http://www.olemiss.edu/mwp/dir/faulkner_william/

Nobelprize.org: William Faulkner
http://nobelprize.org/nobel_prizes/literature/laureates/1949/
faulkner-bio.html

Acknowledgments

From *William Faulkner: A Critical Study,* copyright © 1951, 1952, 1975 by Irving Howe, by permission of Nicholas Howe, Nina Howe, and Ivan R. Dee, Publishers.

Reprinted by permission of Louisiana State University Press from William Faulkner The Yoknapatawpha Country by Cleanth Brooks. Copyright © 1963 by Cleanth Brooks.

From *The Achievement of William Faulkner* by Michael Millgate, copyright © 1966 by Michael Millgate. Used by permission of Random House, Inc.

Minter, David. *William Faulkner: His Life and Work.* pp. 91–112, 282–285. © 1980 The Johns Hopkins University Press. Reprinted with permission of The Johns Hopkins University Press.

Sewell, Richard H. *A House Divided: Sectionalism and Civil War, 1848–1865.* pp. 71–95, 167–172. © 1988 The Johns Hopkins University Press. Reprinted with permission of The Johns Hopkins University Press.

Thadious Davis, from *Faulkner's "Negro": Art and the Southern Context.* © 1983 by LSU press.

Dianne Luce Cox, "A Measure of Innocence: *Sanctuary's* Temple Drake," *Mississippi Quarterly,* vol. 39, no. 3. Reprinted by permission.

Deborah Clarke, "Erasing and Inventing Motherhood: *The Sound and the Fury*' and *As I Lay Dying*" in *Robbing the Mother: Women in Faulkner* (Jackson, MS: University Press of Mississippi, 1994). 19–50, 155–156.

Judith Bryant Wittenberg, "*Go Down, Moses* and the Discourse of Environmentalism," *New Essays on Go Down, Moses*, Cambridge University Press, 1996. Reprinted with permission of Cambridge University Press.

From *The Southern Literary Journal*, Volume 36, number 1. Copyright © 2003 by the Department of English and Comparative Literature of the University of North Carolina at Chapel Hill. Published by the University of North Carolina Press. Used by permission of the publisher. www.uncpress.unc.edu

From *One Matchless Time* by Jay Parini. Copyright © 2004 by Jay Parini. Reprinted by permission of HarperCollins Publisher.

Every effort has been made to contact the owners of copyrighted material and secure copyright permission. Articles appearing in this volume generally appear much as they did in their original publication with few or no editorial changes. Those interested in locating the original source will find bibliographic information in the bibliography and acknowledgments sections of this volume.

Index